BREAKING ICE FOR ARCTIC OIL

Breaking Ice for Arctic Oil

The Epic Voyage of the SS *Manhattan* through the Northwest Passage

ROSS COEN

To Art + Joyce —
All the best!
Ross C

UNIVERSITY OF ALASKA PRESS

Fairbanks

© 2012 University of Alaska Press
P.O. Box 756240
Fairbanks, AK 99775-6240

Printed on recycled paper in the United States

This publication was printed on paper that meets the minimum requirements for ANSI/NISO Z39.48–1992 (Permanence of Paper).

Library of Congress Cataloging-in-Publication Data

Coen, Ross Allen.
 Breaking ice for Arctic oil : the epic voyage of the SS Manhattan through the Northwest Passage / Ross Coen.
     p. cm.
 Includes bibliographical references and index.
 ISBN 978-1-60223-169-6 (pbk. : alk. paper) — ISBN 978-1-60223-170-2 (e-book)
 1. Petroleum—Transportation—Alaska. 2. Manhattan (Tanker)—History.
 3. Tankers—United States—History. 4. Northwest Passage. 5. Oil fields—Alaska.
 I. Title.
 HE595.P4C64 2012
 387.2'45—dc23
                        2011033205

Contents

Foreword

This volume is more than just a great story about a famous ship, the tanker *Manhattan*. It is a complex tale told well about Alaska oil politics, the politics of the Northwest Passage, and sociotechnological risks and choices. This historical review is very timely, since during August 2011 a Suezmax ice class tanker, *Vladimir Tikhonov*, carrying 120,000 tons of bulk liquid, was escorted by two nuclear icebreakers across Russia's Northern Sea Route on an experimental voyage. *Vladimir Tikhonov* is the largest commercial ship to sail the Northern Sea Route, and this voyage is clear evidence that globalization of the Arctic is increasing the use of new marine routes, four decades after the high-profile arctic voyages of the SS *Manhattan*.

Many people wonder why this particular ship was chosen for such pioneering arctic operations. Certainly, Humble Oil did not have time to build a new ship, as the development of a trans-Alaska pipeline was under way at the same time a marine option for oil transport was being explored. An existing ship had to be found quickly and converted to a functional icebreaker. The tanker *Manhattan* was the largest U.S. merchant ship at the time and one of the first supertankers, at 106,000 deadweight tons. The ship was large, powerful, and overbuilt (two-inch-thick hull plating compared with half the thickness used for today's tankers). *Manhattan* also had twin propellers, which were critical for enhanced maneuverability in ice-covered waters. As author Ross Coen notes, it took a half ton of fuel to move this massive ship one nautical mile! Economic viability was obviously not *Manhattan*'s strong suit. However, sheer mass and high propulsion power are required for effective icebreaking, and *Manhattan* had the right mix of both.

There was certainly no shortage of hubris and confidence in Humble's belief that they could literally chop *Manhattan* into segments, send the individual sections to far-flung shipyards (from Maine to Alabama), and then reassemble the pieces at Sun Shipbuilding and Dry Dock Company in Chester, Pennsylvania, to create an icebreaker. It was remarkable that all this was completed in six months, just in time for the ship to operate in the Arctic by September 1969. One can speculate whether American shipyards could do the same job today. This reconstruction story has authority and detail, because the author conversed with several principals, including William O. Gray, Humble's project officer for the conversion. The story of this conversion is fascinating and shows how remarkable it was to accomplish so much in such a short period of time.

It is a little-known fact that the *Manhattan* did not *technically* complete a full voyage of the Northwest Passage. The ship sailed from the U.S. East Coast to the Beaufort Sea, but not into the Pacific. The Northwest Passage is the name generally given to the marine routes between the Atlantic and Pacific Oceans along the northern coast of North America that span the Canadian Arctic Archipelago. Lists of vessels achieving a successful Northwest Passage voyage (even if a voyage took more than one season, such as Roald Amundsen's first voyage in 1903–1906 aboard the twenty-one-meter sloop *Gjoa*) do not include *Manhattan*'s 1969 voyage. But this historical footnote does not diminish any of the ship's accomplishments or detract from the narrative in this superb book. And it is important to note that Humble was consistent in its plans to sail *Manhattan* to Alaska's North Slope and demonstrate a feasible marine transport link with the U.S. East Coast—the primary objective was to bring Alaska crude oil to New York.

The presence of such a large commercial ship smashing through ice in the Canadian Archipelago obviously did not sit well with the Canadian people and their government, then headed by Prime Minister Pierre Trudeau. In an indication of things to come, Canadian Coast Guard icebreakers were sent, without request, to "support" the operation as a matter of sovereign presence and Canadian stewardship of its Arctic. It is safe to say that the *Manhattan*'s voyage of 1969 changed the very nature of governance of the Arctic Ocean. By April 1970 the Parliament in Ottawa had passed the Arctic Waters Pollution Prevention Act, which would be used to regulate marine activity in the waters of the Canadian Archipelago—all of which we now know to be declared by Canada as internal waters. The debate continues today as the United States and other nations disagree with Canada over the legal definition of the waters that comprise the Northwest Passage (no one disputes the sovereign rights of Canada over the islands of the Canadian Archipelago). Thus, one of the significant legacies of *Manhattan*'s operations in the Arctic is a geopolitical outcome full of policy implications regarding how to protect the arctic marine environment while exercising the sovereign rights of an arctic coastal state. These issues are still being sorted out, for example, by application of the articles of the United Nations Convention on the Law of the Sea and ongoing development of a mandatory Polar Code of navigation at the International Maritime Organization in London.

This book is full of anecdotes and stories about the operational aspects of *Manhattan* in ice-covered waters. One did catch my attention: it is reported that *Manhattan* was ramming at fifteen knots into a massive wall of ice—I suspect most mariners with icebreaker experience would cringe at this technique! The variability of sea ice conditions (hourly, daily, weekly, seasonally, and annually) in the Canadian Arctic, and the vagaries of icebreaking alluded to in the narrative, are very real and are well presented. Perhaps not so remarkable, the Arctic Ocean remains a complex place to operate ships despite the extraordinary changes in arctic sea ice observed during the past forty years. Most of the operational challenges the *Manhattan* faced have not disappeared, and the Arctic Ocean as an operating theater remains as unforgiving as ever.

It is important that this new volume about such a key event in arctic maritime history has been published early in the twenty-first century. Ross Coen has done a great service researching the background of the tanker *Manhattan* and its forays into the Arctic. It is a highly relevant story today as the emerging uses of the Arctic Ocean gain prominence in arctic and global affairs. Enjoy the voyage!

Lawson W. Brigham, PhD
Distinguished Professor of Geography and Arctic Policy,
University of Alaska Fairbanks
Captain, U.S. Coast Guard (Retired) and Commanding Officer,
USCGC *Polar Sea* (1993–1995)
September 2011

Acknowledgments

This book could not have been written without the contributions of many people. First, I would like to express my deepest thanks to Terrence Cole, Mary Ehrlander, and James Gladden, all of whom provided invaluable direction from start to finish and guided this project into areas I otherwise would have failed to consider. Their mentorship is greatly appreciated. I also thank Judith Kleinfeld, director of Northern Studies at the University of Alaska Fairbanks, for her inestimable support. Others at the University of Alaska who assisted with this project are Rick Caulfield, John Heaton, Mary Mangusso, Gerald McBeath, Julia Parzick, Terry Reilly, and Jonathan Rosenberg.

Those who graciously consented to interviews or provided feedback on the manuscript as it evolved include Charles Baker, John Bockstoce, Lawson Brigham, Ted Catton, Sharon Cissna, Richard Fineberg, Hugh Gorman, William Gray, John Havelock, Walter Hickel, Jack Hicks, Virgil Keith, Tom Kelly, Joe LaRocca, Dan Lawn, Mike McCloskey, Dan O'Neill, Jack Roderick, William Smith, Mead Treadwell, and Richard Voelker. Special mention goes to Merritt Helfferich and Ed Clarke, who sailed on the *Manhattan*, and Mike Dorsey, who served on the *Northwind*. The able-bodied seamen proved more than generous in talking about the subject at length and also in providing me with photographs and copies of their personal scrapbooks of the expedition.

Special thanks to Joan Braddock and the outstanding staff at the University of Alaska Press, and to Shelagh Grant and Ken Coates, who reviewed the manuscript. Excerpts of the text were previously published in *Oil-Industry History*, the journal of the Petroleum History Institute. I would like to thank the journal's editor, Bill Brice of the University of Pittsburgh at Johnstown. For providing me with the opportunity to present papers on this topic I thank the Alaska Historical Society, especially Jo Antonson, Jim Ducker, Katie Oliver, and Katie Ringsmuth; Jonathan Anzalone and the American Society for Environmental History; Mary Barrett and the Petroleum History Institute; as well as the moderators, commentators, and attendees at those conferences for their questions and comments. A huge thank you to Krista Wright and BJ Kirschhoffer at Polar Bears International for opening to me the extensive archive of photographs taken by the late Dan Guravich. Thanks also to Rick Britton, who drew the map of the Northwest Passage that appears in the book. For authorizing the reproduction of copyrighted materials I thank Jim Calvesbert, Earle Gray, Dan Seckers at Exxon Mobil Corporation, Maxine Trost at the Lawrence Livermore National Laboratory, Rob Doolittle at General Dynamics, Bill Whitelaw at *Oilweek* magazine, Katherine Hertel-Baker and Marilyn Knapp at the Anchorage Museum at Rasmuson Center, and Sharon Palmisano, Lynn Hallquist, and Rochelle Welch at the *Anchorage Daily News*.

Any historian conducting library and archival research depends on assistance from many people, and I am no exception. For this I thank Bridget Burke, Anne Foster, Rose Speranza, Caroline Atuk-Derrick, and Deb Knutson at the Rasmuson Library, University of Alaska Fairbanks; Paul Johnston at the Smithsonian National Museum of American History; Robert Shindle at the Steamship Historical Society of America; Heather Long and Maureen Boulianne at the Transport Canada Library in Ottawa; Scott Price of the U.S. Coast Guard; Matthew Darby at the Center for American History, University of Texas; Theresa Salazar at the Bancroft Library, University of California, Berkeley; Marjorie McNinch at the Hagley Museum and Library in Wilmington, Delaware; Linda Robinson and Walter Parker of the Prince William Sound Regional Citizens' Advisory Council; Suzzallo & Allen Libraries, University of Washington; Lisa Rosenthal and Dave Goff at the International Organization of Masters, Mates & Pilots; Katie Breen and Derek Mueller; Barb Hameister at the Center for Global Change; Alison York and Wendy Warnick at the Arctic Research Consortium of the United States; University of Alaska Fairbanks Graduate School; University of Alaska Foundation; the family of James Cook; and Association of Canadian Universities for Northern Studies.

Finally, there is the Bauer family. My thanks to them requires a bit of explanation. One winter evening several years ago, while entering the Gruening building on the campus of the University of Alaska Fairbanks, I passed an individual wearing a dark blue parka. The official *Manhattan* insignia on the left breast first caught my eye. I stopped short upon noticing the name "S.B. Haas" embroidered above the patch, then instinctively reached out and asked, "Where did you get that coat?!?" Eric Bauer could have been forgiven for running away from this breathless stranger, but he explained that the coat belonged to his grandfather, Stanley B. Haas, who happened to be the Humble Oil executive in charge of the *Manhattan* expedition. Serendipity is the only word that appropriately describes my bumping into the grandson of the very man whose career I was researching at that moment. Eric stated that his grandfather had passed away some years before, which I knew, and that he'd left two steel trunks filled with all manner of *Manhattan* papers and paraphernalia in a garage in Florida, which I most certainly did not. Charla Bauer, Haas's daughter and Eric's mother, and her husband, Delane, keep his personal papers at their home in Floral City, Florida, and with their permission I viewed the entire collection in March 2004. It is no exaggeration to say that the breadth and depth of this project was expanded immeasurably by this fortuitous discovery. I wish to express my deepest thanks to Charla, Delane, and Eric Bauer. I only hope that the process of discovery was as thrilling for them as it was for me. And I would be remiss to move on without thanking Stan Haas himself, a man I never had the privilege to meet but nonetheless feel that I know, having absorbed the material legacy of this project that meant so much to him. I gathered from his personal collection of papers, especially handwritten notes and letters, that he one day intended to write a book about the *Manhattan*. That he never did is unfortunate, but I hope this book goes some distance to filling that void.

Ross A. Coen
July 5, 2011

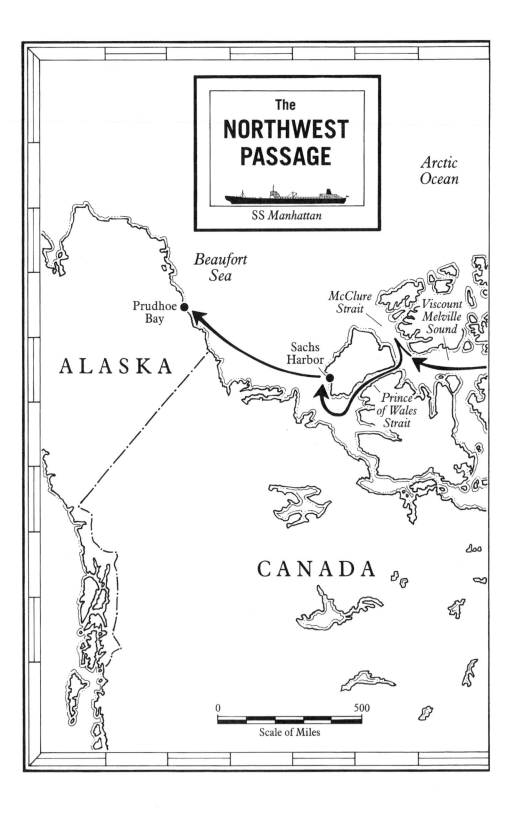

The
NORTHWEST PASSAGE

SS *Manhattan*

Arctic Ocean

Beaufort Sea

Prudhoe Bay

McClure Strait

Viscount Melville Sound

Sachs Harbor

ALASKA

Prince of Wales Strait

CANADA

0   500

Scale of Miles

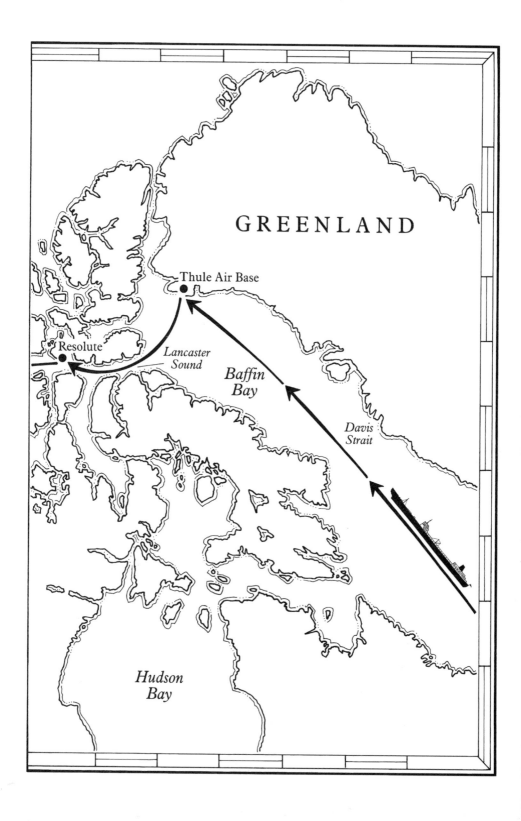

GREENLAND

Thule Air Base

Resolute

Lancaster
Sound

Baffin
Bay

Davis
Strait

Hudson
Bay

Introduction

The first barrels of crude oil lifted from the Prudhoe Bay field on Alaska's North Slope entered the Trans-Alaska Pipeline in June 1977, and spent the next five and a half weeks on an eight-hundred-mile journey to the south. Destined for Port Valdez, an ice-free deep-water harbor capable of accommodating tankers ready to ferry the crude farther south to refineries in Washington and California, the oil followed the meandering twists and turns of the pipeline over three mountain ranges and across hundreds of streams and rivers. Those first barrels represented the vanguard of billions more, discovered nearly a decade earlier, a true bonanza waiting deep beneath the ground. The line's operators kept this initial flow at a glacial pace, their restraint designed to slowly ease the complex system into full operation. By the end of July, the inaugural flow of crude emptied into holding tanks at the terminus of the line.[1]

A few days later, an intricate series of feeder lines, valves, and loading arms completed the transfer of some 824,000 of Prudhoe Bay's first barrels into the ARCO *Juneau*, a glistening, brand-new tanker designed and constructed specifically for the Alaska trade. The coming months and years would witness a steady parade of tankers at Valdez—the Sohio *Intrepid*, Mobil *Arctic*, Overseas *Alaska*, and countless others—with thousands of separate loadings totaling billions of barrels of crude oil. The presence of these mammoth vessels would eventually become so routine as to merit barely a passing glance from locals across the harbor. The novelty was at its peak that summer, however, and curious onlookers marveled at the continuous line of gleaming tankers in the *Juneau*'s wake. The local newspaper printed their names and kept track of each arrival, loading, and departure.

But not every vessel in the harbor shone so brightly. Those in Valdez who lifted their eyes to the loading docks in mid-October saw a tanker quite unlike the *Juneau* and her sleek contemporaries.[2] This tanker did not shine at all; rather, a coating of rust covered her every external surface. Large flecks of white paint peeled from the deckhouse. Remnants of mismatched pipe and hose were stacked here and there on the deck. While modern tankers such as the *Juneau* featured automated, computer-controlled oil-loading systems, this vessel had to be loaded by manually operated deck valves so imprecisely calibrated that spillage from overfilling the tanks was almost a given. Anyone able to step inside one of her cabins would have discovered pails on the floor, kept there to catch rainwater that leaked from the deck. Though only fifteen years old, this vessel was clearly past her prime—if, in fact, she'd ever had one at all. Compared to the ultramodern tankers of the trade, one observer thought she resembled "a great lady fallen on bad times."[3] The state's lead environmental regulator boarded the vessel and expressed bewilderment at how her owners had "really let her go."[4] The tanker wouldn't have been in Valdez at all—she had been sitting for the last year and a half in dead storage in New Jersey—except that a temporary lack of available tonnage in the Alaska shipping fleet made her employment necessary. A two-week refitting operation in Japan got the vessel seaworthy again, but even the fresh coat of gray paint on the deck piping was already peeling and couldn't mask the toll wrought by years of service in the pounding seas and salty air.[5]

She was the SS *Manhattan*, at the time of her 1962 christening the largest merchant vessel in the American fleet. To a world not yet familiar with supertankers, the *Manhattan*'s sheer bulk left mouths agape. Longer than three football fields and weighing over 105,000 deadweight tons, the tanker claimed a spot in the first edition of the *Guinness Book of World Records* as the largest ship in the history of the world. Newsmen marveled at the fact that the behemoth, which drew forty-nine feet when fully loaded, couldn't even dock in the harbor of her namesake. On her maiden voyage to New York, the vessel had to anchor well offshore at sufficient water depth and allow smaller barges to ferry her cargo bit by bit into the city.[6] The *Manhattan* set more records in her first few years of operation. In spring 1963, she carried 105,000 tons of grain, her full cargo capacity and the largest quantity of wheat ever loaded onto a single vessel. That same year she transported Persian Gulf crude oil to Fawley, England, along the way becoming the largest ship ever to transit the Suez Canal.[7]

The grandeur of the impressive vessel, however, belied the sad fact that from the very day of her launching the *Manhattan* was a white elephant. Greek shipping magnate Stavros Niarchos built the tanker as little more than a gimmick and a tax write-off. At the time, Niarchos held six T-2 tankers under American registry, which he hoped to withdraw and sail under foreign flags with more favorable tax structures. But U.S. shipping regulations required him to replace the cargo capacity of the withdrawn tankers with new vessels of equal tonnage. Reasoning that it would be cheaper to build one enormous tanker than another six smaller ones, Niarchos contracted with the Bethlehem Steel Company of Quincy, Massachusetts, to build a tanker like no other in the world. The shipyard responded with a 940-foot leviathan costing an exorbitant $28 million.[8]

Even before the *Manhattan* first tasted the salt of the ocean shipping analysts predicted the vessel would be too costly to operate at a profit. Robert T. Jones, president of the Niarchos subsidiary that owned the ship, admitted her future prospects were bleak. Quite simply, the *Manhattan* was a supertanker built before anyone knew how to build supertankers. Shipbuilding is an exact science that demands precise calculations of strength and power balanced against the costs of operation. A tanker's hull must be packed with enough steel to withstand the pounding of the sea but not so much that it weighs down the vessel and becomes a drag on the engines. The line between too much steel and too little is remarkably fine, and with little practical experience to draw upon Bethlehem Steel's naval architects and engineers made the mistake of overbuilding the *Manhattan*. She featured two-inch steel plates on her hull (a modern tanker's hull is half as thick) and a remarkable forty-five separate cargo tanks, each braced by a redundant network of bulkheads and steel beams. What the *Manhattan* gained in strength and sturdiness she lost in the incredible expense of fuel and manpower to keep her afloat. The tanker's turbines required an astounding half ton of fuel to power the vessel exactly one mile. Her non-automated systems necessitated a crew of at least fifty men, all drawing the usual high wages and overtime pay. The best the *Manhattan*'s owner could hope for was simply to break even.[9]

Less than a year after Niarchos took delivery of the *Manhattan*, he sold her to Seatrain Lines for $265,000—not even one-hundredth of the cost to build her—and earned himself an extraordinary tax write-off. The tanker settled into a workmanlike routine, alternately hauling grain to Asia, Middle East oil back to the U.S., or simply sitting in dry dock when her owners couldn't find anyone desperate enough to pay her charter costs. In 1973, she sailed to Bangladesh and was promptly anchored as a floating grain silo during famine-relief efforts. When the aged vessel lumbered into Port Valdez in October 1977, the arrival marked yet another chapter in her legacy as the white elephant of the seas, called into service out of equal parts necessity and desperation. She hauled a few loads of Alaska crude oil that year, followed by the odd shipment of grain in foreign ports. She once crushed a dock in the Mediterranean when an inexperienced captain misjudged her size. The *Manhattan* soon found herself back in dry dock and before long disappeared from the seas altogether.[10]

The story of the *Manhattan* begins and ends with such ignominy—but one middle chapter of her life worked to secure her place in history. The setting was again Alaska.

Two days after Christmas 1967, a drilling crew on the desolate North Slope, at the very top of the North American continent, tapped into an oil and gas reservoir of mammoth proportions. Prudhoe Bay contained untold quantities of crude oil. The first conservative estimate said five billion barrels. Later guesses pegged the figure at twenty billion. Before long, the contagious optimism ran unimpeded by either facts or logic, and people who should have known better let their imaginations run wild—forty billion, fifty billion, perhaps one hundred billion barrels of crude oil! In those heady days following the strike—well before the pipeline, the *Juneau*, or even the *Manhattan* herself called on Port Valdez—three of the world's largest oil companies sat atop the Prudhoe Bay oil field and began devising some transportation method to bring those vast reserves to market. Everyone first thought of a pipeline. One company, however, Humble Oil and Refining, looked at a map of the Arctic and envisioned a different method altogether. Humble knew that shipping oil by tanker was nearly always more cost effective than by pipeline, and even a cursory glance at Alaska's position atop the Earth revealed circumpolar marine shortcuts between North America, Asia, and Europe. First conceived as a trade route to the Orient for silks and spices, the Northwest Passage now held promise for Alaska crude. The prospect of an all-marine tanker route from Prudhoe Bay to the East Coast of the United States proved immediately tantalizing to Humble.

The irony of the Northwest Passage, of course, was that despite being the shortest line on a map the route itself coursed deep within the Arctic, where massive sheets of ice blocked every channel and choked every strait. In order to determine whether oil could be shipped across circumpolar waters. Humble required a test vessel to smash through the ice and collect scientific data along the way. The assignment called for something much stronger and more powerful than any conventional tanker. Without the luxury of time to design and build a custom-made vessel from the keel up, the company was forced to choose the best candidate from available tankers in the U.S. fleet, one with an already-sturdy frame that could accommodate additional layers of steel. In short, Humble required the largest tanker it could find to be converted into an icebreaker.

Thus the *Manhattan*, for one glorious shipping season at least, would be a white elephant no more. The very characteristics that made her so costly to operate on the open sea—her immense size, weight, and overbuilt hull—made her the ideal candidate for the Humble experiment. A transit of the Northwest Passage would certainly encounter heavy ice, including floes and pressure ridges dozens of feet thick, and the *Manhattan*, once bulked up even further with an icebreaking bow and reinforced hull, was almost certainly the only ship in the world that might successfully smash a pathway through to Prudhoe Bay.

The tanker sailed in August 1969 from Chester, Pennsylvania, to the heart of the North American Arctic. World attention turned to the vessel, fed by a retinue of journalists who, despite the inordinate challenge of filing stories from the isolated Arctic, documented every mile of the voyage. Dozens of men volunteered for the privilege of serving on her crew, and no fewer than three captains walked her bridge. The huge tanker smashed through enormous ice floes no ship in history had ever bested. In the romantic language of the sea, her historic voyage had been five centuries in the making. This was no wooden ship of stouthearted men fighting off scurvy, starvation, and death, yet the *Manhattan* would still achieve the holy grail of polar exploration, a prize that for centuries had eluded the best of mariners—including Franklin, Frobisher, and Hudson. On September 15, 1969, just seven weeks after a human being first set foot on the moon, the *Manhattan* closed another chapter in the annals of exploration when she became the first commercial vessel to complete a transit of the Northwest Passage.

Our understanding of history is continually framed by the cataloguing and examination of past events, yet that study may be enriched as much by analyzing those events that did *not* happen. As historian Roxanne Willis writes in her study of Rampart Dam, a proposed hydroelectric project in interior Alaska that was never built, "[T]hings that never happen move history along in profound ways. Nonevents may not shape the way a landscape looks, but they inevitably shape the ways in which a landscape is imagined."[11] That the *Manhattan* successfully transited the passage but failed to establish a regular tanker transportation system in the Arctic— Humble abandoned the project in October 1970—need not automatically relegate the event to an isolated episode whose connection to the overall context of Alaska oil development is lost.

Alaska occupies a unique place in the American imagination. Popular conceptions of the "Last Frontier" are based in part on the extreme environment and hardy pioneers who, with equal parts determination and sweat, built a society in the wilderness. It is the mythology of Alaskan exceptionalism. Correspondingly, the history of oil development is often presented as a heroic tale. Wildcatting for crude oil, according to this particular frontier mythology, requires bold action on the part of even bolder men operating in (and thus subduing) one of the most challenging environments on the planet. A representative example is the legendary tale of Bill Bishop, geologist for Richfield Oil Company, leading a convoy of bulldozers into the Swanson River area in late 1956, digging his boot heel into the ground, and saying, "Drill here."[12] The discovery that followed was the largest in Alaska to date, some 250 million barrels of crude oil. Bishop's boots were later bronzed and are now on display at the Anchorage Museum at Rasmuson Center. Swanson River not only propelled Alaska into the realm of major oil-producing states but also ignited an exploration frenzy that a decade later would result in the Prudhoe Bay strike. That discovery also conforms to the heroic myth in many ways. Nearly every written account emphasizes the Arctic's harsh climate that challenges (but rarely, if ever, defeats) the oil industry's inestimable technological capabilities. Historian Peter Coates has noted that many Alaskans who participated in the Trans-Alaska Pipeline debates of the late 1960s and early 1970s used sweeping historical analogies to place North Slope oil development in the same category as the Transcontinental Railroad, Hoover Dam, Alaska Highway, and other industrial megaprojects of earlier eras that transcended mere functionality and brought about widespread societal change.[13] In this context the discovery and production of oil in Alaska almost assumes an aura of inevitability.

The history of oil, however, in Alaska and elsewhere, is more often than not marked by frustration, false starts, and failure. For every Swanson River and Prudhoe Bay, there are dozens of dry holes dotting the landscape. For every Bill Bishop and his bronzed boots, there are countless men (wildcatters are almost without exception men) who toiled in the country for years without finding so much as a surface seep of crude. For every Trans-Alaska Pipeline, which in its first three decades of operation delivered fifteen billion barrels of oil to market, there is an SS *Manhattan* that today is largely forgotten. Contrary to the above-mentioned myth, an oil strike requires more than simply oil in the ground, men with a daring spirit, and state-of-the-art machines at their disposal. A more useful historical paradigm might be social constructivism, as the phases of oil development—exploration, discovery, production, and transportation—always occur within a particular set of political, social, economic, and historical circumstances whose cumulative influence equals if not exceeds the mere physical nature of the operation.[14]

This is a book about the SS *Manhattan*, the frontier mythology that so conveniently framed its voyage through the Northwest Passage, and the ship's place within the historical context of industrial development in the North American Arctic. Non-events such as the *Manhattan* provide an important perspective. Inasmuch as we can understand the evolution of Alaska as an oil state, and resource development in the circumpolar regions more generally, the history of development schemes that did not pan out may prove as instructive as those that did.

From the perspective of environmental history, landscapes shape both our interactions with and attitudes toward the natural world in many ways. In the case of the *Manhattan*, the constant presence of ice in the Northwest Passage served as the dominant theme that informed the approach to development taken by the oil industry. The specific details of that approach—in this case, icebreaking tankers—then framed the disparate views of the expedition as a romantic conquest of nature, the triumph of human ingenuity in the form of science and technology, and an unwarranted intrusion of humankind into wilderness. On both a literal and metaphorical level, the point of contact between the ship's icebreaking bow and the ice floes of the Northwest Passage is the very point from which this history needs to be told. (Today, climate change and the thinning ice pack in the Arctic are resulting in a different interface between industry and environment—and therefore a very different story.) Three specific historical contexts receive attention in this book: the function of science and technology at the forefront of human-environment relationships, the corresponding debates over environmental protection and sovereignty of the Northwest Passage, and how the *Manhattan* figured as a stratagem within the intensely competitive oil industry—one company's development proposal in contradistinction to those of its rivals—and therefore helped to guide Alaska's evolution as an oil state.

The oil industry's general approach to resource development in the Arctic, whether by pipeline or icebreaking tanker or some other inventive transportation option, depended heavily on science and technology. Humble initiated its *Manhattan* experiment with a view of the natural environment as a series of engineering problems, the linear solving of which would comprise a general solution to the overall challenge of industrial development in the Arctic. (Put another way, the industry quickly discovered that producing oil in Alaska presented a whole new set of challenges that Oklahoma and Texas did not.) Measuring the costs of this technological assault against the expected economic return from development of the resource resulted in the commodification of the natural environment, or the assigning of dollar values to resources (usually to the exclusion of other values). With science and technology at the forefront of Humble's interaction with the Arctic, the company largely sidestepped the broader range of social concerns such as the geopolitical and environmental impacts of arctic resource development. It would be left to others—government officials in Ottawa, social scientists at the University of Alaska, even newspaper cartoonists—to take up those questions.

Historian of technology Leo Marx has noted the general public's fascination with machines and its tendency to view them as the primary drivers of social change. This is the type of history regularly taught to schoolchildren. Whitney invents the cotton gin, or Bell the telephone, or Edison the lightbulb, and voilà—the inventor's stroke of genius sets off a lasting transformation of society itself. The steam locomotive, to cite another example, is a powerful image that represents the opening of the western U.S. frontier in the latter half of the nineteenth century. But, Marx is quick to argue, the machine itself is but one part of what he calls a sociotechnological system. In addition to the locomotive, the operation of railroads required ancillary equipment (e.g., rails, bridges, tunnels), corporate entities with huge amounts of capital, specialized technical knowledge, a trained workforce, standardized operating procedures, national and local governments, and so on. Understanding the true historical context of railroads, therefore, requires an analysis of, among other topics, labor trends, political regimes, the development (often on the fly) of government regulation, and the inestimable contributions not of the lone genius inventor hunched over in his laboratory but of factory workers, politicians, passengers, children, immigrants, bureaucrats, military officials, homesteaders, Native Americans, and countless other groups that participated in the full development of the system. In calling technology a "hazardous concept" and cautioning against an overemphasis on the role of machines, Marx writes, "To attribute specific events or social developments to the historical agency of [technology] makes lit-tle or no sense. Technology, as such, makes nothing happen."[15] To return to the SS *Manhattan*, every machine the oil industry deployed in the pursuit of Alaska oil must be studied as part of such broad sociotechnological systems. It's true that only a machine as technologically advanced as the *Manhattan* could have accomplished the feat in that manner—but the machine had help from many other actors worth noting.

Among the social issues trailing in the *Manhattan*'s wake, perhaps none were felt so acutely as those in Canada, where questions of sovereignty and environmental protection stirred passions. For many Canadians, the icebound, sparsely popu-lated region played a not-insignificant role in their very national identity as an arctic state. They were therefore troubled by the prospect of American-flagged tankers sail-ing between two U.S. ports carrying environmentally hazardous cargo through what they believed were their sovereign waters. At the time of the *Manhattan*'s voyage, Canada's only real claims to sovereignty rested on untested legal arguments made decades before and recently passed domestic fishing legislation. Neither Humble Oil nor the U.S. State Department formally requested permission from Canada to make the transit of the Northwest Passage—to do so would be an implicit acknowledgment of Canadian claims. By the same token, the Canadian government did not ask but rather informed Humble it would be sending its own icebreaking ship, the *John A. MacDonald*, to escort the tanker. In the months leading up to the expedition, Prime Minister Pierre Trudeau and External Affairs Secretary Mitchell Sharp explored options for defining the passage as territorial waters, an international legal designa-tion that would empower Canada to regulate its use. In April 1970, Parliament unani-mously passed the Arctic Waters Pollution Prevention Act, signaling to the world that Canada would safeguard the environment on behalf of the world's nations. "Canada regards herself as responsible to all mankind for the peculiar ecological balance that now exists so precariously in the water, ice, and land areas of the Arctic Archipelago," explained Trudeau.[16] A companion piece of legislation, the Territorial Sea and Fish-ing Zones Act, brought the waters of the arctic passage under Canadian jurisdiction. The acts represented an innovative approach whereby Ottawa avoided declarations of outright sovereignty, which would have placed the debate in international forums and resulted in strong resistance from the United States, and instead asserted functional sovereignty by means of environmental stewardship alone. Whatever diplomatic hos-tilities may have existed between Canada and the United States did not extend to the crews of the *Manhattan* and the *John A. MacDonald*, who unfailingly supported one other. Theirs was a single expedition, not two that happened to be operating at the same time and in the same geographic space.

Since the days of John D. Rockefeller, the oil industry has been one of the most secretive and cutthroat in the world. Every company's action represents a chess move of sorts in an intensely competitive game where multiple players struggle for control of a finite resource. Because Prudhoe Bay was held by three of the largest oil companies in the world, none of which possessed absolute control of the field, its development would be the result of uneasy and ever-shifting alliances between entities that both required and resented the others' presence. The voyage of the *Manhattan* may have doubled as a stratagem by Humble to control the pace and form of Prudhoe Bay development, allowing the industry giant to disadvantage, if not outright stymie, its rival companies, who had their own transportation plans in mind. The industry consortium formed to design and construct an Alaska pipeline—first called TAPS (Trans-Alaska Pipeline System) and later renamed Alyeska Pipeline Service Company—depended on its parent companies for both personnel and operating funds. Humble, a stable company with diversified sources of crude all over the world, did not require immediate delivery of its Prudhoe Bay share. Humble executives admitted they felt no sense of urgency when it came to Alaska oil. In practical terms, every dollar the company spent on the *Manhattan* test (or the study of any other transportation alternative, for that matter) was a dollar it could essentially withhold from TAPS, thereby frustrating the plans of British Petroleum and ARCO, its main Prudhoe partners/rivals. Or so goes the theory, which, like the underlying rationale of every action within the oil industry, is notoriously difficult to pin down.

A new player in the chess match was the State of Alaska. Having obtained statehood just a decade before, Alaskans were novices at not just resource policy but policy in general. The Prudhoe Bay discovery guaranteed a financial windfall to the state's three hundred thousand residents, but the need to establish taxation and regulatory regimes to protect the state's interest put state officials at the low end of a very steep learning curve. By the fall of 1969, the State of Alaska had held its Prudhoe Bay lease sale, which brought $900 million to state coffers in a single day, and was planning for the eight-hundred-mile pipeline everyone expected to be constructed shortly. State officials duly visited the *Manhattan* when the tanker arrived in Alaska waters, knowing her expedition was part of the dialogue between the companies and would somehow affect the eventual development of Prudhoe Bay. Although the Alaskans' extensive experience in northern engineering and development told them icebreaking tankers in the Arctic were not likely to be practical, the officials nonetheless welcomed Humble's attention and investment. This was a place, after all, with a long history of big dreamers and even bigger development schemes, and Alaskans wanted to be ready for anything.

For eleven weeks in the autumn of 1969, the *Manhattan* achieved a measure of glory unique in the annals of polar exploration. One could cite her triumphant arrival at Prudhoe Bay as the pinnacle of her life on the seas—or perhaps the subsequent homecoming to her namesake city where she proudly displayed rusty abrasions and wide swaths of scraped paint, the history of the voyage written on her hull. Then again, one could imagine her crowning moment of glory was the northbound journey itself just in advance of her rendezvous with the ice of the Northwest Passage, a time when expectation hung in the air and all who witnessed her knew this was the ship destined to make history. It was on that outbound voyage to the Arctic when Merritt Helfferich, a scientist from the University of Alaska who joined the crew for the better part of two months, met the tanker in Halifax:

> I knew that I would be boarding a big ship but I had no idea just how big a near quarter-mile of ship looked. She lay at anchor on the far side of Halifax Harbor and seemed to fill the horizon. Ten stories above the waterline officers on the flying bridge looked like dwarfs. The long sloping bow and the great black length overwhelmed me, and any earlier doubts about her ability disappeared. I was...staggered by the size of the ship above me.[17]

Helfferich would not be the last to be astounded by the SS *Manhattan*.

Strike at Prudhoe Bay State No. 1

The Arctic is probably the most misunderstood place on earth. It is even more mysterious than the moon.

—Walter J. Hickel[1]

During his second overland expedition in the summer of 1826, Sir John Franklin and his crew sailed two mahogany boats west along the arctic coast of what was then still Russian America. Ice floes tossed about by strong winds hampered the crew's progress, and at one point a thick summer fog forced the expedition ashore for over a week to a "detestable" locale Franklin appropriately named Foggy Island. On the morning of August 16, the weather broke for a few hours and the men lowered the sails and hurriedly paddled west. The boats soon skirted a shallow bay roughly twelve square miles in area, though, as Franklin noted in his log, the closing weather did not permit them time to explore further:

> The fog returned, and the wind freshening, soon created such a swell upon the flats, that it became necessary to haul further from the land; but the drift ice beginning to close around us, we could no longer proceed with safety, and, therefore, endeavored to find a landing-place.[2]

Just before leaving to find a secure anchorage elsewhere, Franklin named the small bay for an old friend and fellow British naval officer, Captain Algernon Percy, Baron of Prudhoe, later the Fourth Duke of Northumberland.[3] Though barely a footnote in the annals of nineteenth-century exploration, this inauspicious locale called Prudhoe Bay would a century and a half later beckon the largest icebreaker in the world through the very passage Franklin had sought in vain.

Within a decade of Franklin's expedition, Hudson's Bay Company traders discovered surface seeps of oil in the Canadian Arctic. The indigenous peoples, they learned, gathered the crude or cut away chunks of the oil-soaked tundra, which they burned for cooking and heating. Military and whaling expeditions in Alaska in the latter half of the nineteenth century also discovered surface pools of crude oil on both the coast and inland river valleys.[4] While hunting with a friend near Cape Simpson in 1886, Charles Brower, the first white man to live with the Inupiaq on Alaska's North Slope, also discovered lakes of oil: "No sooner had we reached the top of the rise than a small lake spread out before us, its water curiously dark and ranging from a liquid center to an asphalt-like substance around the edge."[5] Geologist and cartographer Ernest de Koven Leffingwell explored the eastern North Slope from 1906 to 1914—his expedition, ironically enough, partly funded by John D. Rockefeller, founder of Standard Oil. In a groundbreaking report on the Canning River region that would be cited by geologists for decades afterward, Leffingwell noted the location of surface petroleum seeps and widespread evidence of subsurface oil formations. Quantities of oil clearly lay beneath the North Slope tundra; whether such reserves would prove recoverable and economically viable were questions compounded by the region's inaccessibility and hostile climate. As Leffingwell presciently put it in 1919: "Even if an oil pool were found in this northern region, there is serious doubt as to its availability under present conditions…though it might be regarded a part of the ultimate oil reserves that would someday be developed."[6]

In February 1923, President Warren G. Harding withdrew by executive order some twenty-three million acres on the North Slope and established the parcel as an oil reserve. The Naval Petroleum Reserve No. 4 (or Pet-4, as it came to be known) encompassed an area larger than many states and was to be appraised for its potential as a fuel source for the U.S. Navy, which was then converting its ships from coal-fired engines to oil. At the behest of the navy, the U.S. Geological Survey (USGS) immediately undertook a five-year survey to map the geology and topography of the region and to perform chemical analyses of samples from the many surface pools. In its very first field report the project team also delved into what it called the "broader economic principles" of potential oil development. USGS personnel did so not from any degree of expertise in that area but only because they recognized how easy it would be for an engineer or businessman in a comfortable office far from the Arctic to completely misjudge the region and its many challenging features. According to the USGS:

> The region is most assuredly not one where anybody can get rich quick in oil without enormous expenditures of capital for development, and no one should risk funds whose loss will seriously embarrass him, because development of oil in this region is distinctly a wildcat undertaking of the most speculative charac-

ter, and at the same time the development can be successful only if undertaken on a large scale.[7]

The USGS effort confirmed the potential of significant oil and gas deposits on the North Slope and further recommended an exploratory drilling program be conducted at the most promising locations. Such a program began in 1944, by which time the navy was not alone in its interest in the Arctic. That same year, Wallace Pratt, a pioneering petroleum geologist who had been influenced and encouraged by the initial USGS field studies, penned an article in which he confidently predicted a future for the Arctic as an oil-producing region: "One of the most impressive manifestations of petroleum in the Western Hemisphere is situated near Cape Simpson, east of Point Barrow, on the Arctic coast of northernmost Alaska.... Geologically [the region is] ideal for important accumulations of petroleum."[8] Widely regarded as a visionary within the industry, Pratt steadfastly maintained that the harsh arctic climate need not be an impediment to development in the area. The navy's nine-year exploration program in Pet-4, however, did not immediately vindicate Pratt's optimism. The USGS, again operating on behalf of the navy, drilled dozens of wells and analyzed hundreds of core samples, which added significantly to the geological understanding of permafrost and the Arctic. Yet despite the discovery of deposits of both crude oil and natural gas, the difficult climatic and environmental conditions of the region dampened enthusiasm for production of these modest finds.[9]

Industry attention still remained focused on the northernmost reaches of Alaska. Peter Cox, the head of exploration for British Petroleum (BP), believed that the topography of the North Slope so closely resembled that of Iran that the region simply had to contain crude oil. BP geologist Peter Kent described the North Slope in terms identical to those used by Wallace Pratt: "Alaska is probably the world's last major oil province available for exploration."[10] BP's interest in Alaska was based on a desire to establish operations in politically stable regions of the world. The company's turbulent experiences in the Middle East in the 1950s, in particular the Suez Canal crisis, convinced executives in BP's London headquarters of the need to diversify its crude supplies internationally. Cox successfully sold the Alaska program to the company's board with a classic argument—the advantages of being first. "Unless our entry into [Alaska] is secured at this relatively early stage in the country's exploration," he wrote, "the cost of entry later will be high if commercial production on a substantial scale proves feasible within the next ten years."[11]

BP obtained its entry by joining forces in 1958 with Sinclair Oil, an independent company already with Alaska holdings in Cook Inlet. Two years later, the partnership secured two hundred thousand acres of North Slope leases located primarily in the foothills of the Brooks Range. The true prize, BP and Sinclair believed, lay on the coastal plain farther to the north. At a December 1964 lease sale where the State of Alaska put up this coastal acreage for competitive bid, the BP–Sinclair partnership acquired large tracts of an area identified by company geologists as an arch adjacent to the Colville crest. The exploratory drilling program that followed had to be initiated in the winter as the spongy summertime tundra could not support heavy equipment or vehicle travel without turning into a muddy bog. The subzero temperatures and gale-force winds left no doubt as to the incredible difficulties any oil development in the Arctic would face. A company history of BP described the steep learning curve posed by an arctic winter: "Metal became brittle and snapped, lubricants solidified, drilling mud froze and simple matters, like having to wear mittens, hampered straightforward operations like tightening and loosening bolts."[12]

That these redoubtable efforts produced only six dry wells in the Brooks Range foothills region proved even more discouraging. A seventh well, this one farther north on the newly acquired Colville crest, also came up dry. Sinclair had had enough and withdrew from Alaska. BP was left to bid alone on acreage at another lease sale in the summer of 1965. The company secured some eighty thousand acres in the Prudhoe Bay structure at an average cost of $17.80 per acre. After seven dry holes, however, BP was content to sit on its leases and let another company try its luck on the North Slope.

RICHFIELD

Two small, otherwise unremarkable petroleum companies based in Los Angeles consolidated their interests in 1911. The three owners of the Kellogg Oil Company agreed to jointly finance a corporate partnership with the three owners of the Los Angeles Oil Company. The men constructed a small refining plant next to a railway depot known as the Richfield Station, and the Richfield Oil Company was born. Over the next few decades the company would negotiate a series of mergers and acquisitions, and diversify its operations to include every aspect of the oil business, including exploration, refining, and marketing. By the 1950s, the small independent company had grown into the Richfield Oil Corporation. Despite its still relatively small size, Richfield used an aggressive exploratory program to compete with the industry giants.[13]

If a corporation tends to take on the collective personality of the people leading it, then much of Richfield's aggressive style can be traced to its president, Charles S. Jones, and its head of exploration, Rollin Eckis. The two men witnessed the ever-increasing volatility of international markets and, like BP and other industry competitors, embarked on a strategy to secure new, cheaper supplies of crude. "Convinced of the absolute need to discover more new reserves," Jones wrote in his memoir, "we went north to Alaska."[14] Company geologists ventured to the Kenai Peninsula south of

Anchorage and grabbed a seventy-thousand-acre lease, a small holding compared to the acreage already being explored by major industry players such as Phillips Petroleum, Shell, and Standard Oil of California. A federal government ruling in 1954 had opened the Kenai National Moose Range to oil exploration. Richfield focused on the thickly forested Swanson River area where, in July 1957, the company struck an oil field containing 250 million barrels of crude oil. It was by far the largest oil strike in Alaska to date.

The Swanson River discovery proved an economic boon on several levels. For Alaska, then still a territory inching toward statehood, revenues and royalties from Kenai oil development brought in $300,000 in 1957. Six years later the burgeoning oil industry would pump $84 million into state coffers. Some Alaskans believed the Swanson River strike helped convince Congress the territory could support itself economically and thus tipped the scales in favor of Alaska statehood. The Richfield Oil Corporation, after years of declining revenue, no longer struggled in financial dire straits. Only a few weeks after the Swanson River strike, the company sold half its interest in the Kenai leases to Chevron for $30 million.[15] Emboldened by the influx of capital, Richfield continued to explore for oil in Alaska, this time turning its attention farther north.

Drawing on recently released USGS data from Pet-4, Richfield first sent its survey teams to the foothills of the Brooks Range. By summer 1963, the crews, operating with a fair amount of autonomy from Richfield management, turned their attention to the promising structures on the coastal plain. A memo that summer from Gil Mull and Gar Pessel, two company geologists working the Sagavanirktok River area on the North Slope, conveyed their great optimism to Richfield's Los Angeles headquarters: "We have a good section of excellent reservoir possibilities, and positive proof of the petroliferous nature of these sands. If one cannot get an oil field out of these conditions, I give up!"[16]

Richfield approached the December 1964 North Slope lease sale with four seasons of survey and map work under its belt. The company had great confidence in the region's potential. But the exploratory work had proven expensive—the total outlay for those four seasons of work approached $3 million. And despite the company's Swanson River success, it still lacked the deep pockets to finance a full operation in such a remote area. Richfield first approached Standard Oil of California with an offer of partnership in Alaska. The company declined the offer, much to Charles Jones's surprise. He then sent Rollin Eckis to negotiate a deal with Humble Oil, the Texas-based affiliate of the largest oil company in the world, Standard Oil of New Jersey. Humble had its own history in Alaska, one marked by disappointment and failure. The company had closed its Alaska exploration office four years earlier following the shut-in of a $7 million dry hole. In getting Humble to agree to a jointly financed

North Slope partnership, Richfield's Eckis would have to do more than sell the suitor on the region's potential. He would have to convince the Humble executives to reinvest in a place the company had already abandoned once before—essentially get them to take another bite of a dish they knew to be bitter.

HUMBLE'S BOOM AND BUST

The sequence of events that led to the Humble Oil and Refining Company's entry to Alaska can be traced back to the dissolution of the Standard Oil monopoly in 1911. Citing the monopolistic nature of the company's operations, the U.S. Supreme Court affirmed the antitrust action initiated by the Theodore Roosevelt administration two years earlier and forced the breakup of the company newspaper cartoonists invariably depicted as an aggressive octopus. Of the handful of large companies and dozens of smaller ones carved from John D. Rockefeller's empire, the largest by far was Standard Oil of New Jersey (Jersey). In addition to keeping the famous Standard Oil headquarters at 26 Broadway in Manhattan, the company maintained its extensive (and hugely profitable) network of refineries and retail outlets around the world. If Jersey had any shortcoming at all it was that the company possessed minimal crude reserves of its own and instead depended on numerous smaller companies, including several of its new Standard sisters, for its supply of oil. The situation provided exactly the impetus for Jersey to launch an aggressive pursuit of crude, which it did both by exploration/production and by simply buying up smaller companies that were already producing.[17]

One such company was a small but promising Texas independent called Humble Oil, which faced the opposite problem as Jersey—it had plenty of crude reserves but no means to refine and sell the product. The company had been named for Pleasanton Humble, an Englishman who in the late nineteenth century founded an eponymous town just north of Houston (actually pronounced *umble* with a silent "h"). In 1918, William Stamps Farish, one of Humble's five principal owners, traveled to New York in pursuit of a buyout by a larger company with so-called downstream assets. He soon telegraphed his partners back in Texas about a promising lunch meeting with a man he called "the father of them all."[18] The cryptic message referred to Walter Teagle, the head of Jersey and one of the industry's most powerful executives. Jersey soon bought a controlling interest in Humble for $17 million, making the upstart its largest (and soon to be most profitable) domestic affiliate.

Humble was then producing about 16,500 barrels of oil per day, a number that would steadily climb over the years as a result of continued exploration and capital investment. Among Jersey's many subsidiaries, Humble enjoyed a special degree of autonomy. Independent oil producers in Texas had a long history of open resentment toward the Rockefeller empire, and the Jersey board proved wise enough to keep a low profile and vest nearly all operational control with the Houston-based Humble. The parent company exerted control only by voting its majority shares at the annual shareholders' meetings. Jersey had little reason to meddle, however, as Humble's highly competent exploration and production divisions consistently developed new oil fields. By the time of the postwar oil boom, Humble was the country's largest producer of crude oil at 110 million barrels in 1950.[19]

Demand for petroleum skyrocketed following the end of the Second World War. The number of automobiles in the United States jumped from twenty-six million in 1945 to forty million just five years later. Gasoline consumption nearly doubled in that same period and steadily grew throughout the 1950s.[20] In a message to Humble shareholders in the company's 1954 annual report, President Hines Baker and Board Chairman L. T. Barrow noted that increasing demand required "a long-range point of view with respect to petroleum investments" regardless of the adequate crude supplies at present.[21] The company had made large capital expenditures in 1954, Baker and Barrow reported, and would continue to do so throughout the decade in order to maintain Humble's profitable and competitive position in the industry. "Humble plans to continue an aggressive program of exploration and capital expenditures in the belief that such enterprise is necessary to meet the tremendous demands for oil and gas foreseeable over the next ten to twenty years," the company informed shareholders in 1955.[22] In that year, U.S. demand grew by over 650,000 barrels per day, a margin that was met primarily by increased domestic production. A large reserve producing capacity of two million barrels per day stood to fill any gaps between demand and supply. Most of this reserve was located in Texas, where limited market capacity kept wells operating at only fifty percent of their maximum rate of production.

Despite these seemingly adequate supplies, Humble believed exploration and the drilling of new wells were not expanding quickly enough to keep pace with the steadily increasing demand. Proven domestic reserves had increased by ten billion barrels since 1948—but should have increased by 13.5 billion barrels in order to match the demand curve. Continuation of this trend, Humble believed, would result in an ever-increasing dependence on foreign imports.[23]

The volatility of the world oil markets came into sharp focus for Humble and its industry rivals in November 1956 with the closing of the Suez Canal by Egyptian President Gamal Abdel Nasser. The crisis emphasized the risks of continued dependence on imports from the Middle East. While major companies such as Humble and smaller independent producers in Texas were in a position to increase production and offset the lost Mideast supplies in Europe, the latter group feared the ramp up would create a glut of supply in certain domestic markets and send prices falling. With the support of the independents, the Texas Railroad Commission, a regulating body whose focus was exclusively local, refused to lift restrictions on production. On January 3, 1957, Humble took the bold step of increasing its posted price for Texas crude oil by thirty-five cents a barrel. The move encouraged independent producers to similarly raise prices and increase production to the extent that European needs were largely met.

It was against this backdrop—steadily increasing domestic demand and the instability of world supply structures—that Humble sought to diversify its sources of domestic production. From 1947 to 1956, the number of producing wells operated by Humble jumped from 8,976 to 13,145. Expenditures for drilling in the same time period more than doubled from $50.5 million to $127.5 million. Although most of this activity took place in Texas and the Gulf Coast, Humble also expanded its operations on the West Coast in the hopes of securing crude oil for its new refinery in Benicia, California.[24]

The company also turned north to Alaska.

When Wallace Pratt joined the Jersey board as vice president in 1942, he immediately began recommending the company undertake geological surveys in Alaska. His bullish outlook on the North Slope extended to another region he believed had even greater potential, the equally remote stretch of land in the southwest that jutted out from the mainland toward the Aleutians:

> Another promising region is the Alaska Peninsula. Its accessible southern coast exhibits seepages of petroleum at Cold Bay.... Three successful test wells have been drilled on the peninsula ranging in depth between 5,000 and 8,775 feet. Obviously further exploration is justified in this region.[25]

Pratt retired from Jersey in 1945, and therefore wasn't present a decade later when Humble chief geologist J. Ben Carsey decided to follow his mentor's recommendation and send geological and aerial survey crews to the Alaska Peninsula. In the summer field seasons of 1954–1956, the Humble crews focused on the eastern shore of the Cold Bay region near the boom-bust town of Kanatak, which had seen numerous oil exploration efforts going back to the turn of the century.

In 1900, an independent prospector named Jack Lee found seepages of oil on the surface of the ground at Kanatak and learned that the region's indigenous population had long been using the fuel to cook food and heat their homes. The discovery set off an oil boom that included rampant land speculation and the drilling of a few shallow wells with crude steam-powered rigs. The boom turned quickly to bust when no significant deposits of oil were found. A second boom at Kanatak occurred in 1920, when Congress passed the Mineral Leasing Act, which reopened previously withdrawn lands to resource development. Three hundred people landed at the once-deserted town, including those who worked for oil companies that had acquired leases on the peninsula, as well as numerous independent wildcatters intent on scouring the region for oil. Kanatak soon boasted stores, restaurants, hotels, saloons, a post office, and a government weather station.[26]

One of Humble's sister companies, Standard Oil of California (Chevron), drilled the region's first deep exploration well twelve miles northwest of Kanatak in 1923. It was abandoned at 5,033 feet after minimal shows of crude oil. Another Chevron effort in 1938 reached a depth of 7,596 feet, at the time the deepest well in Alaska history, where it encountered numerous shows of oil and gas, but none in commercial quantities. No fewer than four additional wells drilled in the area in those years similarly failed to strike oil.[27]

Despite this history of failure, Shell Oil Company began acquiring leases around the largely abandoned Kanatak in 1954. The company obtained acreage from the U.S. Navy, which was then returning withdrawn lands to the public domain, and from many Alaska residents who had snapped up leases on their own and now assigned them to Shell in return for cash and future royalties. Four separate Shell field crews explored the area over the next few years by boat, horseback, and helicopter. The parties focused on the Bear Creek region and its prominent anticlines (sedimentary beds believed to hold crude oil within their porous structures).[28]

Attracted by the same geological formations, Humble also began exploring the region. The company was brand-new to Alaska, drawn there as much by the territory's oil potential as by the need to expand its petroleum sources and keep pace with rival companies then doing the same. Geologists Dean Morgridge and Alex Osanik conducted aerial surveys in different parts of Alaska in 1954. Bernold M. Hanson explored the Cold Bay coastline the following year and observed an outcrop of Upper Triassic carbonates, a particular formation of exposed layers along the Bear Creek anticline whose angular unconformity suggested the subsurface geology might be an ideal trap for crude oil.[29] "When we tested the area which we thought was the most desirable and the easiest, we had mounted quite an exploration effort," explained Humble's Carl Reistle in an interview years later. "We had a lot of information north of the Aleutians."[30] That Cold Bay was readily accessible by sea would facilitate transportation of any discovered crude oil and made the region all the more attractive to Humble.

On April 25, 1957, Humble formed a partnership with Shell, agreeing to drill three wells on Shell's leases at Bear Creek, Ugashik Creek, and Wide Bay in return for a fifty percent interest in the entire 250,000-acre field. The two companies spent the summer building a port at Jute Bay, the nearest anchorage to the Bear Creek field and a five-mile road to the drill site. More than eight thousand tons of supplies were barged to the remote location. Drilling on the Bear Creek No. 1 well began on

September 23 on a lease held by Earl Grammer, one of the independent prospectors from the 1920 Kanatak boom and the last to still hold leases in the area.[31] The well had reached a depth of 6,585 feet by the end of 1957. Humble's annual report that year summed up the effort in a single sentence: "The remote location, severe cold, and high winds have presented unusual difficulties."[32]

Humble president Morgan Davis spoke to the Anchorage Chamber of Commerce on August 30, 1958, and expressed his belief that Alaska had "real promise" as an oil-producing state. He cited the Bear Creek operation as proof of Humble's confidence in Alaska and its willingness to "have a try at the riskiest and most expensive kind of hunting your state has to offer: wildcatting for oil." Davis's visit came just four days after the 1958 primary election at which voters overwhelmingly approved the state-hood act. (Alaska would officially become the forty-ninth state on January 3, 1959.) Alaskans were poised to assume greater control of their natural resources under state-hood, and they were eager for long-term economic development. The Humble chief told them just what they wanted to hear. Referring to the Bear Creek campaign as a "long-range project," Davis told the assembled Anchorage business leaders, "Our company's policy has never dictated that we enter into an area such as Alaska on a short-term basis, nor that we pull out if our first ventures prove unsuccessful."[33]

As drilling at Bear Creek continued in 1958, it appeared the venture would indeed test Davis's claim. Cores from the well compared favorably with those from the nearby Chevron well drilled two decades earlier in that both revealed the presence of hydrocarbons throughout their respective depths. Of five total drill-stem tests con-ducted at different depths, however, only one recovered a consistent show of crude oil. Humble geologists came to suspect that the Bear Creek No. 1 well did not penetrate the Triassic strata associated with the exposed outcrop at Cold Bay.[34] When continued drilling in winter 1959 failed to recover any further shows of oil, Humble and Shell agreed to abandon the prospect and terminate the partnership. The remaining two wells planned for Ugashik Creek and Wide Bay would not be drilled. The well at Bear Creek had reached a depth of 14,375 feet when it was plugged in March 1959. Humble had spent $7 million on the operation, making Bear Creek No. 1 the most expensive dry hole in company history. Reistle explained the effort in the most suc-cinct terms: "We made a bad choice there."[35]

"The year 1958 presented many difficult problems for the domestic petroleum industry," wrote Morgan Davis in a message to Humble shareholders the very same month of the Bear Creek shutdown. "Weak demand, large inventories, and excessive imports," he continued, "created downward pressures on prices of both products and crude oil." This downturn led to a corresponding decline in exploration and drill-ing by Humble. The company's exploration expenses dropped from $235.4 million in 1957 to $154.9 million in 1958, while the number of completed wells decreased from

867 to 557 in the same period. Humble seemed to be walking back the aggressive exploration program announced just a few years before. That the company was now drilling for oil in new, high-risk regions such as Alaska was reflected in the "dry hole costs," which accounted for a record forty-five percent of total drilling expenditures in 1958.[36]

On July 19, 1960, Humble announced it was closing its Anchorage office and sending eleven of its twelve employees back to Houston. A lone scout would remain in Alaska to monitor the progress of the other oil companies exploring in the state. "I can't deny this indicates a definite downgrading of interest in Alaska by Humble," stated geologist Fred Sollars.[37] He cited the region's high operating costs and the downturn in world oil demand as the main reasons behind the move. Sollars nonetheless insisted that Humble remained interested in Alaska and might continue to support field crews in future summer seasons. Two parties were in the field at that moment, he noted—one on the North Slope and another on the Porcupine River in the southern foothills of the Brooks Range. Humble also planned to retain mineral leases for an iron ore deposit it had located north of Dillingham. (The company would abandon that prospect two years later.)

If Humble's official position on Alaska was lukewarm, some individuals within the company remained optimistic about its prospects. J. R. Jackson, of Humble's Los Angeles office, continued to assign geologists to Alaska field campaigns in the early 1960s. With the backing of Merrill Haas, vice president of exploration, and other Humble executives in the minerals department, Jackson lobbied the Humble board of directors to invest in seismic exploration on the North Slope and attempt to secure leases the State of Alaska was then putting up for competitive bid. Perhaps still reeling from the Bear Creek failure, Humble declined to commit any significant resources to Alaska.[38]

The company's hesitation also may have been a function of its changing relationship with Jersey, its parent company. In late 1958, Jersey made an offer to Humble shareholders: it would exchange five shares of Jersey stock for four Humble shares. Many accepted the deal. The swap increased Jersey's ownership share of Humble to more than ninety-eight percent.[39] At the same time, Jersey consolidated Humble and a number of other domestic affiliates into a single corporation, a move designed to give the Jersey board of directors and executive committee more direct control. (The company believed its many small affiliates lacked the comprehensive vision necessary to compete in the rapidly changing global oil industry in the 1950s.) The result, according to Jersey historian Bennett H. Wall, was the intended standardization of overall policy making—but also the creation of an administrative bottleneck at the company's highest levels. "More and more problems [moved] up the administrative pyramid to the Board for resolution," Wall noted. "This altered the ability of the operating affiliates, and of the company as a whole, to quickly and effectively resolve urgent problems."[40] The entrepreneurial and even freewheeling spirit that had guided Humble since its very beginning was being replaced with Jersey's more conservative approach, one that emphasized comprehensive study and cautious deliberation at every level of the company. The running joke around company watercoolers was that no issue was too small to require an internal committee and preparation of a written report. Wall notes that Humble's Alaska champions felt stymied time and again by Jersey's unwillingness to invest in Alaska exploration.[41]

It was this corporate climate that Rollin Eckis of Richfield encountered when he approached Humble with an offer of North Slope partnership in early 1964. With the state's next lease sale scheduled for that December, Richfield knew that its limited capital resources would almost certainly prevent it from securing significant acreage. Industry giants BP and Sinclair also had field crews exploring the region and were likely to bid aggressively for leases. Eckis brought his chief geologist, Harry Jamison, to meet with J. R. Jackson and his exploration staff in Humble's Los Angeles office. In addition to the usual maps and geological data, Eckis and Jamison brought actual samples of oil-saturated sand from the Sagavanirktok River. Most impressively, Richfield possessed survey data from a North Slope seismic line that showed exactly the type of folded geologic formations in which crude oil might be trapped. Jackson was sold. He recommended that Jersey approve the partnership with Richfield. Humble paid $900,000 for a fifty percent share in Richfield's leases, plus another $1.5 million for exploration work in summer 1964. Humble committed another $3 million to future exploration and up to $15 million for the 1964 lease sale. The terms of the deal also included a gentleman's agreement of sorts between the equal partners—neither company could sell its Alaska interests without offering the other the right of first refusal. This seemingly innocuous condition would later complicate the intense wrangling over the Prudhoe Bay oil field.

Wall, the official Jersey historian, attributes the company's sudden willingness to invest once again in Alaska to the impressive field work of Richfield.[42] In addition, Jersey's directors may have seen the sizable investment its industry rivals were then making in Alaska and believed the partnership with Richfield represented an affordable hedge against being left out in the event of a discovery. Despite the move, Jersey still pinched its pennies when it came to supporting Humble-Richfield operations on the North Slope. In advance of a July 1965 lease sale, the board denied Humble's request for an additional $1 million when it appeared Richfield would be unable to match the contribution. Merrill Haas would later claim that had Jersey come through with those additional funds the company would have outbid its competitors and secured nearly every tract on what became the Prudhoe Bay oil field.

STRIKE AT PRUDHOE

The Richfield-Humble partnership entered the 1964 lease sale and, though outbid on most tracts by BP, still secured enough North Slope acreage to continue its comprehensive exploratory program. The following year at the Prudhoe Bay lease sale, the partnership bid a then-unheard-of $94 an acre for some tracts and grabbed two-thirds of the available leases. With three thousand tons of drilling equipment in Fairbanks and a chartered Hercules C-130 transport plane ready to go, Richfield was eager to explore its leases.

The company would have to wait, however, as by this time Richfield was beset by financial problems and embroiled in an antitrust lawsuit brought by the U.S. Justice Department. Justice charged that Richfield, Cities Service Company, and Sinclair Oil—three companies linked by corporate reorganizations dating back to 1937—did not provide a sufficient level of competition and thus disadvantaged consumers in six western states. The lawsuit weakened Richfield in the eyes of shareholders and industry analysts. Its practical effect was to force Richfield to seek a merger with a stable company. Among its many prospective suitors, Atlantic Refining Company of Philadelphia emerged the victor. In early 1966, the two companies merged to form the Atlantic Richfield Company, or ARCO.[43]

In February that year, ARCO hauled its drilling rig north and began working the Susie No. 1 well located sixty miles south of Prudhoe Bay. Ten months and $4.5 million later, it was plugged and abandoned as a dry hole. The failure of Susie disappointed the company greatly. Many Richfield employees were already upset by the merger, believing their hard work for the scrappy company would be overlooked when the larger ARCO assumed credit for any success. That Susie came up dry proved another bitter disappointment, and some in ARCO advocated the company follow its industry competitors and pull out of Alaska altogether. Robert O. Anderson, a self-described wildcatter and the head of the newly formed ARCO, recognized that with the drilling equipment already on the North Slope much of the capital expense was out of the way. It would cost relatively little to drill another well, only the cost of moving the rig, and he convinced ARCO's board of directors to give Alaska one more shot.[44]

The ARCO team moved farther north in April 1967, and began drilling the Prudhoe Bay State No. 1 well, surely their final attempt if this too turned up dry. In late December that year, the drilling crew reached a depth of around seven thousand feet when a tremendous rumbling from the well attracted the attention of curious field workers. Among them was Gil Mull, the very geologist whose impressive survey work a few years earlier had convinced Richfield to gamble on the North Slope. Mull later recalled the scene at Prudhoe Bay that day:

It was about 30 below zero and there was a thirty knot wind blowing. We could hear the roar of natural gas like four jumbo jets flying right overhead. A flare from a two-inch pipe shot at least 30 feet straight into the wind. It was a mighty encouraging sign that something big was down below.[45]

ARCO initially attempted to keep the discovery under wraps, though with a gas flare burning twenty-four hours a day and drilling personnel rotating on and off the site, the secret could not be kept for long. Company press releases downplayed the significance of the find, yet within weeks Alaska newspapers boldly trumpeted the events occurring on the North Slope. ARCO next drilled a second step-out well seven miles to the southeast that confirmed the Prudhoe Bay structure held an enormous quantity of crude oil and natural gas. By the summer of 1968, ARCO called in the Dallas-based petroleum consulting firm DeGoyler and MacNaughton who, in a report prepared for ARCO but fully intended for public release, announced the Prudhoe Bay oil field likely held between five and ten billion barrels of crude oil. Even this admittedly conservative estimate made Prudhoe Bay the largest oil field on the continent.

The discovery did not leave the industry suddenly scrambling for ideas on how to bring the crude to market. Each company knew before ever setting foot on the North Slope that any potential discovery would require an innovative (and expensive) transportation system. The capital-intensive exploration programs these companies had undertaken since the 1950s were initiated only after some rudimentary number-crunching demonstrated just how much oil would have to be found to justify the expense of bringing it out. As early as 1924, the USGS speculated in its study of the resource potential of northwest Alaska that a thousand-mile pipeline would have to be built to develop any petroleum finds in the region. Twenty years later, Wallace Pratt, the sage of arctic oil development, agreed that a North Slope discovery would necessitate a pipeline south to Fairbanks. Such a line across Alaska had always been the default option underpinning each company's exploration on the North Slope.

Within weeks of the strike, both ARCO and Humble formed in-house teams of engineers to begin preliminary work on pipeline design, going so far as to conduct aerial and ground surveys of different routes south from Prudhoe Bay. Both companies had been exploring the concept of an Alaska pipeline for at least two years. The Humble engineering team had established a very rough project outline even before the first confirmation well in March 1968 validated Prudhoe Bay's awesome reserves. Their first choice of routes would take the pipeline from Alaska diagonally through Canada to Chicago and on to the East Coast, where Humble's downstream operations—refineries, chemical plants, gas stations, and other retail outlets—were located. When the Humble team first came together with its counterpart at ARCO, however, the latter group displayed cursory interest in delivering the oil to Chicago but certainly not any farther east. ARCO maintained its own downstream operation primarily on the West Coast and therefore desired a pipeline to a port on the Gulf of Alaska, Valdez perhaps, where tankers would ferry the crude to Washington, Oregon, and California. This meeting of engineers marked the first of many subsequent struggles over the destination of the oil.

By the summer of 1968, the Humble-ARCO teams were ensconced in Anchorage offices working on pipeline design. The effort soon included BP, and in October the three companies announced the formation of the Trans-Alaska Pipeline System (TAPS), an organization charged with designing and building a pipeline from Prudhoe Bay to Valdez.[46] Yet while TAPS ramped up operations in late 1968, Humble maintained a separate in-house team of engineers working on an all-marine route whose only pipelines would be feeder lines to load crude into tankers directly off the arctic coast.

2

No Cream Puff

The geographical origins and expertise [of the oil industry] had encouraged a special breed, cut off from the centres of politics and diplomacy; the shanty-towns of Pennsylvania and the swamps of Texas sent forth rugged, confident men who knew they had transformed the world around them.
—Anthony Sampson, *The Seven Sisters* (1975)[1]

Stanley B. Haas was working in the transportation division of Standard Oil of New Jersey in 1960 when a casual conversation with two geologists helped define the next decade of his career. The three men discussed the state of world oil exploration, and the geologists agreed that the next (and possibly last) discovery of a world-class oil field, an "elephant" in industry terms, would likely happen in Alaska. But, the geologists continued, there was simply no practical and cost-effective method for bringing any North Slope crude to market. The region was one of the most isolated on the planet, enclosed by mountains and roadless tundra, hundreds of miles from the nearest ice-free harbor and thousands of miles from any large cities. "This seemed like a terrific challenge," Haas would later recall, "and nobody was doing anything about it."[2] He returned to his division eager to tackle the problem. Humble Oil, Jersey's main domestic subsidiary, held no leases in Alaska at the time—the company having abandoned its Bear Creek prospect the year before—yet Haas was able to convince Jersey management to authorize a study of transportation systems in the Arctic. Haas enlisted the support of George McCammon, an engineer then only months from retirement, and the two men quickly collected a modest amount of baseline data from available arctic experts.

There the matter sat until 1964, when Richfield approached Humble with its offer of partnership in a joint program of Alaska exploration. Like every other oil company with interests in Alaska, Humble first had to consider under what circumstances a potential crude discovery would justify the cost of developing it. Planning for a trans-Alaska pipeline from the North Slope proved problematic when so many variables remained unknown. The size of a potential reservoir, composition and weight of the crude, and of course the location of the deposit itself all would bear greatly on the eventual cost of a pipeline. The crude's destination was clear from Jersey's perspective—its East Coast refineries—but the possible pipeline routes also remained indeterminate. A direct pipeline thousands of miles in length could stretch from Alaska through Canada all the way to New York. Alternatively, a pipeline could cross Alaska to tidewater on its southern coast and be followed by a fifteen-hundred-mile tanker route to Washington or Oregon, which in turn would be followed by another three-thousand-mile pipeline across the country to New York.

But tankers? Shipping oil by tanker is nearly always less expensive than by pipeline and, even taking into account the fact that the forty-five-hundred-mile ocean route between Prudhoe Bay and New York remained blocked by ice year-round, a straight comparison between the two methods could be made. Stan Haas, by this time part of Humble's marine division at its Houston headquarters, revived the arctic study and put together a preliminary analysis of an all-marine tanker route through the Northwest Passage. It was not unreasonable for him to posit that an all-tanker route could lower the per-barrel transportation costs considerably. These were all what-if scenarios based on a hypothetical oil field that hadn't yet been discovered, but the economics and engineering behind both pipelines and tankers appeared credible enough to convince Humble that Alaska was worth the risk.[3] The company agreed to an Alaska partnership with Richfield.

When the Prudhoe Bay State No. 1 well struck oil a few years later, Haas suddenly found himself engaged in hypothetical scenarios no longer. He now had actual numbers to work with. In August 1968, Humble tapped Haas to chair the Arctic Marine Task Force, a group charged with providing hard data on the feasibility of the all-tanker route. Haas was a native of Missouri and had served in the air force during World War II. After the war, he earned a degree in chemical engineering from Iowa State University and joined Humble in 1949. His first assignment took him to Humble's Bayway Refinery in Linden, New Jersey, after which he quickly worked his way up the ladder to managerial positions with Jersey and Esso Marine in London. Joining Haas on the Arctic Marine Task Force in Houston were Abraham (Bram) D. Mookhoek and Walter Devine, both naval architects, and Captain Robert Stap. Within a few months, two other men would join the core team: R. L. Vukin, another naval architect, and A. McKenzie, who joined Stap in operations coordination.[4] The men assumed the seemingly straightforward yet complex task of determining whether a fleet of icebreaking tankers could ferry crude oil from Prudhoe Bay to New York via the Canadian Archipelago. How many tankers? How big? What icebreaking design criteria would be required for such vessels? What sort of terminal/docking system could safely load the tankers at Prudhoe Bay? And, most importantly, even if the project proved feasible from a purely technical standpoint, would the economics work out? Such questions would have to be answered in great detail before Humble invested billions in developing its Prudhoe Bay reserves.

The efforts of Haas and the task force coincided with the industry-wide pursuit of an Alaska pipeline in which Humble played a significant role. Yet the various engineering teams assembled in those heady months following the discovery were more complementary than exclusionary. Where the oil industry once debated whether a North Slope discovery would justify the expense of any one transportation system, it now considered the possibility that the giant Prudhoe Bay field could support two operating simultaneously. By the summer of 1968, the oil companies had confirmed the structure likely held up to ten billion barrels of crude, yet industry analysts knew this to be a conservative estimate and suspected the actual total to be much higher. Until BP drilled its own confirmation wells on its Prudhoe Bay leases—something it did not accomplish until that winter—the exact definition of the field could not be known. In the meantime, the estimate of ten billion barrels figured in industry calculations and suggested production at Prudhoe Bay could reach two million barrels per day. That Humble threw its support behind both a pipeline project and the all-tanker route says a great deal about the strategic maneuverings of self-interested companies in a highly competitive industry, but also demonstrates the company's optimism that more than one transportation system would be required for the field's incredible reserves. After further delineation wells had mapped the reservoir and proven its immense quantity of crude, TAPS executive R. G. Dulaney testified before Congress that both an Alaska pipeline and the all-tanker alternative could indeed operate simultaneously.[5]

Haas now plugged the figure of two million barrels per day into his calculations and found that shipping crude forty-five hundred miles—again ignoring the arctic ice—would cost roughly sixty cents per barrel. Pipeline estimates came in at $1.20 per barrel or more, suggesting a daily savings of $1.2 million by the tanker method. Multiply that figure over an entire year and the savings reached nearly half a billion dollars. Though still only estimates the numbers at least had some quantifiable basis, and Haas needed only to pull out a calculator to convince naysayers the concept was at least worth looking into. The logistical challenge of operating tankers in icebound waters was certain to increase costs to some degree, yet an annual margin of half a billion dollars between the tanker and pipeline systems left Haas plenty of room to maneuver.

The Arctic Marine Task Force first needed to bring together all available data in order to create a comprehensive scientific picture of the arctic environment. Only then could the team begin to address specific issues such as the design requirements for an icebreaking vessel and the development of a docking and oil loading terminal on Alaska's arctic coast. With respect to tanker design parameters, Mookhoek and Vukin soon organized the overall research plan under four primary objectives: establish speed and power requirements for continuous motion through (1) uniform ice of various thickness and (2) ridges of various thickness; (3) establish forces, accelerations, motions, and impact loads in various ice conditions; and (4) evaluate maneuvering capability of a long tanker with parallel sides in uniform and broken ice.[6] The team quickly found abundant information on the ice itself in the Arctic, but to their great disappointment discovered few data regarding the behavior of ships in ice. What information did exist invariably referred only to small, noncargo icebreakers such as those sixty-five-hundred-ton vessels operated by the U.S. and Canadian Coast Guards. No one had ever before attempted sailing a tanker through ice. No one had even given thought to the circumstances under which icebreaking tankers might be needed. Humble would have to set the baseline.

Rear Admiral A. H. G. Storrs of the Canadian Department of Transport, who would later act on Ottawa's behalf as an official observer on the *Manhattan*, identified some icebreaking cargo vessels in the Gulf of St. Lawrence, such as the ten-thousand-ton *Imperial Acadia*. Using this vessel as a model, Storrs was able to compare the ice thickness of the St. Lawrence relative to the Northwest Passage and thereby project a theoretical size of the vessel required for the latter environment. He and the Humble engineers worked up a rough design of an icebreaking tanker on the order of 250,000 tons. "From 10,000 tons to 250,000 tons is a big jump," Storrs wrote, "and on the way up the curve can drift off in all sorts of directions, so obviously [Humble] had to get a base a little closer to the eventual ship that could make a better jumping off point for calculations."[7] Haas increasingly began to feel that he could not go before the Jersey board of directors and advocate a multibillion-dollar investment based solely on laboratory studies and mathematical models. They would have to actually build their own vessel and send her through the passage.[8]

ARCTIC TANKER TEST

Humble convened a conference in Washington, DC, in September 1968, where dozens of scientists, academics, naval specialists, and military officials, all with expertise in the Arctic, assembled to listen to the company's pitch. Haas opened the conference with an ambitious statement of purpose: "We hope to build a ship that will be able to sail year-round through the Northwest Passage."[9] Standing before a roomful of bemused smiles, he then described the concept in more detail. Humble proposed to construct an icebreaking tanker weighing 250,000 deadweight tons with an engine room capable of 100,000 horsepower. Such a vessel would be the largest of its kind in history. If the test vessel demonstrated both the technical and economic feasibility of an arctic transportation system, Haas stated, Humble would follow with an *entire fleet* of tankers of comparable size and power.

Haas would later say it was at that moment he observed a sudden shift in the atmosphere of the room. Barely concealed smirks gave way to open mouths. Once they realized Humble was indeed serious, the wide-eyed attendees eagerly pledged support. German and Milne, the Montreal-based naval architectural firm that designed icebreaking and ice-strengthened ships for the Canadian Coast Guard, was one of the first to sign a consulting contract with Humble. In remarkably short order the company produced a two-volume report with hundreds of recommendations for arctic tankers, covering everything from the metallurgy of the propellers to the type of heater that would keep the windows on the bridge from icing over.[10] The U.S. Army Cold Regions Research and Engineering Laboratory (CRREL) agreed to provide data on the thickness, strength, and composition of sea ice. From the U.S. Navy and the Coast Guard the company obtained assistance in charting possible marine routes through the Arctic, as well as aerial reconnaissance data and radar analyses of present-day ice conditions in the Northwest Passage. These entities rightly assumed that the Houston-based Humble knew almost nothing about sea ice, and they started at the very beginning with a report that described how ice forms. They explained the difference between winter ice and polar ice, the former a smooth sheet formed during the previous year and unlikely to survive the summer melt, the latter being two or more years old and typically displaying ridges, hummocks, and other deformations caused by lateral pressures. The first reports delivered to Houston contained comprehensive glossaries with definitions for every polar term the oilmen were likely to encounter. For Humble's purposes, probably the most salient feature of polar ice was its unpredictability. This was a complex environment with heterogeneous ice in constant motion. Scientists could—and did—put together charts, graphs, tables, and diagrams that showed the observed history of ice in the Northwest Passage. But reliable predictions of future ice conditions depended on hydrographic, oceanographic, and meteorological data that simply did not exist. The U.S. Naval Oceanographic Office agreed to supply Humble with ice forecasts from forty-eight hours to thirty days, but included a disclaimer that all forecasts were basically mathematical extrapolations using incomplete data. Whatever plots the ice experts came up with would provide useful design data for the naval architects, but would be too oversimplified to be of navigational use during an actual voyage. Any ship in the Northwest Passage would have to conduct on-the-spot analyses of whatever ice lay directly ahead of the bow. When it came to vessel design, Humble contracted with the U.S. Naval Undersea Warfare Center in San Diego to conduct small-scale model tests of different hulls that would help determine the best icebreaking configuration. One team of Humble engineers subsequently traveled to a lake in the foothills of the French Alps to test 1-to-20-scale model ships in real-world ice conditions. The models were not toys. Each steel-hulled model measured sixty feet in length and weighed forty tons.[11]

On December 4, 1968, Haas went before the executive committee of the Jersey board of directors with the task force's findings to date:

> [We have] evaluated a number of possible alternatives for transporting Alaskan North Slope crude oil to market and concluded tentatively that the possibility of moving ice-breaking tankers through Arctic waters (the Northwest Passage) appears to have substantial economic advantages over other alternatives, providing such movement is feasible.[12]

In touting the potential economic benefits of the tanker route, Haas proved fully aware that corporate boards tend to focus on the bottom line. He could also boast of the assembled team of arctic specialists who for months had been working on the scientific and technical details of the expedition. Emboldened by his team's findings and confidence, Haas suggested to the Jersey board that the project would indeed prove feasible, and he recommended sending a test vessel from New York to Prudhoe Bay via the Canadian Arctic. The executive committee approved the officially named Arctic Tanker Test two weeks later.

The concept of an all-tanker route appealed to Jersey on a number of levels. The potential economic advantages first sold the company on the idea. Now the Arctic Task Force had marshaled scientific evidence suggesting the project was technically feasible. Most importantly, an all-tanker delivery system would bring significant quantities of crude oil to the East Coast, where Humble maintained a strong downstream presence. Here the company could deliver its share of the Alaska bonanza, turn the crude into refined products, and distribute them via its own network of retail outlets. In as volatile and cutthroat an industry as oil, this level of independence would provide at least some stability.

It was this brand of "vertical integration," a business technique pioneered and then perfected by John D. Rockefeller, that made Jersey a dominant force in the world oil market. When Rockefeller founded Standard Oil in 1870, he revolutionized the burgeoning oil industry by bringing production and distribution together under one roof. This alignment of interests—controlling the product from the reservoir in the ground all the way to customers' homes—created an ultracompetitive company able to wield market power in diverse sectors of commerce yet simultaneously insulated from fluctuations in any one market. This and other Rockefeller innovations proved so anticompetitive that in 1911 the U.S. Supreme Court forced dissolution of the Standard Oil monopoly into many smaller entities. Yet the business philosophy of vertical integration remained a dominant pillar in the new companies, of which Jersey was the largest.[13]

The Jersey-Humble merger in 1919 caused the practice of vertical integration to begin anew. Six decades later, the parent company maintained on the Eastern Seaboard a vast network of refineries, chemical plants, gas stations, and other downstream entities, all complemented by Humble's steady supply of domestic crude. When Prudhoe Bay burst onto the scene in 1968, Humble naturally desired to feed its share of the Alaska crude into this distribution network. The simultaneous tanker and pipeline studies commissioned by Humble therefore do not appear contradictory or mutually exclusive; rather, they represent diverse approaches to the same problem— how to get Alaska crude to New York. Humble vice president Russell Venn acknowledged as much to a group of Canadian journalists in Halifax when he claimed the East Coast as the natural market for the crude and projected that by 1980 two-thirds of the Alaska production would have to find its way there. Venn professed an air of indifference to the transportation method, whether tankers or transcontinental pipelines or some combination of the two. All were open for study, he stated. Like a true oilman, he stressed only that the most economical would ultimately be chosen.[14]

While Haas appeared before the Jersey board in December 1968 seeking approval for the tanker test, the question of exactly where the company would obtain a vessel for the experiment remained unanswered. Just a few months earlier, at the Washington conference, Humble had stated its intent to build from scratch a 250,000-ton tanker, the likes of which had not previously sailed the world's oceans. Like schoolboys about to receive a new toy, the task force even brainstormed half a dozen possible names for the marvelous test vessel, all of them steeped in the romanticism of the sea. One suggested name, the *Lewis & Clark*, would recognize the two brave men who explored unknown lands from St. Louis to the Pacific Ocean in 1804–1806. A vessel christened *Sakajawea* would honor the young Shoshone woman who guided Lewis and Clark on their famous expedition. Still other suggestions—the *Aurora Borealis* and the *Polar Bear*, for example—connected more strongly with the Arctic. Incredibly, the team also considered the name *Hamilton*, which, according to the memo, would honor "Sir John Hamilton who made several trips to the [Alaska] North Slope area in the years 1825–27." The name was an error in two ways. First, the explorer's name was not Sir John Hamilton but rather Sir John *Franklin*. Second, it would have been a public relations disaster of the highest order. Franklin was not remembered for his 1825–1827 expeditions but for the disastrous one he led two decades later. His ships, the *Terror* and the *Erebus*, remained beset in ice for three years, and those crew members who did not die of starvation perished on a desperate overland trek in search of rescue. At some point the crew resorted to cannibalism, a charge the Royal Navy vehemently denied at the time but that forensic evidence, especially tool marks on recovered human bones, has proven beyond dispute. Franklin is the ultimate tragic figure in the history of arctic exploration—hardly the sort of romanticized image Humble hoped to conjure with its own daring voyage.[15]

The privilege of naming a brand-new oil tanker failed to materialize, however, along with the very ship itself. Humble calculated that to build an icebreaking tanker to its exact specifications would take at least two years. At least one test voyage would be required, followed by modifications to the ship's design, then construction of perhaps twenty or thirty ships—all of which would push the schedule of the tanker system well into the mid-1970s. But plans for the Alaska pipeline were proceeding at a more rapid pace. Construction was scheduled to begin in summer 1969, with the first crude oil expected on the market just three years later. Time was not on the side of the Arctic Marine Task Force. Haas and his men would have to surrender their dream of a custom-built vessel if they wanted to keep pace with the pipeline. The team instead decided to find an existing tanker in the U.S. fleet, one that closely resembled its ideal design and could be quickly renovated for the arctic journey. This led Haas to the SS *Manhattan*.

THE ARCTIC TANKER

Since the *Manhattan*'s construction in 1962, other foreign-flagged tankers had surpassed her in total size, yet the Jones Act of 1920 stipulated that any commercial cargo shipped between U.S. ports had to be carried by a vessel built, owned, and registered by an American. Among the available ships in the U.S. fleet, the *Manhattan* was still the largest and the ideal candidate for the Arctic Tanker Test. Converting the vessel into an icebreaker would require strengthening her hull with many tons of steel—a load the modern class of relatively light supertankers could not accommodate, but one the *Manhattan*'s overbuilt structure could. Her power and maneuverability also proved tremendous assets to Humble. At the time of her design and construction the U.S. Navy had asked Niarchos Shipping, the tanker's owner, to make the *Manhattan* capable of achieving seventeen knots so as to be available during wartime to refuel ships at sea. Thus the vessel featured twin propellers, which not only made her more maneuverable than traditional single-screw ships but also boosted her total forward output to 43,000 horsepower. Straight off the rack the *Manhattan* already possessed many characteristics of a good icebreaker. She was powerful enough to thrust her bow atop the ice pack and large enough that the weight of her massive hull would easily cleave a pathway through the ice. The ship, according to one Humble official, was "no cream puff."[16] Seatrain Lines, the company that owned the *Manhattan*, eagerly leased the vessel to Humble for a period of two years.

In late January 1969, Haas returned to the Jersey board with a progress report. He presented background information on the recently chartered *Manhattan*, along with the task force's plans for modifying the vessel. The bulk of his presentation focused on the ongoing studies of arctic ice, the definitive variable that would influence virtually every decision made for the duration of the project. Along with Bram Mookhoek, the team's ice-testing program coordinator, Haas informed the board that the U.S. Navy and the Canadian government had already performed what they called "ice reconnaissance"—actual measurements of ice thickness, its multiseasonal growth, rates of drift, and migration patterns along the entire route the *Manhattan* expected to follow. Once the vessel actually reached the passage, a U.S. Coast Guard C-130 operating out of Thule Air Base in Greenland would fly hundreds of miles ahead each day and use side-looking airborne radar to "photograph" some two thousand square miles of ice. The plane's crew would then airdrop the film to the vessel for onboard navigational planning. Humble planned to commission from the Canadian Coast Guard a second aircraft equipped with infrared cameras to similarly make daily photographic surveys of the route ahead.

First-year ice contains more salt than multiyear ice, reflects more heat, and appears as a distinct shade of gray on the infrared projections. Salinity of ice drops precipitously as it ages, which makes multiyear ice harder than first-year ice. Any other vessel on a conventional transit through the Canadian Arctic would use these data to identify weak spots in the ice and plot the safest route through the passage. Paradoxically, the men behind the *Manhattan* intended to do the opposite. They planned to seek the most difficult passage through the hardest, thickest multiyear ice. The disquieting nature of such a mission went against every mariner's instincts, according to Captain Frederick Goettel of the U.S. Coast Guard: "For years a sailor is told to avoid anything in the ship's path bigger than a baseball bat. And then one day he is made captain of an icebreaker and told to ram into floes bigger than football fields made of ice as hard as steel." Such unnatural nautical maneuvers were altogether necessary in order to gather crucial data that would assist the design of the next generation of icebreakers, ships capable of defeating the worst possible ice conditions.[17]

Haas went on to describe to the Jersey executive board the vessel his team had chosen for the test. The *Manhattan* was considered the ideal candidate for the project because of her extra-heavy construction, high horsepower, and twin-screw propulsion system. Humble had signed a letter of intent with Sun Shipbuilding and Dry Dock Company of Chester, Pennsylvania, to undertake the many modifications identified by the task force as essential for a successful voyage, including hull strengthening around the engine room, installation of machinery collision chocks, new propellers, new tailshafts, protection for rudders, ice-testing and photographic laboratories, installation of communications and navigation equipment, and a heliport at the ship's stern capable of accommodating two helicopters. Haas provided a list of the vessel's characteristics—including her deadweight tonnage of nearly 115,000 and displacement tonnage of 145,000—but he was quick to remind them that if and when the full tanker program was implemented the tankers would likely be much larger:

> We are keeping very much in mind that we're really conducting a model test. It just happens to be on a larger scale than most. But the ship we would build to use on the route on a year round basis would be more than twice the displacement and probably about twice the power. Our primary mission will be to obtain operating data of reliable quality which can be used to check the validity of math and small model test results and which can be scaled up to a 250 MDWT [thousand deadweight tons] tanker size with a minimum of error.[18]

Robert Stap and A. McKenzie further briefed the assembled executives on the ongoing selection and training of the ship's officers, a program being conducted with assistance of the U.S. Coast Guard and the U.S. Navy.

If the presentation by Haas and his task force lacked for detail on any one issue it was the mooring facility and loading terminal that would have to be constructed at Prudhoe Bay. Haas mentioned only vague plans for a test structure to be built the following summer. He candidly observed, "We have not progressed as far in the development of the [terminal] project but we are in the process of gearing up to a major effort.... However, this program is not fully developed and it is probably premature to expand on it at this time."[19] The construction and operation of a secure docking facility in the harsh winter environment of the Beaufort Sea presented probably the most difficult challenge the Humble team would face. Haas noted that the two studies—tanker and terminal—would operate along largely separate tracks, the latter entirely dependent on the success of the former. It was one thing for Humble to build an enormous ship capable of smashing its way through the ice, but quite another to design infrastructure that would have to remain stationary, resist the pressures of the unpredictable ice pack, and generally coexist with the arctic marine environment rather than subjugate it by sheer force. Such a system, presumably anchored offshore, would be subject to migrating ice layers, which the strong arctic winds continually roll and pile atop one another. Additionally, a terminal that would receive tankers on the order of those twice the size of the *Manhattan* required significant ocean depth, yet the shallow seabed of the continental shelf extended for many miles offshore.

Haas then submitted the latest cost estimates for the Arctic Tanker Test, which, not unexpectedly, had been revised upward in only the few weeks since the board granted its official go-ahead. The Humble team no longer planned to construct its own icebreaking tanker (a huge cost savings to be sure) but the modifications to the *Manhattan* still stood to cost $17 million. The estimated total cost of the test now came to just over $26 million. Costs would go even higher if Humble elected to send the vessel on a second voyage to the Arctic in 1970, a prospect the company deemed exceedingly likely. The Jersey board assented to the proposed budget for the summer 1969 voyage, but made clear its intent to appropriate no additional funds for other future work. The board also pressed Humble to obtain some level of financial cooperation from the other oil companies in Alaska.[20]

William O. Gray of Esso Tankers, a division of Jersey's international affiliate, managed the tremendous job of converting the *Manhattan* into an icebreaker. Gray was a mechanical engineer and naval architect who, after service in the navy and a stint designing ships for Bethlehem Steel, joined Jersey and quickly established himself as the company's top tanker expert. He joined the marine task force in late 1968 and immediately informed Haas that the most innovative icebreaking research was then being conducted in Finland. He wanted to bring on Wärtsilä, a Helsinki-based shipbuilding company and international leader in the field, as a project partner. Wärtsilä rejected Gray's invitation at first, then later agreed. "You guys don't know what you're doing," Gray recalled the Finnish company telling him, "and if you screw this up it's going to give icebreakers a bad name."[21]

Between Thanksgiving and Christmas, Gray worked with Sun Shipyard to devise an ambitious schedule to have the *Manhattan* ready for a voyage the following summer. The most contentious point during the negotiations involved not the renovation work itself but rather Sun's fee. The job of renovating the *Manhattan* was like nothing that had ever been attempted before. No one knew precisely what it was going to cost, and Sun proved unwilling to commit to a hard figure that might later cause the company to lose money on the project. Gray admitted they were dealing with "back of the envelope" figures in those first few weeks.[22] Humble finally agreed to a graduated cost-plus contract in which Sun's percentage was guaranteed.

On February 26, 1969, the tanker steamed up the Delaware River to Sun's Dock No. 3, the largest floating dry dock in the country and the only berth at the yard capable of accommodating her. Once in place, the tanker blocked three entire piers. The job of lightening the ship and lifting the dock took two full days, but in time the *Manhattan* was high and dry. Long before the tanker's arrival Gray knew this one shipyard could not have the vessel ready for the target July 15 sailing date, less than five months away. The volume of steelwork and sheer number of man-hours alone could not be met even if Sun halted work on every other project and assigned its every laborer to the *Manhattan*. (Humble actually did pay Sun to stop work on two other shipbuilding projects in order to devote more personnel to the *Manhattan*.) Gray instead had the tanker cut into four sections and literally parceled the work out to different shipyards around the country. The bow and stern remained in Chester, the afterbow was towed to the Newport News Shipbuilding Company in Virginia, and the Alabama Drydock and Shipbuilding Company in Mobile took charge of the midship section. Haas joked at the time that the *Manhattan* was truly the longest ship in the world, stretching from Pennsylvania to Alabama.[23] Naval architects on the Humble task force saw the tanker in four pieces and dreamed up a unique experiment. They proposed removing three cargo tanks altogether, shortening the vessel by perhaps 120 feet. Following the maiden arctic voyage of this mini-*Manhattan*, the tanks would be reinserted and the vessel sent on another expedition at its full length. The benefit to the architects was obvious—full-scale variation of length-to-beam ratio with real-world data on lateral ice resistance for different ship lengths. In other words, they would get two experiments for (just slightly more than) the cost of one. Senior Jersey management dashed their hopes. "Having chartered an entire 106,000 DWT [deadweight tons] ship," Gray noted, "we were to use an entire 106,000 DWT ship—end of discussion."[24]

The discovery of oil at Prudhoe Bay excited the American shipbuilding industry nearly as much as it did the oil companies. Whatever transportation method ARCO, BP, and Humble ultimately chose (the all-land pipeline through Canada excepted), contracts for new ships would undoubtedly keep every yard in the country busy. If the Humble experiment proved successful, as many as thirty icebreaking tankers would be needed in the coming years at a total expenditure approaching $1.5 billion. And if the trans-Alaska pipeline came to fruition, an entire fleet of U.S.-made vessels would be needed for the run from Valdez to the West Coast. So certain was ARCO in the future of an Alaska pipeline that the company immediately began construction of a refinery in Cherry Point, Washington, and placed orders for several tankers designed for and dedicated to the Pacific route. The shipbuilding industry, having suffered through many lean years, eagerly welcomed this jolt of activity. The conversion of the *Manhattan* turned out to be the largest shipbuilding operation in the country since World War II. Over ten thousand workers put in 2.5 million man-hours on the job.[25]

In drawing up plans for the tanker renovation, Gray and Sun Shipyard drew extensively from the recently completed model tests conducted at the U.S. Naval Undersea Warfare Center. One model in particular, a prototype named IT-1, had proven its efficacy with bow and hull configurations that would now be replicated on the *Manhattan*.[26] Sun, Newport News, and Alabama accordingly acted in tandem to produce an "ice belt" around the ship's hull—a thirty-foot-high sheet of 1.25-inch high-tensile steel capable of absorbing three hundred pounds of pressure per square inch. The belt covered the hull from the bow to the engine room, eight feet above the waterline to twenty-two feet below, with an outward sloping angle of fifteen degrees. Inside the hull, welders attached a network of K-shaped braces made of one-inch steel I-beams. The hull renovations also included a heeling system composed of twelve water tanks, six on each side of the vessel, connected by two seven-foot-diameter pipes. The system's powerful diesel engines needed only sixty seconds to pump two thousand tons of seawater from the port to the starboard, a shift in weight that would induce a lateral rocking motion of roughly three degrees designed to break the ship free when stuck in ice. Humble initially planned to outfit the bow with a "bubbler"—a recently invented mechanism that used air compressors beneath the waterline to send bubbles rising along the hull to reduce friction between the ice and the tanker—but time constraints and lack of necessary equipment prevented its implementation. Sun constructed a double hull around the engine and boiler rooms to reduce the likelihood of flooding in the event ice somehow punctured a hole at that spot. Such a breach would likely mean the end of the voyage, as the vessel would require major repairs.

Another piece of equipment vital to the entire expedition was the twin-screw propulsion system. Workers replaced the conventional propellers with two bronze-nickel alloy models nearly thirty feet in diameter with blade tips five times thicker than normal. Anticipating the powerful impact torques that would be sustained by the shafting and gears when ice struck the blades, engineers developed a coupling with eight shear pins that sat between the rotor and the reduction gears. The pins, essentially six-inch metal rods with a notch at the midpoint, were designed to fail at torque forces lower than the corresponding failure torques of the other system components. In the process of failing, the shear pins would absorb and then dissipate the brunt of the impact. The coupling was easily accessible so that spent pins could be replaced quickly.

To house all the data recording, computing, and analyzing equipment, the Newport News Shipyard constructed an instrumentation van, basically a steel box forty feet long and ten feet wide, that was placed on the starboard side of the bridge deck. The van featured its own power source since being tied into the ship's electrical system would periodically subject the instrumentation equipment to damaging voltage fluctuations, such as during engine start-up. All deck piping had to be insulated and outfitted with either steam or heated glycol lines to keep them from freezing. Finally, on a tanker accustomed to a crew of at most fifty, the renovations included additional staterooms ("winterized" for the northern voyage) for the dozens of scientists, reporters, VIPs, and other guests who would be tagging along.[27]

The most innovative and visually distinctive renovation to the tanker was its brand-new icebreaking bow. Constructed by Bath Iron Works of Maine, the bow was made of steel capable of withstanding up to nine hundred pounds of pressure per square inch and featured a sharp eighteen-degree curve calculated to allow the hull to ride atop the ice for some distance and bring to bear a greater portion of its weight on the ice. In a process known as the down-breaking principle, the sheer bulk of the vessel would apply a perpendicular force to the ice surface, eventually causing tensile failure and a clean split in the ice sheet. The design had its origins in a 1965 doctoral dissertation by Roderick M. White, then a student at the Massachusetts Institute of

Technology and at the time of the *Manhattan*'s voyage a commander in the U.S. Coast Guard.[28] Inside the bow, beams spaced every eighteen to twenty-four inches supported the external plates, while multiple longitudinal and transverse bulkheads made the bow watertight and provided additional bracing. The layout was entirely geometrical, yet one observer who went below the foredeck saw the spider web of steel and commented that it looked as though welders had taken every piece of scrap iron in the yard and tacked them all up wherever there was room. The bow also measured sixteen feet wider than the rest of the ship, with shoulders jutting out eight feet on each side. This arrowhead design would provide adequate clearance for the broken ice to slide past the shoulders without binding the hull. Humble briefly considered an experimental icebreaking bow called the Alexbow, which operated much like a snowplow, where a forward nose under the waterline would exert pressure from beneath the ice, split the ice layer upward, and push the broken slabs aside along the plow's sloped edges. This design was largely untested at the time of the *Manhattan*'s voyage, however, and Humble felt the expedition already contained enough unknown variables not to be adding another, especially one so significant as the ship's icebreaking capability itself.[29]

PIPE DREAMS

While the laborious renovation work on the *Manhattan* continued throughout the spring and summer of 1969, the pipeline partnership known as TAPS operated on its own equally ambitious schedule. In February, the consortium officially announced its plans to construct an oil pipeline across Alaska from Prudhoe Bay to Valdez. The 789-mile pipeline carried an estimated price tag of $900 million and was scheduled to deliver its first barrels of crude oil in early 1972. Within a few months of the announcement—before a single right-of-way or construction permit had been secured, and even before the exact route had been determined—TAPS purchased eight hundred miles of forty-eight-inch-diameter, half-inch-thick steel pipe from three Japanese companies at a cost of $100 million. The order angered American steel companies, as well as some public officials in Alaska, who believed the job should have gone to domestic suppliers. If nothing else, they argued, good will alone should have convinced the oil industry to keep its business in Alaska. Steel firms across the country lobbied TAPS for the pipe contract, some offering to open a plant in Alaska. But such an order was beyond their present capabilities and would require extensive retooling of plants and mills, thus pushing the earliest delivery date back at least a year. With the Japanese suppliers ready to deliver the pipe in a matter of months, and at a cost cheaper than what U.S. firms were offering, the decision proved easy for TAPS. The pipe episode nevertheless demonstrated to the oil companies the necessity of massaging public sentiment and the value of positioning (or at least proclaiming) their own interests as aligned with those of the people of Alaska. It was a practice at which they would become very astute. The pipeline consortium also began staging tons of construction equipment in Valdez, Fairbanks, and Prudhoe Bay. When TAPS finally did apply for federal permits on June 6, 1969, the companies dutifully submitted the right-of-way application, a check for ten dollars to cover the permit processing fee, and a note to federal regulators that blithely advised, "If you have any additional questions concerning this Application or if you desire any further information, please wire or call collect."[30] Confident executives believed approval was only weeks away. Former Alaska governor and fervent industry supporter Walter Hickel had become secretary of the interior that January, and it did not appear unreasonable to TAPS to request official authorization of its plans by the end of the month. Stated ARCO's Robert O. Anderson, "[We believed] it was a done deal."[31]

If the industry's pipeline efforts seemed coordinated and well planned from the outside, the speed and confidence with which they operated belied a thorough lack of understanding of and appreciation for the development challenges ahead, especially regarding construction techniques and environmental protection in the Arctic. The industry initially planned to bury the pipeline for all but a fraction of the distance from Prudhoe Bay to Valdez. At a congressional hearing in September 1969, George Hughes, TAPS project director, declared that its team of arctic experts had determined soil conditions along the proposed route would permit burial of the line without irreparable damage to the terrain. Critics quickly pointed out exactly the opposite, that Prudhoe Bay crude oil would come out of the ground at over 150 degrees Fahrenheit, and that a "warm line" buried in the permafrost (permanently frozen ground found in all but the most southern parts of Alaska) would quickly turn the frozen tundra into a muddy swamp. When asked to provide a detailed account of the industry's research into the planning and design of the pipeline, TAPS chairman R. G. Dulaney submitted only a thin twenty-page summary.[32] With so many questions left unresolved, many members of Congress advocated the pipeline push be slowed down. Senator Gaylord Nelson of Wisconsin asked, "Why not put in some pilot projects in a half-dozen places and experiment with them for a year before we put in the pipeline? Then we will know [the environmental effects].... Why do we have to rush into this?"[33] Senator Henry M. Jackson of Washington similarly advised caution: "[T]here is, in the last analysis, no substitute for experience. It seems to me that you can make predictions up to a certain point, but then you do get involved in unknown factors."[34] Even Interior Secretary Hickel, who staunchly believed the oil industry possessed the expertise to meet every technical and environmental challenge, had to admit that their performance to date did not inspire confidence.[35] The permit TAPS believed was imminent would actually be years in coming. The eight hundred miles of steel pipe, on which the industry had received such a good deal from its Japanese suppliers, was now stacked in storage yards and would cost the owners thousands of dollars per month in rust prevention. Although there was no way for Humble to know it at the time, the hurried tempo of the Arctic Tanker Test, which was intended to keep pace with TAPS and which led the Haas task force to forgo its preferred custom-built tanker in favor of the *Manhattan*, also needn't have been so rushed.

In addition, TAPS suffered from a dysfunctional organizational structure in which each of the three participating companies insisted on placing its own representatives in administrative and managerial positions. This triplication of effort resulted in decision making by committee, always a cumbersome process. When TAPS expanded in February 1969 to include five additional companies with Prudhoe Bay interests, the organization contained multiple redundant layers of executive and management committees, all of which had to be in total agreement for even the most basic decisions. The companies ostensibly cooperated with each other to build the pipeline, yet each naturally placed its own interest ahead of the partnership's. This tension made for uneasy and ever-shifting alliances in the competitive wrangling over the Prudhoe Bay riches. The inefficiency of a system in which paradoxically everyone and no one is calling the shots would plague TAPS for the duration of the project. One frustrated project manager spelled out his concerns in a letter to supervisors: "[T]here appears to be no decision making authority.... Even minor design changes require weeks to resolve and it is impossible to obtain immediate answer[s] to everyday problems that arise." Wally Hickel took an equally exasperated, albeit lighthearted view: "By the time all the principals could be telephoned in Texas, New York, California and London, it could take weeks just to get an agreement on what color to paint the toilets in the construction camps."[36]

To make matters worse, TAPS did not even have a staff of its own, but rather borrowed employees from the parent companies or hired consultants as the need arose. With TAPS entirely dependent on its owner companies to furnish personnel as well as its operating funds, the organization was essentially a hostage to the strategic and often obstructionist maneuverings of the companies relative to one another. For example, ARCO, whose preferred transportation method had always been a trans-Alaska pipeline, proved eager to approve budgets for TAPS and invest whatever funds it deemed necessary to expedite pipeline construction. Other companies proved far less willing to loosen their purse strings. In January 1969, as cost estimates for the pipeline began creeping steadily upward, the Humble/Jersey executive board voted to withhold funds until a more complete picture of both the eventual cost and each company's financial obligations emerged. For the next few years, as ARCO continually motioned for budget approvals and disbursements of funds, the other companies alternately backed away from such commitments or outright blocked such action, thereby leaving TAPS with neither funds nor direction and exacerbating the difficulties faced by its already inefficient operation.[37] Such counterintuitive behavior—oil companies actually *hindering* the development of Alaska crude—appears explicable only in the context of individual companies strategically positioning themselves for some real or perceived advantage over their competitors. This brand of cutthroat competition, the most basic operating premise of the very industry itself, would permeate every decision and action in Alaska and must be the context through which such events are examined, the wrangling over transportation options included. As Robert Douglas Mead wrote in his study of the pipeline: "Oil does not make for comfortable bedfellows, but TAPS was the bed in which the partners would have to lie."[38] British oil magnate Calouste Gulbenkian put it much more vividly: "Oilmen are like cats. You can never tell from the sound of them whether they are fighting or making love."[39]

3

Submarines, Blimps, Trains, and Ships

The icebound Arctic coast is not an insuperable obstacle to the development of this promising prospect. Oil in the Arctic awaits the advance of civilization upon this, the last of our geographical frontiers.

—Wallace Pratt (1944)[1]

Both the Alaska pipeline and arctic tanker proposals faced innumerable technical challenges never before encountered by American industry. In the quest to bring Prudhoe Bay crude oil to market the oil companies met a steep learning curve, one that would require more ingenuity and innovation than anyone initially guessed. And because the industry found conventional methods of oil production so obviously untenable in the unique arctic environment, any proposal—no matter how unconventional—received at least some attention. In the years following the North Slope discovery no idea seemed too outlandish. Government officials, private individuals, engineers, environmentalists, businessmen, and everyone in between hatched innovative transportation schemes.[2]

General Dynamics proposed a fleet of nuclear submarines that could silently ferry Prudhoe Bay crude under the polar ice cap to markets in the U.S. and abroad. The industry giant promoted the idea by touting its efficacy over conventional ships in difficult surface conditions. Roger Lewis, the company's president, also invoked the standard economic argument: "Our work shows that the submarine tanker will achieve substantially lower costs for moving the oil to the United States East Coast than those attributed to projected pipeline projects."[3] Preliminary designs called for rectangular-hulled submarines, nine hundred feet in length, of between 170,000 and 250,000 deadweight tons. General Dynamics calculated that the task required a fleet of thirteen to eighteen vessels, each making one trip daily between Prudhoe Bay and southwest Greenland, where the oil would be transferred to surface tankers. The vessel designs even provided for the comfort of the forty-nine-person crew with individual staterooms, library, recreation room, and hobby shop.[4]

If the submarine proposal seemed at the time like cutting-edge technology, the concept actually was first articulated in 1648 by Bishop John Wilkins, cofounder of the Royal Society of London. Wilkins described arctic submarine traffic in his volume *Mathematical Magick*, where he extolled the benefits of such travel including safety from "ice and great frost which do so much endanger the passages toward the Poles."[5] More than three hundred years later, Lawrence R. Jacobsen of General Dynamics sounded an identical refrain in his description of the advantages realized by submarines over surface vessels:

> [T]he submarine cruises below the ice canopy in a protected environment which is essentially stable and at constant temperature with but small variations throughout the entire route. It sails clear of ice, fog, wind, subfreezing temperature, storms and waves—exposed to a minimum of environmental hazards.[6]

General Dynamics acknowledged the same major difficulty facing Humble's Arctic Tanker Test—the design, construction, and operation of an offshore loading facility at Prudhoe Bay. A submarine terminal that would allow for either surface or subsurface loading required three hundred feet of water, a depth not found anywhere near Prudhoe Bay for dozens of miles from shore. General Dynamics proposed laying fifty miles of underwater pipelines from the producing oil fields to an offshore terminal located at sufficient ocean depth. The high cost of the submarines and logistical difficulties of the terminal ultimately doomed the proposal.[7]

The concept lingered in the minds of some, however, and in 1975 the U.S. Department of Commerce commissioned a study, titled "Arctic Submarine Transportation System," which found that nuclear submarine tankers "can provide the necessary transport momentum for an effective Arctic oil delivery system."[8] Undertaken when construction of the Trans-Alaska Pipeline had already reached its peak, the report recommended an approach largely similar to that of General Dynamics a few years before. A fleet of between twelve and thirty submarines, each measuring one thousand feet in length and capable of carrying two million barrels of crude oil (roughly a single day's production at Prudhoe Bay), would ferry the cargo either directly to the U.S. East Coast or to a transfer terminal for shipment by surface tankers. One such transfer terminal could be based in Norway, the report noted, thereby circumventing the Jones Act and enabling the use of foreign-flagged vessels.

The report's authors played up what they called "attractive economics" while downplaying the system's many logistical difficulties. At one point they blithely suggested that an arctic loading dock "can be designed and constructed by methods similar to those now in use." Recognizing the need to massage diplomatic relations with Canada—a lesson no doubt learned in the aftermath of the *Manhattan*'s voyage—the authors made note of the political and diplomatic risks. The report optimistically suggested that any international questions, including those related to the fleet's right of innocent passage, would prove easy to resolve. For readers left wondering why such a system with so many advantages and so few drawbacks had yet to be implemented, the report likewise expressed bewilderment:

> Presumably...its technical feasibility and economic viability have not been apparent to prospective users. Compared with pipelines and surface tankers (even Arctic pipelines and icebreaking surface tankers) the submarine has been looked upon as being "unnatural." In reality, its characteristics are uniquely compatible with the Arctic transportation environment.[9]

That this particular submarine proposal received such favorable treatment was perhaps explained by the makeup of its study team: Newport News Shipbuilding, Westinghouse Electric, Bechtel Incorporated, and Mobil Shipping and Transportation—all companies that stood to receive lucrative contracts in the event such a transportation system was implemented.[10]

Most in the burgeoning environmental movement opposed the Alaska pipeline on the grounds that it would irrevocably harm the fragile ecosystems and wilderness character of the regions it crossed. They also decried the potential for tanker accidents and oil spills on the marine route between Alaska and the West Coast. Those environmentalists with a more pragmatic streak who were not steadfastly opposed to oil development altogether tended to favor crude oil transport via a railroad corridor from Alaska through Canada to the Lower 48. The sentiments of David Brower, the one-time Sierra Club director who split off to form the more radical Friends of the Earth, largely summed up those of the environmental movement: although he preferred that Prudhoe Bay remain undeveloped altogether and advocated an emphasis on alternate (less polluting) energy sources, he nonetheless recognized the inevitability of Alaska oil production and therefore favored an overland railroad through Canada. Friends of the Earth aligned with the Wilderness Society and Environmental Defense Fund to submit four volumes of public comment to the U.S. Interior Department stating their opposition to oil development in general, as well as tepid support for the trans-Canada alternatives.[11]

In 1971, the Interior Department evaluated the railroad and other transportation alternatives in its Draft Environmental Impact Statement (DEIS) for the Trans-Alaska Pipeline, the first such document produced in accordance with the recently passed National Environmental Policy Act (NEPA). Critics pounced on the meager analysis found in the DEIS. The document ran a scant 256 pages, with only eight devoted to the project design of the entire pipeline. Its cursory approach notwithstanding, the DEIS found the railroad concept unfeasible. Moving two million barrels of crude oil per day across Alaska alone necessitated sixty-three trains of one hundred cars each. A rail system all the way to the Lower 48 would require even more. The DEIS also noted the prodigious amounts of gravel needed to construct a rail bed, not to mention the substantial earth fill and excavation necessary to provide suitable grades for mountain range crossings. Railroad advocates disputed the Interior Department's numbers, but the concept went no further. Representatives from the oil industry itself stated that they gave serious consideration to railroads, but a trans-Alaska pipeline proved preferable for a number of reasons.[12]

Some industry observers suggested that conventional tanker trucks could move Prudhoe Bay crude oil. This concept quickly proved nearly impossible from a technical standpoint and so economically marginal that it had no strong supporters. The estimated fleet size to move a single day's Prudhoe Bay production numbered sixty thousand vehicles, nearly the same amount of semitrailer trucks operating in the entire United States at that time. The system would require more than ten thousand daily shipments and two hundred separate loading and unloading facilities at each end of the line. Round-the-clock travel of tens of thousands of trucks would necessitate an eight-lane, all-weather paved road south from Prudhoe Bay. These logistical difficulties, not to mention the notorious Alaska weather and certainty of highway accidents, ruled out any serious consideration of the tanker truck method.[13]

Cargo aircraft had long been the workhorse of the oil industry in the Arctic. The C-130 Hercules, for all its remarkable payload capacity, still required roughly two hundred trips to supply a single drilling rig. In the winter construction season following the Prudhoe Bay strike, one Fairbanks freight carrier held enough contracts to fly five Hercules aircraft twenty-four hours a day for the entire winter. The takeoffs and landings on the North Slope at this time numbered one thousand per day.[14] With so many airplanes constantly in the air proving their utility, both Lockheed, the maker of the Hercules, and Boeing decided to explore the feasibility of using cargo airplanes to fly crude oil out. In 1972, Boeing unveiled the design of a mammoth aircraft with twelve jet engines, a 478-foot wingspan, and an eighty-three-foot tail. Two wing-mounted removable pods measuring 150 feet long and twenty-six feet in diameter would hold the crude oil. The plane's gross takeoff weight would be an astounding 1,750 tons.[15] Other proposals called for the use of dirigibles, nonrigid balloons, and hovercrafts. In its evaluation of pipeline alternatives, the Interior Department dismissed such suggestions with a mere two sentences, one noting that a single day's production at Prudhoe Bay equaled thirty times the total tonnage of freight carried by every U.S. domestic airline in 1968.[16]

One of the more inventive transportation proposals came from Bud Brown Enterprises, Inc., of Scottsdale, Arizona. The system utilized steel towers, spaced at 800-to-1,500-foot intervals, with an aerial tramway mounted on the upper half of the towers and an oil pipeline suspended on the lower half. The tramway would facilitate movement of people and cargo by self-propelled vehicles hanging from dual parallel cables. The pipeline design included in the proposal was remarkably similar to that ultimately employed by the oil companies—a forty-eight-inch steel pipe wrapped in heat insulation with a network of valves and pumping stations.[17] The proposal touted the perceived advantages over a traditional pipeline. The tramway, the inventor claimed, would reduce ground disturbance by eliminating the need for a maintenance road. It would also provide year-round passenger and cargo transportation along the line, as opposed to a roadway that could be rendered impassible by snowstorms. Byron "Bud" Brown, the president of the company, could be given to overstatement in his project description, as when he blithely claimed that operation of both the tramway and pipeline would not be affected by the weather, earthquakes, or landslides. Brown, apparently sensing by mid-1972 that his idea had not yet received the appropriate consideration by either the oil industry or the federal government, filed a series of affidavits with the Interior Department. He stated that his permit applications for construction of an aerial tramway and oil pipeline had been submitted in November 1970, that he held patent applications for said pipeline system, that an independent engineering analysis confirmed the feasibility of the system, and that a Wall Street bank was prepared to loan Bud Brown Enterprises $2 billion for the project. Despite winning three honorable mention citations for engineering innovation from the Petroleum Engineer Publishing Company, Brown's proposal met with incredulity from the Interior Department. The DEIS dismissed the proposal outright, noting the exceptionally high cost of elevating both a pipeline and tramway for eight hundred miles. Interior also refuted the system's supposed invulnerability to weather when it observed that winds over one hundred miles per hour were not uncommon on the North Slope. The aerial tramway proposal went no further.[18]

In the end, each of the above schemes for bringing Alaska North Slope oil to market proved too expensive, too logistically difficult, and often too outlandish to merit more than passing consideration. Only Humble's Arctic Tanker Test would receive significant attention as a viable complement/alternative to the Alaska pipeline. Perhaps the best analysis of these schemes as viable alternatives is made by Robert Douglas Mead, a journalist who reported on the construction of the Alaska pipeline in the mid-1970s:

[A]ll depended on technologies that did not yet exist to replace one that, even granting all its possible fallibilities, was at least known from a century of experience.

Most suffered also in presentation from bad arithmetic which converted misplaced decimal points and too many zeroes (a billion for a million, say) into forceful argument for economic feasibility. What counted finally was that the oil companies were not prepared to invest money in any of these possibilities, and it was, on the whole, their money that was at issue.[19]

The many proposals for transporting North Slope crude oil to market fell squarely into the tradition of the Alaska "booster," defined by environmental historian Peter A. Coates as one who advocates the immediate and total development of natural resources with assistance, not interference, from the government.[20] Boosters do not necessarily have to live in Alaska, Coates noted, as the state's frontier image lends itself to dreamers far and wide who believe Alaska's wide open spaces can accommodate industrial projects of a scale no other region possibly could. The booster tradition is further marked by a willingness to apply scientific and technological solutions to subdue, if not outright defeat, the natural environment. This is especially true when adaptive measures prove either not possible or more expensive to achieve. That only a select few of the proposals mentioned above were deemed meritorious at all merely reflects the basic economic limitations of transportation systems in the Arctic. Given the nature of boosterism in Alaska, where entrepreneurs believe the natural world possesses no obstacle that cannot be conquered by human daring and ingenuity, one should not be surprised by the number and inventiveness of the proposals or the seriousness with which some were promoted.

PREPARING FOR THE VOYAGE

Throughout the spring of 1969, Stan Haas and his team had every reason to grow more anxious. Sun Shipyard, the primary contractor on the *Manhattan* and the yard where the icebreaking bow was to be installed, fell weeks behind schedule. In early March the shipyard revised its production and engineering schedules, which had first been hammered out the previous December, before the *Manhattan* had even arrived. Aiming still for a July 15 completion date, Sun discovered its steelwork would have to be ramped up to four times the present rate, a near impossibility. The eventual rejoining of the tanker's sections was estimated to take five weeks, with just a single additional week allotted for full installation of the electrical, navigation, communication, and instrumentation systems. If Sun had any doubts about the ambitious schedule it did not let on to an increasingly skeptical Haas. Sun did inform Humble it would surely incur budget overruns, something project manager William Gray of Esso called a "disturbing situation."[21] The Humble team had already abandoned its hope of having the *Manhattan* ready for a June sailing, and now it appeared the July 15 target date would almost certainly slip by as well. Even with three different shipyards working round-the-clock shifts, the job of modifying the tanker was proving big enough to challenge every timetable and bust every budget.

Humble initially wanted to have the *Manhattan* reach the Arctic by June 1, while the strong winter ice remained intact. The ice would begin to decay about that time under the constant summer sunlight and warmer air temperatures. As the weeks slipped away it became increasingly apparent to Humble the vessel would not reach the Northwest Passage before July or even August, precisely when the ice would be in its weakest condition. Haas remained confident that even at that late date the team could find isolated pockets of winter-type ice, perhaps by steering the tanker even farther north toward the polar pack. If nothing else, Haas decided, a voyage in late summer would supply badly needed data on the ship's performance in ice, period. A second voyage in the spring of 1970 could then establish feasibility in the harshest climatic conditions. Haas naturally wanted delivery of the ship as soon as possible.

William Gray held a series of meetings with Sun representatives the first week of April at which he pulled no punches. Gray first bemoaned that Sun, despite having the *Manhattan* in dry dock in February, had still not fully ramped up its steel work. Charlie Zeien, Sun's vice president of engineering, countered that a number of design modifications over the previous several weeks required an additional eleven million pounds of steel, an order that could not be expected overnight. Sun further noted that every design modification, from the hull configuration to tailshaft materials to the searchlights to be installed on the forecastle, had to be certified by the U.S. Coast Guard and the American Bureau of Shipping. And while those agencies were turning applications around quickly, in just three or four days, the sheer number of open items on the checklist was staggering. Gray granted these points, but expressed frustration that Sun was still using planning and engineering schedules geared toward the July 15 target date when the material shortages suggested this timeline was completely unrealistic. (Gray's own staff calculated that at its current pace Sun would be lucky to have the vessel finished by the first of September.) He questioned whether Sun appreciated the magnitude of a problem so basic—planning and operations schedules that seemed to be in conflict—and in fact whether the shipyard even knew which was the "real" schedule.[22]

Following the meetings, Gray informed Haas of these problems. After weeks of badgering, he had finally gotten Sun to admit that the work would not be completed before August. Showing Haas a Sun memorandum from the April meetings, Gray vented his frustration: "This is the first written notice of any type which I have seen from Sun indicating other than the 15 July date." He assured Haas that at a follow-up meeting he would press the Sun team for a "realistic basis of what they currently consider the completion date."[23] The strain on Sun's workforce was relaxed a short time later, when the shipyard subcontracted with the Bath Iron Works to construct the ice-breaking bow, a task Sun originally planned to complete itself. The move saved Sun an estimated one hundred thousand man-hours and actually enabled the shipyard to complete the K-struts supporting the ice belt ahead of schedule.

The public relations department at Humble also had a busy spring. By March, various media and community relations personnel within the company had established the rather formal-sounding Public Information Task Force. Led by Arch A. Smith II, the group was charged with disseminating information about the expedition while being careful to protect proprietary data. Haas and his engineers had identified five categories of information they instructed the PR team not to reveal to the public either during or after the voyage: strength measurements of ice, velocity of the tanker through different types of ice, power plant performance, forces on the tanker's hull, and ship motion data. Hank Rosenthal, an affable, lanky New Jersey native with Texas credentials as a football star at Sam Houston College, was tapped to be the onboard media liaison for the voyage. Rosenthal liked to joke he got the assignment because he was the only man in the Humble press office who had an active seaman's card (as a teenager he'd been a cook on his father's fishing boat in the Gulf of Mexico). Among Rosenthal's first duties was arranging travel, accommodations, and other logistics for the scores of reporters who had requested passage on the tanker. This would prove a challenge that exercised all of Rosenthal's organizational and diplomacy skills. With limited cabin space on the tanker, the PR team decided that reporters would only be allowed onboard for between two and ten days at a time, whereupon they would be asked (ordered, really) to rotate off the ship and make room for others. Rosenthal would find himself in the difficult position of trying to accommodate each reporter's particular area of interest before he had to kick him off the ship. In addition, the Canadian Arctic was not exactly replete with airstrips, hotels, and other basic services, and devising a schedule for the actual transfer of press on and off the vessel caused many headaches for Humble.

The PR team received hundreds of requests from reporters asking to tag along for the entire expedition, this on a vessel normally suited for a crew of about fifty. One such application came from Elizabeth Rogers of the Sierra Club, who requested passage on the *Manhattan* to write a series of articles about the environmental impacts of oil development in the Arctic. Humble politely declined Rogers's offer.[24] William Smith of the *New York Times* talked himself on to the *Manhattan* by approaching Humble chairman Mike Wright and convincing him that only an outside reporter with full access, not a Humble staff writer, would bring credibility to the project. In addition to Smith, the company granted full passage to Bern Keating of *National Geographic* and hired Dan Guravich as the official expedition photographer.

In designing an expedition logo that would appear on press releases, magazine ads, posters, and other promotional materials, the PR task force employed the Esso Tiger of the famous "Put a Tiger in Your Tank" advertising campaign. In 1959, a young marketing trainee named Emery Smyth recalled a short-lived series of ads for Esso Extra, a brand of gasoline marketed by Standard in Great Britain, that featured a leaping, ferocious tiger. Smyth knew that recent market research had shown consumers equated premium gasoline with power, and he revived the mascot and added the soon-to-be-famous slogan. Executives at Jersey liked the idea but were put off by the savage, wild-eyed beast. Artists in the company's marketing division gave the mascot a complete makeover, turning him into a friendly, cartoonlike figure. This was the finishing touch on what would become one of the most famous advertising campaigns in history. For the *Manhattan* logo, Humble positioned the grinning tiger in front of the tanker, between the U.S. and Canadian flags, and outfitted him with earmuffs, a sartorial flourish perfect for the journey to the Arctic.[25]

In early June, the Humble PR team officially kicked off its public information campaign with "Operation Northwest Passage," a closed-circuit, one-hour TV news conference held simultaneously in New York and Washington, DC (a state-of-the-art event in 1969). Humble president Charles F. Jones and Jack Bennett, general manager of supply, spoke and took questions from the Overseas Press Club in New York, while board chairman Mike A. Wright and Stan Haas did the same from the Madison Hotel in Washington. Some three hundred reporters from the U.S. and as far away as London, Sydney, and Tokyo participated in what Humble later boasted was, according to some newsmen, "the most impressive and complete such conference they had ever attended."[26]

While the speakers relayed many scientific and technical details of the imminent voyage, the PR team who put the show together knew full well that engineering data did not necessarily make for the best news copy. The history and romanticism of the fabled Northwest Passage, however, would certainly capture the public's interest, and Humble proved savvy enough to frame its *Manhattan* expedition as a milestone in polar exploration. The company produced maps of the Northwest Passage in a vintage, antiquated style that resembled the nautical charts one might find in a nineteenth-century London map office. In his remarks at the news conference, Humble chairman Mike Wright invoked the names of past explorers like John Cabot, Martin Frobisher, William Edward Parry, and Roald Amundsen as he described the five-hundred-year quest for a passage to the Orient. Wright further romanticized the voyage by comparing it to another frontier of exploration then making headlines around the world—NASA's Apollo program, which in a matter of weeks would land astronauts on the moon. Calling each voyage a "point where dreams, fantasies and hopes gave way to possibility and foreseeable reality," Wright left reporters to ponder how two institutions from Houston,

Texas—Humble Oil and NASA—were simultaneously closing separate chapters in the annals of exploration.[27] It was a PR man's dream.

The lofty rhetoric now concluded, Humble's other representatives at the news conference handled the nuts and bolts of the expedition itself. Jack Bennett explained to the assembled journalists that while Humble was fully behind the proposed trans-Alaska pipeline, Prudhoe Bay's estimated daily production of two million barrels of oil stood to create a glut in West Coast markets. Surplus crude, Bennett claimed, would somehow have to be delivered to the East Coast. He noted that Humble had considered other options, such as transcontinental pipelines and tanker routes through the Panama Canal or even all the way around Cape Horn, the southern tip of South America. Humble had dismissed these routes—Cape Horn for its incredible distance and the Panama Canal because its relatively narrow channel could not accommodate large tankers. In the end, Bennett explained, the Northwest Passage seemed the likeliest candidate for success.[28]

Haas took the podium next and described the icebreaking tanker, emphasizing its ongoing renovation and many awe-inspiring characteristics. By this point Humble knew full well there was no hope of having the *Manhattan* ready by the target date of July 15—yet the company had announced that date in earlier press releases and Haas was now loathe to admit otherwise in front of the TV cameras. He stretched the truth with a straight face: "If all goes to according to schedule, mid-July should find the *Manhattan* ready, willing, and able to become the first commercial vessel ever to conquer the Northwest Passage."[29]

After Haas traced the tanker's planned route on a map, it was left to Charles F. Jones to place the *Manhattan* and Alaska oil in the larger context of the domestic oil industry and international markets. Jones first granted that pure economics and corporate self-interest underpinned the Arctic Tanker Test, yet he also asked the public to remember what he called the project's "broader implications." Prudhoe Bay development, the Humble president noted, would have a significant impact on the nation's energy supply and go some distance to establishing petroleum self-sufficiency. He characterized the Northwest Passage as an international trade route that might profoundly influence both industrial development of the Arctic and patterns of international trade. The Canadian Arctic, for example, held vast storehouses of minerals such as iron ore, copper, nickel, lead, and zinc—what Jones referred to as "waiting wealth"—that might be developed should the *Manhattan* succeed in opening the route. In many ways what Jones anticipated was the centuries-old promise of the passage as a commercial route between the western and eastern worlds. From there his argument took a short and logical step to the geopolitical interests of the United States. The U.S. military had long recognized the strategic importance of the Arctic, and the Humble press kit duly contained a map that showed that a point near the western entrance to the Northwest Passage was roughly equidistant from New York, London, and Tokyo. These central facts led Jones to reflect on Humble's role in global trade:

> History teaches us to expect the unexpected. It teaches us that new sea routes have frequently had unforeseen consequences; that they have affected the rate of development in various parts of the world; and that they have actually altered the relationships and balance between nations. When the Passage becomes an accomplished fact, we are truly in the hands of history.[30]

For the head of a company that exuded such confidence when it came to the technical details of oil development, Jones struck many as candid when he acknowledged the problematic nature of the *Manhattan*'s voyage: "If the Northwest Passage is opened, overnight the business, governmental, and educational communities will be confronted with great opportunities and difficulties for which they are not now prepared."[31] The socioeconomic, political, and legal effects of these developments had not been adequately studied at the time of Jones's comments, and while he stopped short of identifying environmental impacts, those too would have to be examined by all interested and affected parties as the project moved forward. That Humble confined its focus exclusively to the scientific and technological issues related to the *Manhattan* test was hardly surprising. This simple experiment, however, would surely compel others to consider the many other impacts related to the opening of the Arctic.

The fifteenth of July came and went, and still no *Manhattan*. Humble pushed the departure date to the end of the month, and almost immediately moved it back again to sometime in August. The process of bringing the ship's various pieces back together had been agonizingly slow. In late May, the finished midship section had been towed from Alabama to Newport News, where it was joined with the afterbow. This segment then found its way back to the Sun yard a month later, where welders reattached the stern. Finally, on July 28, the vessel received its new icebreaking bow, and the *Manhattan* was a complete ship again.

Ever quick to seize upon an additional PR opportunity, Humble hosted an "open ship" at Sun Shipyard on August 11, where the general public toured the vessel, met her officers, and enjoyed refreshments on the ship's fantail. The completed vessel awed observers who were free to roam her decks. The *Manhattan*, courtesy of the new bow, which added to her overall length, now measured just over one thousand feet—nearly one-fifth of a mile. The many layers of additional steel brought her displacement tonnage up to over 150,000, but actually dropped her deadweight capacity (the amount of cargo a vessel can carry) to 105,000 tons. Everything about the *Manhattan* was huge. Her anchors weighed thirty-five tons apiece, while each individual link of the anchor chains clocked in at 180 pounds. In order to emphasize the scientific nature of the expedition, Humble personnel directed the visitors' attention to the hundreds of pressure sensors installed inside the hull for its entire length. The sensors would measure just how the hull flexed under the strain of the ice pack, recording data at a rate as high as thirty pulses per second, while a select number of weather gauges noted the air temperature at various locations around the hull. These data points would then be tagged with the corresponding rudder angle, position of the ship, and exact time of day so as to establish how each variable interacted with one another to affect the tanker's performance. To round out the data-gathering system, a dozen closed-circuit-TV cameras pointed at different sections of the hull would provide Humble engineers with a visual record of the ship's icebreaking capabilities. A series of white crosses had been painted six feet apart in a vertical line on the hull to provide scale for the observers. The Humble PR department happily entertained the public on the tanker, fully aware that the event represented the first time anyone could comprehend that the Northwest Passage project was actually going to happen. Roughly half of the day's one thousand guests were journalists, most of whom had arrived at the shipyard on a Humble-chartered airplane from Houston or buses from New York. Media inquiries thereafter sharply increased.[32]

Before the *Manhattan* could embark on her history-making voyage, the ship's captains had to take her out for sea trials. No captain in history had ever sailed such a vessel, let alone through ice-covered waters. Humble accordingly tripled the amount of experience on the bridge by assigning three captains for the expedition. Roger A. Steward, a graduate of the Massachusetts Maritime Academy and certified master for over two decades, served as the shipmaster. Donald Graham and Arthur W. Smith, both masters in their own rights, were named staff captains. In the months leading up to the voyage, the three captains underwent extensive icebreaker training. They sailed on both the U.S. Coast Guard icebreaker *Staten Island* and the *John A. MacDonald* of the Canadian Coast Guard fleet. They also attended classes at Canada's Department of Transport in Halifax, the U.S. Navy's Ice Forecasting School in Maryland, and the Satellite Navigation School in California. Stan Haas had been frustrated by the lack of available data on the *Manhattan*'s original 1962 sea trials following her construction by Bethlehem Steel and launching at Quincy, Massachusetts. All Haas knew was that the tanker's initial sea trials had lasted just two days and consisted only of speed tests, turning maneuvers, and maximum and normal boiler operation. More information on the tests certainly would have been useful for Humble, although the icebreaker modifications to the *Manhattan* essentially resulted in a brand-new tanker that would have to undergo baseline trials anyway.

When Captain Steward finally got the tanker in the water on August 2, 1969, he discovered that, in the words of one observer, "the ship could float and very little else."[33] The heeling system could not be tested because a starter motor in one of the pumps failed. Helicopter landing tests had to be canceled when the navigational equipment wouldn't work. Even the lowering and raising of the anchors failed to go smoothly. When it was discovered that a seam between hull panels on the afterbow had not been welded properly, engineers knew the defect would not inhibit the handling of the ship during the sea trials—but that photographs showing an obvious crack down the side of the tanker would be a public relations disaster. Until they could fix the weld, they simply covered it with huge amounts of masking tape and a touch-up of paint.

The most serious problem occurred in the port engine, where a three-quarter-inch steel nut had passed through the gear train and caused a not-insignificant amount of damage. Where the loose nut came from was never determined, but frustrated engineers suspected the snafu resulted from an oil change they believed was entirely unnecessary. In the *Manhattan*'s first seven years of operation, her engines had been lubricated with products from an oil company that was not Humble. "No way are we going to let Brand X get any credit," huffed one senior executive in ordering the entire propulsion system be flushed.[34] Changing to Humble-brand lubricants proved a time-consuming exercise with no mechanical advantage whatsoever—and now it appeared the operation had left at least one misplaced nut and who knows what other debris rattling around the system. Thankfully for an expedition already weeks behind schedule, repairs to the port gear took only a few days.

Haas shrugged when the vessel completed her first day of sea trials. "We didn't sink anyway."[35] The official date of departure was now set for Sunday, August 24—a date, naturally, Humble would miss by two days.

4

"*Bienvenu dans ces eaux.*
Welcome to Canadian waters."

No machine has ever possessed the incredible mass, momentum, and physics of a modern oil tanker, and few other machines are capable of such environmental damage.
—Eric Nalder, *Tankers Full of Trouble* (1994)[1]

On the very same weekend the *Manhattan* was completing her sea trials in Chesapeake Bay, a continent away the University of Alaska convened its twentieth Alaska Science Conference in Fairbanks under the banner "Change in the North: People, Petroleum, Environment." By this time, some eighteen months after the discovery of oil at Prudhoe Bay, Alaskans had begun to appreciate that the developments on the North Slope stood to alter their lives in numerous ways, some of which they could scarcely imagine. The conference brought together more than a hundred scientists, oil industry representatives, environmentalists, economists, and roughly one thousand members of the general public to discuss Alaska's future as an oil state. Conference chair and university professor Victor Fischer explained the goals of the meeting:

> We hope that from the conference will emerge answers to questions that haven't been answered, such as the importance of Alaska's crude oil on the American market and issues pertaining to Arctic ecology. We don't expect to answer all the questions about oil impact on the state, but this conference should provide information needed for decision-making in economic, social, and environmental issues.[2]

The conference coincided with an awakening environmental consciousness in Alaska and nationwide. For many, the impending oil development at Prudhoe Bay raised concerns about ecological preservation and the value of wilderness. Edgar Wayburn, vice president of the Sierra Club, noted that the very theme of the conference acknowledged more than the obvious economic value of Alaska's resources. "Alaska," he explained, "is one of the last unspoiled places on earth, a Last Frontier where there are great decisions still to be made, where we still have the chance to study the values of an area, to weigh these values, and to make intelligent choices as to their highest use."[3] For Wayburn and the burgeoning environmental movement, Alaska, with its millions of acres of ostensibly untouched land, was the perfect ideological construct in which society could weigh largely intangible environmental values against the more quantifiable economic gains of resource development—a comparison groups like the Sierra Club confidently believed the environment would win. Wayburn was not the first to make such arguments about Alaska; John Muir had done so half a century before, and he was followed by such pioneering conservationists as Charles Sheldon, Robert Marshall, Starker Leopold, and Olaus and Mardy Murie. The Arctic National Wildlife Range (later renamed Refuge), a federally protected, ecologically diverse region that sat immediately to the east of Prudhoe Bay, had been established in 1960 at the urging of environmentalists and sportsmen both inside and outside Alaska.[4] Now Wayburn framed his comments in the same context of wilderness preservation and the idea that such "unspoiled" places remained essential to the spiritual health of all humankind.

Humble vice president James H. Galloway represented the company in Fairbanks and spoke of the oil industry's commitment to environmental protection. (Stan Haas, who obviously couldn't attend the conference because his presence that week was required on the bridge of the *Manhattan*, submitted a short paper on the Arctic Tanker Test that was included in the conference proceedings.) Galloway used the example of Alaska's Kenai National Moose Range, where ongoing oil development had not adversely affected wildlife habitat, to illustrate the careful approach the industry would take on the North Slope. He further referenced the previous two hundred years of development in Alaska, including rampant resource exploitation by Russian fur traders, gold mining, the buildup of U.S. military facilities, and construction of the Alaska Highway. All represented an invasion of the wilderness, noted Galloway, yet he differentiated these historical antecedents from the current effort on the North Slope by emphasizing the industry's deliberate and premeditated approach to development. Where those developers of earlier eras bulldozed their way across the land with little to no planning whatsoever, the oil industry would use its technological know-how to preserve the environment to the greatest possible extent. For Galloway, the prospect of oil development and its attendant environmental impact was a given—the only question was what precautions the industry would gladly take to minimize that impact.

While the environment figured prominently in many conference debates, the larger theme underpinning every discussion was Alaska's sudden leap into the international realm of major oil-producing states. To what extent could this brand-new state, still characterized by its frontier mentality and a largely transient population, prove politically astute enough to play such a high-stakes game with some of the most powerful corporations in the world? The largest oil field on the continent lay in Alaskans' backyard, and if the imminent financial rewards to the state seemed too spectacular to comprehend, so too did the accompanying social and political issues that all citizens would be forced to engage.

A general warning call was sounded by Robert Engler, a professor of political science at Sarah Lawrence College and fierce critic of the oil industry's worldwide power. Noting the lack of what he called a "social philosophy" in governments where revenues are so directly tied to oil industry profits, Engler left no doubts as to his views of the perils facing Alaska: "Wherever the industry has functioned, its concentrated economic power...has been forged into political power over the community. Law, the public bureaucracies, the political machinery, foreign policy and public opinion have been harnessed for private privileges and the immunity from public accountability of the international brotherhood of oil merchants."[5] Engler challenged Alaskans to develop a new democratic philosophy that would emphasize the public interest over private entrepreneurship.

Oilmen and industry advocates responded to Engler's charges with incredulity. "I thought I worked in the international petroleum industry," stated Geoff Larminie of BP, "but as [Engler] carried on with his list of original sins I began to think I was in some Mafia-like organization." Tom Kelly, the state's resource commissioner, took exception when Engler questioned the integrity of public officials who had been recruited from industry and planned to return to it following their stint in government—a practice Engler disparagingly referred to as the "revolving door." Himself a former oilman, Kelly replied, "I find it inconceivable to say that a man entrusted with mining policy should not be a mining engineer or geologist."[6]

The harshest rebuke—not only to Engler, but to every so-called expert who offered advice at the conference—came from Alaska Senator Ted Stevens, who, in an impromptu speech to conferees, thundered, "I am up to here with people who tell us how to develop our country."[7] Stevens resented the outside influence of Washington bureaucrats and national environmental groups. He believed their proposed regulations on oil development represented just another form of economic paternalism that prevented Alaskans from determining their own future. Alaska's senior senator went so far as to call any environmental controls "absolutely stupid." (When asked to respond to Stevens's comments, Edgar Wayburn of the Sierra Club stated, "I don't think I need to. It was one of the most convincing speeches in favor of conservation I have ever heard.") However intemperate his remarks, Stevens accurately reflected the sentiments of most of his constituents, who longed to see North Slope crude flowing to market. Those Alaskans with conservationist sensibilities might have been horrified by their senator's inflammatory rhetoric, yet these individuals represented the minority opinion within the state. Alaska had entered the union as the forty-ninth state only a decade before, and in that time had seen her already unsteady economy rocked by the Good Friday earthquake of 1964, followed by a devastating Fairbanks flood three years later. Both events attracted federal disaster aid that provided a major economic boost. For a state so rich in natural resources, Alaska still could boast only a relatively small population, almost no industrial activity, and an annual state budget too meager to adequately cover the public service needs of citizens scattered over such a large, mostly roadless area. The Prudhoe Bay discovery was a godsend. It embodied for many the very fulfillment of Alaska's destiny. This would be the economic bonanza that Alaskans had long believed was their due. Any perceived impediments to that development—the environmental regulations Senator Stevens railed against, for example—represented nothing less than the denial of the Alaskan way of life.

So many debates, both at the science conference and in the ensuing years, turned on myth and ideology before fact and reality. Alaska was either a pristine, unspoiled wilderness that required protection for the benefit and spiritual health of all humankind—or a bleak, empty landscape devoid of any real value except for its extractable resources, upon which the very progress of civilization depended. The frontier image figured prominently in the way Alaskans viewed their home, yet again few could agree on the *meaning* of that frontier and whether it existed to be conquered or preserved. The same historical analogies regarding the nineteenth-century western frontier found employ in Alaska by both development forces and wilderness advocates. For the former, the settling of this new frontier called Alaska would reinforce the ideal of Frederick Jackson Turner by forging in its people a unique and distinctly American character. For the latter, the new Alaska frontier also stood as a defining national trait, but as a second chance, an opportunity to learn from past mistakes and prevent the wilderness from vanishing in a flurry of economic development.[8]

The often-heated debates at the Alaska Science Conference ultimately proved Professor Fischer correct in that none of the substantive questions received satisfactory answers during that single week in Fairbanks. Outside the halls of academia, the actual progress of Prudhoe Bay oil development marched inexorably forward. With permit applications on file with state and federal agencies, and construction equipment already staged along the proposed pipeline route, the oil industry now awaited delivery of eight hundred miles of steel pipe. In addition, by the time the Alaska Science Conference adjourned, the SS *Manhattan* was already in the water, steaming her way north.

THE VOYAGE BEGINS

At 11:12 a.m., on the bright, already hot summer morning of Tuesday, August 26, 1969, Master Roger Steward stood on the bridge of the largest icebreaker in the world and gave a simple command: "Let go fore and aft, slow astern." With that, the *Manhattan* gave a long, resounding blast from her whistle and left Pier No. 2 at the Sun Shipyard in Chester, Pennsylvania. Two tugs helped the vessel maneuver from her slip and guided her into the Delaware River. From there she sailed downriver to the south, rounded Cape May at the southern tip of New Jersey, and turned north into the Atlantic. Although the *Manhattan* had technically completed her sea trials two days before, a handful of systems were still being tested as the voyage began. Eight mechanics from Sun Shipyard would remain onboard as far as Halifax for machinery tune-ups. A series of baseline speed and maneuvering tests had also been scheduled to take place during the outbound voyage.[9]

The *Manhattan* boasted a crew of fifty-four, hand-picked from the Humble/Esso tanker fleet. Hundreds of men had put their names forward for the prestigious assignment. Those chosen represented the best on the company's roster of able-bodied seamen. Joining them on the ship were seventy-two others, including scientists, navigation specialists, helicopter pilots, communications experts, and "scientific observers"—a catchall term for reporters, photographers, public officials, oil industry representatives, and other nonessential personnel. All received from Humble a handbook of general information that included safety regulations and emergency procedures. The book also contained more mundane details, such as the location of laundry facilities and how to procure a toothbrush.[10] Many stepping onboard for the first time noticed the clocks were all set to the wrong time. Humble personnel informed them the expedition would operate on Houston time. The synchronization with Humble's land-based headquarters in Texas made sense from a logistical perspective, but nearly always resulted in confusion when dealing with any other entity in the outside world. Humble provided for the comfort of those onboard by outfitting the vessel with a library, movie theater, commissary, and recreation room that featured jogging machines, stationary bicycles, punching bags, a full 150 square feet of wrestling mats, and a Ping-Pong table with ten paddles, four nets, and a gross of balls. Wärtsilä, the Finnish company advising Humble on icebreaking operations, had recommended the installation of one sauna for every fifteen crew members (the suggestion was not followed). The absence of saunas aside, Humble provided the wide range of recreational activities on the advice of its arctic consultants. Experience had long shown that those who thrived on lengthy expeditions in extreme environments were the ones with hobbies that occupied their off hours. The reverse was also true: idle crew members were always the first to break. The doctor on the Canadian icebreaker *John A. MacDonald* was in the habit of visiting every crew member at the start of a mission in order to predict, based on his hobbies or lack thereof, his likely mental and physical state four months hence, a skill in which over the years he had developed some acuity. "A misfit in the Arctic is harder to bear than a misfit elsewhere," one officer stated.[11]

The *Manhattan* sported three lounges—but no alcohol. Humble originally planned to allow some controlled social drinking on what was certain to be a long voyage. The company also knew the many dignitaries who planned to visit the ship upon its arrival in Alaska would appreciate a beverage during the celebrations. The serious nature of the high-stakes expedition, however, convinced Humble to maintain its long-standing company policy that banned alcohol on oil tankers. One observer quipped that the policy broke a maritime tradition that went back thousands of years to the Phoenicians. The policy was not really enforced, and nearly every man onboard, including Stan Haas himself, had a number of bottles stashed away here and there. William Smith, the *New York Times* reporter, appropriately brought Canadian whiskey, sweet vermouth, bitters, and a jar of Maraschino cherries—all the makings for a Manhattan.[12]

Humble also knew that nothing proves as vital to maintaining high morale among the crew as good food. The company accordingly gave Chief Steward Leo Oliveira carte blanche to order whatever supplies he deemed necessary. Oliveira, who himself claimed to eat only one meal a day, did not hold back. Told to plan for a four-month voyage, Oliveira brought enough food for six. The immense store of provisions included seventy thousand pounds of canned food, fifty-one thousand eggs, forty thousand pounds of fruits and vegetables, six thousand pounds of coffee, fifty-six hundred quarts of milk, three hundred watermelons, and two hundred pounds of peanut butter. The meat locker contained four thousand pounds of chicken, three thousand pounds of prime rib, and, stashed in the rear of the freezer in case the vessel was still at sea on Thanksgiving, 764 turkeys.[13] With a total of twenty-five tons of meat onboard, each crew member could have eaten five full pounds of meat every day for the duration of the voyage. Across five hundred years of polar exploration starvation had always been a primary concern. Early expeditions faced the challenge of carrying food that would not spoil, and enough of it to feed a hardworking crew for years. Even then most expeditions depended on support ships with relief supplies, as well as Inuit hunters who supplied them with fresh meat. But on the *Manhattan*, the vessel that would finally achieve the centuries-old dream of commercial traffic in the Northwest Passage, every crew member could stuff himself daily with as much grub as he wanted—the mess was open twenty-four hours a day—and no one was in any danger of contracting scurvy. The dinner menu from September 16, 1969, is representative: salad, grilled sirloin steak, fried onions, macaroni and beef, steamed hickory sausage, sauerkraut, buttered fresh broccoli, corn cream style, okra and tomatoes, fried potatoes, pineapple sundae, cake, fresh fruit, coffee, tea, milk, fruit drink, and hot chocolate.[14]

Humble also gave every crew member the requisite "Arctic Parka" and other cold-weather gear. Those on the vessel already with experience in the Arctic, such as the contingent from the University of Alaska, scoffed at the flimsy parka the Houston-based company believed would be adequate. This was a summer voyage, however, with temperatures that while certainly colder than those in Texas did not present any real danger to the crew. Most would remain indoors anyway except for short sojourns to the deck to look at the ice. The parkas did not seem to elicit further complaint.[15]

The expedition handbook described in exact detail those areas of the ship where non-Humble personnel would not be allowed. The bridge and engine room, instrumentation van, analysis room, dark room, satellite navigation room, ice laboratory, and ice office were all strictly off-limits. Every person who set foot on the tanker had to sign a contract agreeing not to divulge any proprietary information, which, in all likelihood, none would be privy to anyway. Some arctic veterans felt put off by Humble's secrecy. Charles Swithinbank, an esteemed glaciologist taking part as one of BP's official representatives, was accustomed to expeditions where scientists willingly shared data with one another in the cause of intellectual collaboration. "This [Humble's security measures] was a rude slap in the face," noted Swithinbank.[16] Humble countered that it was making a significant investment in the Arctic Tanker Test—not just the monetary expense of the expedition but also a claim to the very form and pace of Prudhoe Bay development itself—and the company took seriously its exclusive hold on whatever data the voyage produced. The Teletype machines and radiophones utilized scrambling codes that garbled every transmission. Only the receivers at Humble's Houston headquarters could decode the messages. BP and ARCO, Humble's Alaska rivals, each put up $2 million in support of the expedition, an investment for which the companies received passage for two representatives on the tanker and a technical report to be produced following the voyage. "Nothing else," noted Ralph Maybourn of BP. "Not even a smile."[17]

The *Manhattan*'s officers received many congratulatory telegrams on the day of departure. A. E. Gibson, maritime administrator with the U.S. Department of Commerce, bid best wishes to the ship with a telegram steeped in the mythology now so familiar to the vessel: "Throughout our history, American ships, the skilled craftsmen who built them, and the intrepid men who sailed them have played a vital role in opening new paths of trade and progress to our nation."[18] Admiral Willard J. Smith, the commandant of the U.S. Coast Guard, sent his regards to Humble chairman Mike A. Wright, congratulating the company for the daring and ingenuity behind the experiment. The Coast Guard had taken a keen interest in the *Manhattan*'s voyage from day one, readily supplying all manner of baseline scientific data on the North American Arctic and providing extensive icebreaker training for the tanker's crew. Now that the *Manhattan* was in the water, the Coast Guard assigned one of its icebreakers, the *Northwind*, to rendezvous with the tanker two weeks hence in the Canadian Arctic and accompany her through the Northwest Passage.[19]

Another telegram came from Ian Watson, the chairman of Canada's Committee on Indian Affairs and Northern Development: "Your daring voyage through the Canadian Arctic Archipelago will stir the imagination of people everywhere who are interested in Arctic development. Bienvenu dans ces eaux. Welcome to Canadian waters. We wish you God speed. Bon voyage."[20] The wording was not accidental. Ottawa firmly believed the waters the Humble tanker would be crossing were Canadian. The voyage provoked intense reaction in Canada with regard to environmental protection, economic security, maritime safety regulation, and ultimately the very question of who owns the Northwest Passage.

"WELL, PARTNER, WHAT DO YOU THINK WE OUGHT TO DO?"

A cartoon in the October 7, 1969, issue of the *Christian Science Monitor* depicted a hapless Canadian Mountie and his horse standing on an ice floe while the *Manhattan* surges past. "Well, partner," says the horse, "what do you think we ought to do?" It was a good question, one that had occupied public officials in Ottawa and the general citizenry of Canada for some time.

Humble Oil did not request advance permission from the Canadian government before sending its tanker north. Neither did the U.S. Coast Guard in the case of the *Northwind*, nor the U.S. State Department regarding the entire expedition. To formally ask for permission would be to acknowledge that the waters of the Northwest Passage indeed fell under Canadian jurisdiction. American officials instead believed the route qualified as an international waterway. Canadian Prime Minister Pierre Trudeau initially proved rather oblique on the question of the passage's status as territorial or international waters. When the *Manhattan* expedition was first announced, he stated his intent to assert "stewardship, if not sovereignty" over the Northwest Passage, though it remained unclear precisely what that meant.[21] The soft language angered some in Canada, including members of Trudeau's own government, who desired a firm stance on the issue and possibly a showdown with what they perceived as the arrogant neighbor to the south. Yet Mitchell Sharp, secretary of external affairs, similarly advised restraint:

> This is not a time for wide-ranging assertions of Canadian sovereignty in the Arctic made without regard to the international political and legal considerations [and] there is no necessity for us to make sweeping assertions to reinforce our position. That might satisfy our ego but would not add a whit to the international acceptability of our position.[22]

The seemingly equivocal nature of Trudeau's and Sharp's comments actually belied a firm resolve to assert functional sovereignty over the Canadian Arctic by assuming environmental stewardship of its waters. In announcing plans to send the *John A. MacDonald* as escort on the expedition, Ottawa signaled its intent to pursue an overall strategy of cooperation designed to avoid an immediate and direct confrontation with the United States, and allow time to develop an internationally defensible plan for achieving de facto control.[23]

Sharp further argued that the collaborative nature of Canada's response only underscored its ability to effectively control the passage. That the *Manhattan* likely would not be able to complete the transit without assistance from the *John A. MacDonald* demonstrated, according to Sharp, that the waters remained under Canadian jurisdiction. In addition, Humble had previously asked the Canadian Coast Guard for information about ice conditions. Though not an explicit request for permission to enter the Canadian Arctic, the overture further established Ottawa's operational control of the passage. And where international law failed to address certain unique regional geographical features—like ice-covered waters—Sharp argued individual states had the best claim to contribute to the development of such law.[24] In an October 1969 address that outlined his government's official policy with regard to the Arctic, Trudeau took the innovative step of basing limited sovereignty claims on grounds of environmental security. In proclaiming Canada a "trustee" for the region's unique environment, Trudeau stated, "We do not doubt for a moment that the rest of the world would find us at fault, and hold us liable, should we fail to ensure adequate protection of that environment from pollution or artificial deterioration."[25] With the *Manhattan* at that very moment crossing the Northwest Passage, the prime minister announced that neither economic development nor supposed rights of free passage would supersede environmental protection. Trudeau, himself an accomplished scuba diver with a keen appreciation for the world's oceans, made clear that Canada would not hinder development or even prohibit marine shipping through the region, but would implement a policy designed to protect the land and water from pollution. This policy took formal shape in April 1970, with the passage of the Arctic Waters Pollution Prevention Act, a piece of domestic legislation shrewdly designed to advance the argument with respect to international legal regimes of the time.

Individual nations recognized as early as 1909 the necessity of international agreements to safeguard the world's water bodies from pollution. That year, the United States and Great Britain signed the Boundary Waters Treaty, which established a joint commission to monitor the shared waterways between the U.S. and Canada and report on water pollution cases for action by the respective domestic enforcement agencies. The United States passed domestic legislation on marine pollution as early as 1899.[26] By the middle of the twentieth century, the issue of international marine pollution, especially resulting from the transport of crude oil, was receiving widespread attention. The Truman Proclamation of 1945 established sovereign rights to the ocean bottom extending as far as the continental shelf, thereby vesting the U.S. national interest in the protection of its coastal waters.[27] In 1948, the United Nations created a specialized agency, the International Maritime Organization, dedicated to improving the safety of international shipping and the prevention of corresponding marine pollution. Six years later, Great Britain organized a conference that adopted the International Convention for the Prevention of Pollution of the Sea by Oil (OILPOL), at the time the signature document in the field. Additional international conventions and amendments to existing protocols would be adopted over the succeeding decades, particularly following oil spills in international waters. The rapid increase in shipping following the end of World War II occurred during a time when international maritime standards were inadequate, if not altogether absent. Some nations had their own set of laws and regulations, but what international agreements did exist often were endorsed by only a handful of nations directly involved in marine shipping. Some even contradicted each other. By the postwar era there existed a clear need for international conventions that would regulate safe marine operations and pollution prevention, along with some brand of institutional administration and oversight.

Although founded in 1948, the International Maritime Organization (IMO) did not hold its first meeting until 1959. At that meeting in London, the body assumed responsibility for OILPOL, which defined oil pollution of the oceans as contamination by crude oil, fuel oil, heavy diesel oil, and lubricating oil. The convention also held that most marine pollution occurred during normal shipping operations, not from accidents. It mandated that nation signatories adhere to provisions that forbade the discharge of liquids containing more than one hundred parts of oil per million within fifty miles of shore and required the promotion of onshore facilities that could receive oiled water and residues. Certain ships were exempt from the regulations, however, including military vessels and tankers under 150 tons.[28]

Another UN agency, the International Law Commission, had in its purview the responsibility for developing treaties on basic maritime law. At about the same time the IMO was formalizing international agreement with OILPOL, the Law Commission formally recommended that each nation promulgate regulations to prevent oil pollution. The United States resisted this provision at the Geneva Conference on the Law of the Sea, arguing that it was not in the commission's interest to undertake regulation already being considered by other agencies. The U.S. later withdrew its opposition and the resolution was adopted, leaving the technical work to the IMO. That body convened another conference in 1962 to evaluate the effectiveness of OILPOL. Worldwide surveys intimated that more stringent controls were necessary, and the act was amended to broaden its original intent. The fifty-mile nondischarge zones were extended and the convention was made applicable to vessels previously exempted from the 1954 act. The convention still waived its regulatory authority for oil pollution resulting from damage to a ship if all reasonable attempts to minimize the spillage were made.[29] It would take a disaster at sea to illustrate the potential ramifications of this exemption.

In March 1967, the U.S. supertanker *Torrey Canyon* struck Pollard's Rock off the southwest coast of Great Britain. A navigational error resulted in the spillage of her entire cargo of crude oil, more than thirty million gallons, which spread across the shores of Britain and migrated to the coast of France as well. The *Torrey Canyon* disaster was the largest oil spill to date and demonstrated the inadequacy of OILPOL and its subsequent amendments. Marine oil transportation had changed considerably in the intervening years. Tankers were larger, more powerful, and carried volumes of crude oil greater than anyone had anticipated at the time of OILPOL's passage just over a decade earlier. New rules were again required to regulate tanker design, construction, and operation.[30] The IMO responded by convening an emergency session of its council, which recommended further legal and technical research. Two years later, the IMO convened an international conference in Brussels that adopted the International Convention Relating to Intervention on the High Seas in Cases of Oil Pollution Casualties. This document represented a departure from the historical tradition of the "open seas." No longer would international waters be considered wholly apart from an individual nation's sovereign interest. The *Torrey Canyon* was damaged outside the territorial waters of both Britain and France, yet each nation had a vested interest in preventing oil pollution from reaching its respective shores and coastal waters. The 1969 convention, actually another amendment to OILPOL, allowed states to intervene in incidents likely to result in oil pollution of their coastal areas regardless of the tanker's flag. States had to consult with the flag state on actions it proposed to take, though in cases of extreme urgency they were authorized to act unilaterally. The convention also established a system for compensating victims of the resultant oil pollution. Prior to the *Torrey Canyon*, the majority of the world's shipping companies adhered to a private agreement, the Tanker Owners Voluntary Agreement Concerning Liability for Oil Pollution (TOVALOP), which held that tanker owners would assume responsibility for oil spill cleanup caused by their tanker operations and reimburse any nations affected by such spills. TOVALOP capped their financial liability at $14 million per tanker per spill. The 1969 OILPOL amendment retained the relatively meager liability cap and further exempted companies from responsibility if the damage resulted from natural causes of extraordinary character or by the act of a third party. The *Torrey Canyon* had altered its course slightly to avoid small fishing vessels, and while this did not seem to be a cause of the grounding, it could be argued that the owners of the tanker had cause to seek an exemption from liability under the third-party clause. For many, the similarities between TOVALOP and the 1969 OILPOL amendments indicated the influence of the shipping industry on international environmental negotiation.[31]

Another criticism of the 1969 OILPOL was that it preempted existing and future domestic environmental legislation that might be more stringent in its preventative requirements. Canada, for example, believed the amendments reflected little more than the power of the shipping industry to disingenuously package minimal and ineffective environmental regulation as "progress." Mitchell Sharp commented that the Brussels convention "was so little oriented towards environmental preservation and so much oriented in the interests of ship and cargo owning states."[32] The frustration of Canadian authorities about their particular marine protection needs informed Ottawa's imminent response to the *Manhattan*.

THE ARCTIC WATERS POLLUTION PREVENTION ACT

An entrepreneur from St. John's, Newfoundland, named A. W. Harvey wrote to the British Colonial Office in January 1874 with an unusual request. He wanted to purchase land at Cumberland Gulf, a rocky inlet on Baffin Island, and establish a whaling station there. A similar request arrived from a U.S. citizen two months later. The interest surprised British authorities, according to historian Shelagh D. Grant, for it seemed clear that the last three centuries of polar exploration had pretty well established the valueless nature of the region. Lord Carnarvon, British secretary for the colonies, began quietly negotiating the formal transfer of the Crown's arctic possessions to Canada, an action deemed necessary as much to deny the U.S. an opportunity to claim the northern islands as for any possible benefit to Canada. Although Canada had no navy, no coast guard, and almost no administrative infrastructure in the region, the transfer was completed on September 1, 1880, and Ottawa's formal relationship with the Arctic was begun.[33]

The first expression of what might be called sovereignty—independent legal authority over a geographic area—occurred in 1907 in the form of the Sector Principle, which utilized longitudinal meridians extending north to the pole to enclose the region and define its territorial boundaries. Pascal Poirier, a senator from New Brunswick, suggested the declaration could firmly establish Canada's hold on the region. Although rejected out of hand by the United States and never formally declared by Ottawa, the Sector Principle proved easy to understand—not to mention simple for mapmakers to depict—and quickly gained acceptance with the general public in Canada.[34] The actual utility of the country's northernmost islands remained questionable during this period, yet Canada again signaled its determination to hold the region in 1925, when

O. D. Skelton, external affairs secretary, issued the "Statement of Canada's Claims to the Arctic Islands." The document came in response to planned U.S. Navy operations in the Arctic Ocean and the MacMillan-Byrd expedition that featured aerial exploration (including landings) on islands in the Canadian Archipelago. The statement employed the Sector Principle to draw the nation's eastern border at the midpoint between Greenland and Baffin, Devon, and Ellesmere Islands. It also laid out a legal argument for land ownership that included evidence of habitation and administrative actions Ottawa had taken in the area.[35] Both the 1925 statement and the Sector Principle on which it was based represented a broad-brush approach the international community would largely reject for being too overreaching. Interestingly, the statement referred only to the islands of the Canadian Archipelago—an astounding thirty-six thousand of them—not its waterways. With very little marine traffic in the region at the time, and no indication vessels would ever regularly use the icebound waters, Ottawa neglected to use the act to make any claims to the northern waterways.

The onset of the Cold War in the late 1940s and early 1950s finally brought recognition of the Arctic's strategic value. In the interests of continental defense, Canada cooperated with the U.S. on military operations. The Distant Early Warning Line (DEW Line) went into operation in the Canadian Arctic in 1957, and was, despite the premise of joint operations, largely controlled by the U.S. military. That Canada did not perceive this arrangement as being in conflict with control of its own national territory would later cause some officials to worry that they had undermined their own claims of sovereignty.[36] Marine traffic increased in the 1950s as well. The U.S. ships *Spar*, *Storis*, and *Bramble* entered from Alaska in the east, meeting the HMCS *Labrador* in Bellot Strait. That submarines also operated in the region unseen was a secret to no one.

In the early 1960s, even before the Prudhoe Bay discovery, Ottawa was aware that oil exploration in the North American Arctic might one day force its hand. Panarctic Oils, a quasi-public Canadian oil company, was then exploring the region and would, in fact, make a number of significant petroleum discoveries. The Advisory Committee on Northern Development, the nation's leading governmental agency for arctic affairs, recognized that Canada was then in no position to regulate the use of northern waterways, whether by its own Panarctic venture or by a multinational corporation operating in an adjacent state such as Alaska.[37] Humble's 1968 *Manhattan* announcement didn't exactly catch Ottawa by surprise, but it did force officials to acknowledge that Canada had no formal international declaration of sovereignty over her arctic waters, only a piece of domestic legislation limited in scope. The 1964 Territorial Sea and Fishing Zones Act established a three-mile territorial zone around islands in the Canadian Arctic. Except in the narrowest of (easily avoidable) channels where these zones overlapped, the Humble tanker could traverse the length of the passage and claim rights of open sea nearly the entire way.[38] The Trudeau government made clear from the outset, however, that it had no intention of prohibiting industrial activity. Practical cooperation with both Humble on the *Manhattan* test and the U.S. on the development of international law stood to enhance economic opportunities for Canada while simultaneously strengthening its claims to the North American Arctic. The *Manhattan*, Trudeau claimed, was a positive development for Canada.[39]

Many Canadians agreed. In a four-part series titled "Wealth Below the Ice," the Montreal-based newspaper *La Presse* downplayed the American intrusion angle and instead focused on the potential benefits of a successful voyage:

> It matters little whether the telephone was invented by a Canadian or an Ethiopian, provided we all may use it. It matters little whether drugs are discovered by the French or the Russians, provided they are effective healing agents. In the same way, it matters little whether the Northwest Passage is opened by the Americans, provided it becomes possible to develop the resources of the polar regions.[40]

On September 18, 1969, one week after the *John A. MacDonald* had proved its indispensability by rescuing the *Manhattan* from massive ice floes in McClure Strait, Mitchell Sharp declared, "Canada's sovereignty over Arctic waters is being steadily strengthened by developing concepts of international law and by our own activities."[41] Sharp's external affairs department had approached other arctic states to gain their support for special regulations for frozen waters, a condition unique to the polar environment not then addressed in international maritime law. Ottawa's intent to act as steward of the arctic environment—"a trustee to all mankind," in Prime Minister Trudeau's words—had shifted the debate from sovereignty to pollution control, and was receiving widespread international acceptance. In November, Trudeau met with UN Secretary-General U Thant to reiterate that Ottawa would coordinate with the international community on the development of environmental regulations, but that domestic efforts would continue as planned.[42] Events at the OILPOL conference in Brussels that same month strengthened Ottawa's resolve to act, unilaterally if necessary. Among the provisions supported by Canada but voted down in Brussels were those that would more clearly delineate the chain of liability for accidents and include flag states as responsible parties. The defeat of these amendments left Canada to believe that unfortunate coastal states still would bear the greatest cost of environmental cleanup.[43]

As the Trudeau government prepared domestic legislation in late 1969, a number of possible directions emerged. First, the Sector Principle: Ottawa could enclose the entire Arctic with straight baselines. Alternately, the territorial boundary could be extended from the current three miles to twelve (or more, theoretically), thereby establishing jurisdiction over every narrow entrance to the passage while technically retaining free transit on its wider channels within. A third option was not geographical at all, but rather would call for a multilateral conference to formalize the right of states to act according to unique regional circumstances. (Ottawa was then resisting calls by Washington first for bilateral meetings, then for multilateral conferences, because the U.S. had already signaled its inflexibility on Canada's position.) The available options appealed to different governmental bodies in different ways, and it became clear by early 1970 that the pending legislation would include elements from all three.

On April 8, 1970, the government introduced in Parliament the Arctic Waters Pollution Prevention Act (AWPPA). The act extended the territorial zones around all arctic islands from three miles to twelve, effectively enclosing the Northwest Passage as both Barrow and Prince of Wales Straits measure less than twenty-four miles wide. The AWPPA also extended regulatory jurisdiction to one hundred miles from all mainland north of sixty degrees latitude for the purpose of pollution control. Political scientists John Kirton and Don Munton note that the one-hundred-mile control zone had limited functional purpose but was in line with prevailing international legal standards and went some distance to satisfying a Canadian public eager for a declaration of arctic claims. The size of the zone also maintained a distinction between full sovereignty and purpose-specific jurisdiction, an approach that avoided a direct legal confrontation with the U.S.[44] The AWPPA also established standards for ship construction and navigation. Any vessels not meeting those requirements, or those unwilling to accept financial liability for any damage from pollution they caused during transit, could be denied entry to Canadian waters. Additional sector-specific navigational restrictions were applied within sixteen different safety zones.[45]

Finally, the act made provisionary Canada's acceptance of the jurisdiction of the International Court of Justice in matters related to the Arctic. Ottawa wanted to ensure that any international challenge to the AWPPA would require that Canada first accepted the court's authority in the matter before the case could be adjudicated. Said Trudeau: "Canada is not prepared...to engage in litigation with other states...where the law is either inadequate or non-existent.... [C]oastal states are entitled, on the basis of the fundamental principle of self-defense, to protect their marine environment and the living resources of the sea adjacent to their coast."[46] Many historians and political scientists have noted that the unilateral nature of the AWPPA, in particular its reservation from the ICJ, represented a stark departure from the internationalist foreign policy Canada had followed since World War II.[47]

A handful of historical precedents helped shape Canada's position. The 1949 Corfu Channel Case was among the first international legal decisions to provide a definition of an international waterway. Corfu arose from a 1946 incident where two British ships struck mines in waters off Albania, resulting in loss of life and extensive damage to both vessels. In deciding to hold Albania responsible for the accidents, the International Court of Justice ruled that a strait qualifies as international when two conditions are present. First, the waterway has to connect two high seas, or a high sea to a territorial sea for international transit, and must fall outside the territorial jurisdiction of adjacent states. The court determined that although Albania did not set the mines, it must have been aware of their presence in the closely monitored channel and therefore had a legal obligation to warn passing vessels. A state that claims territorial waters takes on the responsibility for monitoring traffic within them. In the case of the Northwest Passage two decades later, Canada assumed operational control the moment it extended its territorial zones from three to twelve miles. The U.S. alleged the opposite, stating that because the Northwest Passage connected the Atlantic and Pacific Oceans—both "high seas" in the court's terms—Corfu demonstrated that the passage was international.[48]

Canada could refute this claim with the court's second condition, which held that an international strait had to show evidence of established use for marine shipping. The court provided no exact definition of what constituted established use, but it was widely taken to mean there had to be a clearly identifiable legacy of the strait as a transportation corridor. While the Corfu Channel witnessed over a hundred crossings per month at the time of the Britain-Albania conflict, the Northwest Passage had been traversed barely a dozen times total when the *Manhattan* sailed in 1969, and never for commercial purposes.[49]

In buttressing its territorial waters claim, Ottawa could also cite the 1951 Fisheries Case, a dispute between Norway and Great Britain, in which the International Court of Justice recognized the right of states to claim historical title to coastal waters. The court held that where an irregular coastline is broken by bays, inlets, and coastal islands, the state can establish territoriality by drawing a straight line from points on the coast to those islands. The AWPPA did precisely that: it enclosed the entire Northwest Passage with baselines drawn around the perimeter of the archipelago. But where the discounted Sector Principle drew longitudinal lines with little regard to the actual sinuosities of the coast, the AWPPA used a more deliberate sectional approach.[50]

On April 3, 1970, just five days before the Trudeau government formally introduced the AWPPA, the *Manhattan* embarked on a second voyage to the North American Arctic. Humble deemed another expedition necessary to evaluate the tanker's performance in winter ice conditions (the 1969 maiden voyage had encountered mostly weak summer ice). Prior to the start of the voyage, Canada's Department of Transport informed Humble that it would inspect the tanker's hull, propellers, and rudders in accordance with the AWPPA—despite the fact that the legislation had not yet been introduced, let alone passed into law. In addition, the official Canadian representative on the voyage, in this case Captain George Burdoch of the *Louis St. Laurent*, the Canadian Coast Guard's newest icebreaker, had the authority to call a halt to the expedition if necessary. These were just two of twenty-four requirements outlined in a March 26, 1970, letter to Humble chairman Mike Wright. A key environmental stipulation was that the tanker could carry only fuel oil, not crude, and that the oil must be stored in center-line tanks remote from the ship's sides (a common-sense provision Humble had already taken during the 1969 voyage and planned to do again in the second expedition). Humble acquiesced to all twenty-four demands, giving Ottawa a successful test of its pending pollution control legislation. The eventual passage of the AWPPA caused the United States to disavow its standing, but other arctic states—Sweden, Norway, Iceland, and the Soviet Union—as well as several other non-arctic shipping states supported Canada in her efforts.

Twelve years later, the UN Convention on the Law of the Sea (UNCLOS) affirmed, at least in part, Canada's earlier efforts at marine pollution prevention. Article 234 of the agreement legitimized the twelve-mile zone for territorial waters and allowed states to establish a two-hundred-mile exclusive economic zone (EEZ) in which domestic regulation could apply. From the standpoint of international maritime law, Article 234 provided for the very type of unilateral action taken by the Trudeau government in 1970:

> Coastal states have the right to adopt and enforce non-discriminatory laws and regulations for the prevention, reduction and control of marine pollution from vessels in ice-covered areas within the limits of the exclusive economic zone, where particularly severe climatic conditions and the presence of ice covering such areas for most of the year create obstructions or exceptional hazards to navigation, and pollution of the marine environment could cause major harm to or irreversible disturbance of the ecological balance.[51]

Article 234 acknowledged the fragile nature of the arctic environment. The polar regions' relatively slow ecological regeneration rates meant that oil pollution stood to contaminate the land, ice, and sea in a more lasting and devastating manner than in the world's temperate climates. In 1954, while advocating unsuccessfully for more stringent pollution controls in regions with unique geographic features, Canada likened the Arctic to a "hemophiliac," in that its environmental wounds heal slowly, if at all.[52] Pierre Trudeau used the same argument in 1970, when rebutting U.S. objections to the AWPPA. The prime minister also took the clever step of timing the April 1970 passage of the bill to correspond with the first Earth Day celebration in the U.S. Officials in Washington would be hard-pressed to complain about Canada's environmental stewardship on the very day they were ostensibly celebrating their own.

That Ottawa claimed only functional jurisdiction over its northern waterways ultimately proved a wise move. The stance put Canada on solid footing during the negotiation of Article 234, and its adoption in 1982 validated the approach. In introducing the AWPPA in April 1970, Mitchell Sharp explained, "The Arctic Waters bill represents a constructive and functional approach to environmental preservation. It asserts only the limited jurisdiction required to achieve a specific and vital purpose."[53] Had Ottawa overreached with an overt declaration of sovereignty, as some ultranationalists and newspaper editors demanded at the time, the action likely would have provoked a legal challenge from shipping states and undermined its standing in the development of UNCLOS.

In 1985—three years after UNCLOS was enacted but nine years before it achieved full ratification by the required sixty countries—Canada faced another sovereignty crisis. The U.S. icebreaker *Polar Sea* transited the Northwest Passage on a supply mission to Thule Air Base in Greenland. Although the expedition took place with the full knowledge and cooperation of the Canadian Coast Guard, and both Ottawa and Washington agreed ahead of time it would have no effect on the standing of either country in the ongoing sovereignty debate, the presence of another American ship in the Canadian Arctic stirred the same worried passions as the *Manhattan* had a decade and a half before. Shortly after the *Polar Sea*'s otherwise uneventful crossing, Joe Clark, secretary for external affairs, announced that a straight baseline would be drawn around the entire archipelago, with the waters within the line formally declared internal. "Canada's sovereignty in the Arctic is indivisible," he stated. "It embraces land, sea and ice. It extends without interruption to the seaward-facing coasts of the Arctic islands." In language noticeably more forceful than that heard in Parliament during the *Manhattan* controversy, Clark continued, "The policy of this Government is to exercise full sovereignty in and on the waters of the Arctic archipelago and this applies to the airspace above as well."[54] Clark's declaration went into effect on January 1, 1986, and resulted in numerous maps depicting what to Canadians must have been a satisfyingly bold line around the perimeter of the northern islands.

If the declaration was meant to be the last word on the matter, however, it failed badly. Not only did the U.S. protest the claim, but what came next repeated the pattern following the end of the *Manhattan* test in 1970. The issue slowly faded from public view, and before long Ottawa slipped into insouciance. *Arctic Front*, a 2008 analysis of circumpolar policy that its Canadian authors admit was written out of collective frustration, concludes with a straightforward statement of that dissatisfaction: "We've been through much of this before. Canada has spouted the rhetoric of Arctic engagement in the past and then done nothing."[55]

Today the issue is far from settled. Protection of the Arctic Marine Environment (PAME), a working group of the Arctic Council, counted some six thousand vessels operating in the Arctic in 2004, the last year in which a full survey was conducted. The governance of shipping activities in the region is, in PAME's words, "a complicated mosaic" of domestic laws, bilateral agreements, and international accords to which not every arctic state is a signatory (as of 2011, the United States has not ratified UNCLOS).[56] Enforcement actions vary according to the different maritime zones described in UNCLOS—internal waters, territorial seas, contiguous zones, exclusive economic zones (EEZs), and the continental shelf—to which, yet again, different nations apply different definitions. "Lack of clearly delimited maritime boundaries for territorial seas and EEZs is of potential concern for future shipping in the Arctic," PAME dryly noted.[57] The group also acknowledged a present-day dearth of mandatory standards for crew training, navigation, and ship construction designed to protect the arctic environment—precisely the issues Ottawa had identified as priorities decades earlier but today remain unresolved.

Although PAME has credited the Arctic Waters Pollution Prevention Act of 1970 for the environmentally sustainable nature of the shipping and resource development that has occurred in the years since, it also noted that the decades-old act has been outpaced by subsequent international law and evolving pollution control technologies, and should be updated. Perhaps the primary factor in keeping the Canadian Arctic from being despoiled by oil pollution to date, however, has been its historically low level of use. The simple fact is that for all the public attention a crossing by the *Manhattan* or *Polar Sea* generates, marine shipping in the region remains a difficult, expensive proposition. For decades traffic has been limited, consisting mostly of small fishing vessels and supply barges visiting northern communities, and almost exclusively directional—where a vessel sails northward for a specific purpose and retreats to the south afterwards—as opposed to trans-Arctic in nature. According to PAME,

> The Northwest Passage is not expected to become a viable trans-Arctic route through 2020 due to seasonality, ice conditions, a complex archipelago, draft restrictions, chokepoints, lack of adequate charts, insurance limitations and other costs, which diminish the likelihood of regularly scheduled services from the Pacific to the Atlantic.[58]

Of the six thousand vessels PAME counted in the Arctic in 2004, not one was a commercial ship that made a full transit of the Northwest Passage.

5

A Floating Laboratory

Science has accomplished such wonders but hasn't been able to duplicate a simple egg, add a little heat and make a chicken.

—Walter J. Hickel (1971)[1]

The first ship in history to feature metal plating on her hull with the specific intent of breaking through ice was the *Pilot*, a small Russian vessel built in 1870 to maintain communication between St. Petersburg and Kronstadt, an island naval fortress some eighteen miles offshore in the Gulf of Finland. The next was the *Bear*, commissioned in 1874 as a sealer and transferred a decade later to the U.S. Revenue Marine Service (now the Coast Guard) for the Alaska service. The 198-foot, seventeen-hundred-ton ship featured a hull of English oak with iron plating. This first generation of icebreakers, including the *Pilot*, the *Bear*, and those used in the Baltic Sea, the Great Lakes, and along the U.S. East Coast, possessed neither the engine power nor the sheer bulk necessary for continuous motion in ice conditions. They also lacked the particular hull curvature that later shipbuilders would discover was essential for moving aside broken slabs of ice.[2]

Icebreaking took a huge leap forward in 1893 with Fridtjof Nansen, the legendary Norwegian explorer, who designed his ship from the keel up to operate in the polar environment. The 128-foot, 420-ton *Fram* featured a barrel-shaped hull, angled at the bow and stern but almost perfectly circular amidship, that would cause the vessel to be forced upward when under lateral ice pressure and thus avoid being crushed. Sixty-eight diagonal braces made of fir distributed the pressure on the hull. Although not a true icebreaker by definition, the *Fram* sported a unique design that directly influenced later shipbuilders. Nansen pioneered several techniques. The *Fram* was divided into three compartments by leakproof bulkheads, which were insulated from the cold by layers of felt, cork, reindeer hair, and open air space. The three-masted schooner also had an auxiliary coal-burning engine with cast-iron propeller capable of achieving six knots in open water. Both the propeller and rudder were housed in well assemblies that could be lifted on deck to avoid being damaged by ice. The *Fram*, with its keel of fourteen-inch American elm and its oak hull up to thirty-two inches thick in places, left Norway on July 21, 1893. Nansen and his crew of twelve would return heroes three years later, his ship having survived every challenge the ice-choked Arctic Ocean could muster.[3]

Nansen's innovations were incorporated in the design of the eighty-seven-hundred-ton *Yermak*, widely considered the first modern icebreaker. Built in 1898 at Newcastle, England, for the Russian fleet, the *Yermak* featured an angled bow and sloped hull designed to reduce binding in ice conditions. She also boasted one-and-a-quarter-inch steel plating along the waterline and a notch in her stern into which another ship could be secured for towing. The *Yermak* remained in service for over six decades. In the 1930s, the Soviets constructed five large *Stalin*-class icebreakers, followed in 1959 by the *Lenin*, the world's first nuclear icebreaker. The evolution of modern icebreaking ships involved numerous modifications, especially in construction materials, from wood to metal plating to steel, and propulsion systems, from steam engines to diesel-electric to nuclear power. The basic configuration of an angled bow and sloped hull, however, remains the standard for ice ships.

The first transit of the Northwest Passage by an icebreaking vessel was achieved in 1954 by the *Labrador*, a Canadian ship under the command of Owen Connor Struan "Long Robbie" Robertson, so nicknamed due to his towering six-foot, eight-inch frame. The transit almost didn't happen. Eager to beat the Americans through the passage, the Canadian Navy rushed the *Labrador*'s construction. Sea trials for the brand-new ship took place on a compressed two-week schedule in July that year, and the ship's engineers were still solving technical failures (including a loss of steering capability) as she steamed into the Arctic on her maiden voyage. Robertson had been given the authority to make an on-the-spot decision as to whether the vessel was ready to attack the passage. He judged that she was, and in September the *Labrador* emerged from the archipelago into Alaska waters to great fanfare throughout Canada. Post-expedition reports for two U.S. ships in the Arctic at the time, the *Northwind* and *Burton Island*, revealed that neither had any intention of attempting a transit.[4] In fact, it would be another three years before the first American icebreaker, the Coast Guard *Storis*, accomplished the feat. (The *Spar* and the *Bramble*, both officially classified as buoy tenders, accompanied the *Storis* through the passage.)

When the *Manhattan* thrust aside her first ice floes off Baffin Island on the morning of September 2, 1969, she not only added her name to this official roster of icebreakers but joined their ranks as the largest such vessel in history. The *Manhattan* was a full seven times larger than the *Lenin*, previously the world's largest. Like every other cargo ship in the world, the *Manhattan* featured flat, vertical sides with almost no curvature, exactly the design mariners going back to Fridtjof Nansen recognized as the worst for polar operations. Humble mitigated the shortcoming somewhat by sloping the ice belt outward, a configuration that in uniform ice conditions would cause upward forces on the ship and downward forces on the ice. It wasn't the barrel-shaped design of the *Fram*, but it was the best Humble engineers could do.

Third Officer Charles D. Hahn spotted the first ice of the expedition, pointing out a large iceberg grounded near the Labrador shore to the port side of the vessel. In so doing the watch officer won the $20 prize for being the first to catch sight of ice. (Other pools with cash prizes officially sanctioned by Humble included being the first to spot a polar bear and correctly guessing the highest and lowest recorded temperatures during the expedition.) The giant chunk of ice dwarfed the *Manhattan*. Ice scientists onboard estimated that it weighed one million tons. Before long, the sea was dotted with bergs of all shapes and sizes, for which the bridge kept a close lookout. The ship's radar operators often could not differentiate between relatively small chunks of ice and massive multi-ton icebergs. All were just blips on the screen. Despite boasting steel-strengthened hulls, icebreaking vessels are designed for attacking stationary pack ice, not ramming into floating bergs that may outweigh the vessel itself. The first pack ice that would put the *Manhattan* to the test was still days away off Cape Dyer (Baffin Island) in Davis Strait.[5]

While still on open water in the Labrador Sea, the ship's officers received a cable from the Coast Guard bearing unpleasant news. A standard review of Sun Shipyard's renovation reports revealed that no internal bracing was in place for some thirty steel plates on the port side of the ship near the bow. Months before, Humble engineers had devised a plan to leave this section of the hull intentionally unsupported in order to test the deformation and provide straight comparisons with the reinforced sections. Watertight bulkheads would be used to seal off these weak spots. After consulting with naval architects, however, Humble recognized that any breach in the hull might inhibit the overall handling of the ship and they ditched the plan. Now, when the tanker had reached the North Atlantic, the Coast Guard realized that workers at Sun had gone ahead and cut away the internal bracing on those panels anyway—perhaps the result of working from one of the outdated schedules Humble had previously complained about. Even worse, they subsequently failed to make the compartment watertight. A simple at-sea inspection of the hull by the *Manhattan*'s crew determined that was indeed the case. A breach was all but certain. The vessel was accordingly deemed unsafe for arctic operations.

Stan Haas hastily convened a meeting with the onboard Coast Guard representatives, the *Manhattan*'s officers, and his own task force. Should the hull be punctured at one of the weak panels it was unlikely the vessel would be in danger of sinking, but the rush of seawater would almost certainly wreak havoc with the ship's electrical systems. The hull pressure sensors and other data-gathering equipment, not to mention cabin lights, would be useless. Without means to collect data there would be little point to continuing the voyage and the entire expedition might have to be canceled. The men quickly identified two options for fixing the problem—turn the vessel around and sail back to Halifax or complete the repairs at sea. No one, especially Haas, cared for the first option. Putting in at Halifax would surely set the already late expedition back at least another week, an unacceptable delay for Humble. Fortunately, with 126 men onboard the tanker, Haas discovered four with welding experience. The repairs would be made at sea. The confined spaces in that section of the hull would accommodate only two men at a time, so the four welders devised swing shifts and had the job completed in only a few days. Frederick Goettel and Virg Keith, the Coast Guard officers on the vessel, inspected the work and recertified the ship in compliance with Coast Guard specifications.[6]

Late on the evening of August 31, while the welding continued belowdecks, the *Manhattan* rendezvoused with the Canadian icebreaker *John A. MacDonald*, or *Johnny Mac* as she was commonly called, under the command of Captain Paul Fournier. The meeting in Davis Strait took place with near-military precision, only three minutes off the appointed time and at the exact latitude and longitude that had been planned weeks earlier. The brightly painted red-and-white ship took up position two miles off the tanker's port bow. She would be the *Manhattan*'s inseparable companion for the next ten weeks. The Canadian icebreaker was built by Davie Shipbuilding in Lauzon, Quebec, in 1960, and featured a diesel-electric power plant of fifteen-thousand-shaft horsepower, including a then-revolutionary triple-screw propulsion system allowing for greater operational reliability and more efficient steering. Fournier, a lifelong sailor from Quebec's Gaspé Peninsula and an acknowledged expert at breaking ice, had already once taken the *Johnny Mac* on a westward transit of the Northwest Passage. "I just talk to the ice and the ship a little bit," was how the modest captain described his inestimable skill.[7] While the *John A. MacDonald* had been assigned to the expedition in part to wave the Canadian flag, the icebreaker, smaller than the *Manhattan* but more powerful and maneuverable relative to her size, would guide the supertanker through the passage, repeatedly rescue her from especially brutal ice conditions, and generally prove indispensable to the entire mission. Fournier described his initial impression of the *Manhattan* as "very favourable":

> She appears to be very sturdily built and looks very sleek. With her harpoon bow and her saddle tanks which extend the whole length of the cargo compartments, she appears to be ready to meet any eventualities that might occur when she

reaches the ice. As the Arctic has no respect for persons or ships, this remains to be seen.[8]

Only a few hours after the rendezvous, the two ships found themselves in calm seas amid a dazzling array of icebergs, the heaviest concentration seen to date. Although it was the middle of the night, many of the crew appeared above decks to gaze at the beautiful yet perilous spectacle. Growlers—chunks of ice the size of automobiles—occasionally rattled along the hull, sending up dull, ghostly, metallic thuds, which frayed more than a few nerves of those on deck.[9] The *John A. MacDonald* steamed ahead of the tanker and cleared a path for both through the treacherous sea. Later that day the *Manhattan* emerged into clear, still water and sailed west toward the coast of Baffin Island. Soon a hazy, uneven line on the ocean's surface came into view. The black of open water met the white of a vast field of ice. This was the Baffin Pack, for centuries notorious as the destroyer of whaling ships and now the first testing ground for the largest icebreaker in history. The *Manhattan*'s officers pulled the vessel to a stop five miles short of the five-hundred-square-mile pack, awaiting confirmation from the engineers that the recently completed welding of the forward hull had sufficiently prepared the vessel for the pending operation. Haas and Tom Pullen flew by helicopter to the *John A. MacDonald*, where Captain Fournier hosted the men for lunch and coordinated their plans for the Baffin Pack. One officer warned it was finally time for the *Manhattan* to "blood herself" on the ice.[10] Steward agreed to hold the tanker overnight and try her against the ice first thing in the morning.

Well before dawn on Tuesday, September 2, the entire officer crew and every Humble official assembled on the *Manhattan*'s bridge. Off-watch hands who normally would be grabbing some much-needed rest gathered on the forward decks and gazed ahead at the ice pack looming in the predawn darkness. This would be a sight no one wanted to miss. Reconnaissance flights the day before had determined that the Baffin Pack ranged from twenty to sixty percent coverage with areas of hard, multiyear ice. The onboard ice scientists estimated the floes ahead to be between three and fifteen feet thick. By the day's first light Captain Steward had already downed at least three cups of coffee. He ordered, "Slow ahead."[11]

The *Manhattan* reached a cautious speed of two knots, and at 7:31 a.m. she collided with the first floe. An ice layer roughly half the size of a football field broke cleanly in two, its fragments tilting skyward with agonizing slowness before being easily thrust aside. Steward kept the tanker idle for a moment, giving technicians a chance to ensure that the instrumentation along the hull was recording data. The *MacDonald* began sailing circles around the tanker, giving some the impression the tiny ship was eager to show the giant how it was done. Captain Fournier had no such ambition; he needed to maintain speed to keep his ship's engines at operational efficiency. The *Manhattan* soon attacked more floes, and all aboard marveled at the up-close sight of these massive sheets of ice being cracked apart, their fragments then rolling and plunging in the ship's wake. More than one observer noted the strangely animate howls and shrieks the ice gave as it scraped the passing hull. Some large chunks remained trapped underneath the tanker, sliding the length of her hull and causing third engineer Al Burns to note, "When that ice hits the props, I feel like a squirrel trapped in a concrete mixer."[12] The men in the engine room placed their hands on the external plates and felt the steel flex, a sensation they likened to maniacs with sledgehammers whacking the hull from the outside.[13] Back up on deck, shouts went up from the previously stunned and speechless crew. No one seemed to mind when a spray of ice-cold water gave all on the deck a good drenching. For a vessel as large as the *Manhattan*, the sudden impact with each ice floe resulted in practically no hesitation and only a slight, imperceptible lift of the bow. Virg Keith recalled his days on the *Westwind*, a much smaller Coast Guard icebreaker, when ramming thick ice meant an altogether perceptible eight-foot rise to the vessel, well enough to knock an unaware man off his feet. Each contact with the ice did send shockwaves down the length of the *Manhattan*—what one observer described as "the feeling of riding a fast train over a poor roadbed"—but for the most part the tanker knifed through its first ice with ease.[14]

Up on the bridge, smiles began to appear on previously nervous faces. The officers grew more confident with each conquered floe. They increased the tanker's speed to a full ten knots and aimed the *Manhattan* towards a square-mile sheet of ice with surface ridges suggesting it measured sixty feet thick in places. All hands clung tightly to rails. One crew member said of the apparent hubris, "They're going to smash their toy first day out of the wrappings."[15] The tanker struck the massive floe, sending plumes of water sixty feet in the air. Almost instantly a wide crack shot far ahead through the very center of the floe. Sheets of ice, no matter how thick, are much like panes of glass—strong in compression but weak in tensile strength. Like a hammer tapping on a window pane, a strong perpendicular force tends to send cracks and fissures shooting from the point of impact. For an icebreaker, it all comes down to the vessel's weight, power, and speed matched against the thickness, hardness, and area of the ice. As Roger Steward put it, "It's only a matter of steel and horsepower."[16]

Martti Saarikangas, a Finnish engineer with years of experience aboard Soviet icebreakers in the Northeast Passage, watched the shattered pieces of this largest floe slide by and noted, "This ship just broke more ice than any ship in history."[17] Tom Pullen, the Canadian government's official representative, agreed: "The *Manhattan* broke ice today better than any ship I have ever seen."[18] Pullen would know. While in command of the *Labrador* in the mid-1950s, he navigated numerous channels in the Canadian Arctic, some that had never before been traversed by deep-draft vessels, and led some of the first hydrographic and oceanographic surveys of the area. "Mr. Arctic" he was sometimes called. Pullen had retired from the Royal Canadian Navy the year before the *Manhattan*'s voyage, but none in the service knew the Arctic better and he'd agreed to serve as Ottawa's representative.[19]

All on the bridge were elated by the ship's performance, perhaps none more so than Stan Haas, for whom the day's efforts represented the culmination of years of research and ambition. Haas knew as well as anyone, however, that the ice conditions that day were not fully representative of what they would encounter even farther north. The Baffin Pack was composed of discontinuous floes, whereas the ice ahead would be one solid pack compressed by wind and tides, sheets on top of sheets that choked the narrow straits of the passage. The day's press release from the tanker celebrated her initial success, yet Haas remained only cautiously optimistic: "We haven't yet proved...that we have a test vehicle that can successfully traverse the Northwest Passage, but we have clearly demonstrated that we're riding on the finest special purpose commercial vessel ever built."[20]

A DATE WITH BOREAS REX

The next afternoon, Captain Steward informed the crew of their imminent rendezvous with Boreas Rex, the King of the North and Ruler of the Arctic Seas, from whom he had received an important message a few days earlier. Carl Thenemann, the ship's radio officer, had discovered bits of seaweed and ptarmigan feathers on the floor outside the radio room. Inside, he found a note on the teletype machine, which he duly delivered to the captain. The altogether serious nature of the *Manhattan*'s voyage was about to be interrupted by complete foolishness.

Boreas Rex, Steward explained, had learned from his intelligence network of ptarmigans, right whales, and mermaids that an awesome vessel making sounds like a honking goose and filled with porthole-peeping interlopers planned to cross the Arctic Circle. The right of safe passage into the Far North could be procured only one way, according to His Royal Majesty: "All blue-nosed creatures on board understand that they must undergo a personal examination by myself and some members of my court before they will be truly welcome in my kingdom as members of the Royal Order of the Polar Bear."[21] In short, any person who had never before ventured into the Arctic had to undergo an initiation of sorts, whether they wanted to or not. The custom, long practiced by mariners around the world, probably originated from the desperate need to break the monotony of months at sea.

Soon after the *Manhattan* crossed 66 degrees, 33 minutes north latitude, "Davy Jones" (a.k.a. Captain Thomas C. Pullen, Royal Canadian Navy [ret.]) appeared on deck in an ill-fitting admiral's coat and ridiculous patchwork pants, waving a cardboard sword. "Hear ye! Hear ye!" he shouted to the bewildered crew shivering in a twenty-knot wind. "Let it be known that Boreas Rex, mighty king of the north, is angry with all the blue-nosed swabs for entering his domain uninvited and breaking his ice." Captain Steward didn't miss a beat: "Welcome aboard. The fate of all offenders is in your hands."[22] Those with previous arctic experience rushed to establish their credentials with Davy Jones, hoping to bypass whatever humiliation lay in store for the others.

Boreas Rex and his queen, Amphitrite (Captain Don Graham and chief ice scientist Dr. Guenther Frankenstein, respectively), then emerged in full regalia—yellow and white robes with glittering crowns. The queen also sported long golden locks, bright red lipstick, and obscenely large breasts that the king happily noted were "52's if they're an inch." To complete the absurd spectacle, Frederick "Beef" Goettel, all 250 pounds of him, appeared as the Royal Baby wearing a diaper and a frilly pink chemise that covered precious little of his pale torso. The royal court plopped in deck chairs and prepared to receive, one by one, the now very nervous crew. "What the hell do these guys think they're doing?" muttered one of the professional mariners, who believed he had signed on for good work and better pay, not some drag show in the Arctic.[23]

A retinue of the king's jesters, wizards, and other helpers then sprayed seawater in each man's face, painted his nose blue, and finally led him to be insulted, ridiculed, or otherwise verbally tormented by Boreas Rex himself. A kiss of the queen's hand was next, though some did not escape her audience until being forced to plant one on the royal bosom as well. As the final indignity, each man was required to kiss the belly of the Royal Baby, which Goettel kept amply smeared with garlic, horseradish, and blue cheese salad dressing. Captain Steward closed the ceremony by providing two glasses of champagne to each crew member, nearly all of whom had gotten into the spirit of things and were enjoying the fun immensely. (The crew should have been grateful they did not serve in the Canadian Coast Guard on the *John A. MacDonald*, where newbies underwent an even more brutal initiation. The offenders were forced to eat a mixture of strawberry jam, mustard pickles, and celery boiled in cod-liver oil. The more fortunate "got rid of it [vomited] at once," according to an arctic veteran who watched the ordeal. The initiates then had their heads shaved and washed with fish oil, only to discover the showers had been turned off for "repairs," leaving the odor to last on their person for days.[24])

The *Manhattan* dropped anchor the next day at Thule Air Base on the west coast of Greenland, the last stop before entering the long-awaited Northwest Passage. The U.S. Department of Defense constructed Thule at the onset of the Cold War—forcibly relocating an entire Inuit village in the process—in order to take advantage of its proximity to the Soviet Union. Located just nine hundred miles from the North Pole, the base was intended as a refueling stop for long-range aircraft and as an early warning station for possible Soviet missile strikes. The *Manhattan* entered Thule via Wolstenholme Fjord on a clear, brilliant afternoon, the seas full of gleaming white icebergs and the sunlight sparkling off the ice blue water. Even for the arctic veterans the sight made for a simply unforgettable day. Those on the crew who hailed from more temperate climes such as Trinidad, Portugal, South Africa, and the Philippines described the experience as bordering on spiritual.[25]

Waiting for the *Manhattan* at Thule was the U.S. Coast Guard Cutter *Northwind* under the command of Captain Donald J. McCann. The Coast Guard had commissioned the Wind-class vessels—the aptly named *Northwind*, *Southwind*, *Westwind*, and *Eastwind*—during World War II, and immediately sent three of them (save the *Eastwind*) to the Soviet Union under the lend-lease program. The three ships would not be returned until the early 1950s, by which time the Coast Guard had contracted with San Pedro Shipbuilding in California to build another identical vessel. This fifth Wind-class icebreaker was also named *Northwind*. The original *Northwind* would be renamed the *Staten Island* upon her return to the U.S. fleet. All five ships measured 269 feet in length and displaced sixty-five hundred tons. Each featured twin propellers, driven by electric motors in turn powered by six diesel engines capable of twelve thousand horsepower. A third detachable forward propeller could also be used to dredge broken ice and create a wash along the bottom of the vessel. The hull of each vessel was composed of one-and-five-eighths-inch high-tensile steel plates that were welded, not riveted, and capable of resisting three thousand pounds per square inch at the waterline.[26] That the *Northwind* met the *Manhattan* at Thule at all was due to schedule delays and unforeseen breakdowns in a few other vessels.

Months before, when Humble announced that the Arctic Tanker Test would commence in midsummer, the Coast Guard made plans to send one of its Wind-class vessels along as escort, but as late as July it was not clear which one would get the nod. Both the *Southwind* and the *Westwind* operated in the Atlantic that summer, making an early rendezvous with the *Manhattan* a possibility. The *Northwind*, on the other hand, was clear on the other side of the continent. She departed Seattle in mid-May, bound for the Bering Sea, where she was to spend the next two months assisting oceanographers from the University of Alaska. Captain McCann's orders then called for the ship to sail into the Beaufort Sea in mid-July and meet the *Manhattan* after the tanker had completed the Northwest Passage. McCann would then escort her the short distance to Prudhoe Bay. (The *Eastwind* had been decommissioned the year before, and the *Staten Island* was in dry dock undergoing repairs for a cracked hull.) Both the *Southwind* and *Westwind* became disabled that summer, however, rendering them unsuitable for such an arduous voyage. Furthermore, with the *Manhattan* delayed by her extensive renovations and still in port in July, the crew of the *Northwind* found themselves in the Arctic in midsummer with neither operations nor orders. Captain

McCann soon received revised orders to make for Thule, wait there for the *Manhattan*, and then provide escort back to the west through the Northwest Passage.[27]

While the *Manhattan* remained at Thule overnight, divers from the *MacDonald* made an inspection of the tanker's hull, propellers, and rudders. All appeared in pristine condition. Even the paint marks left on the propeller blades by workers at Sun Shipyard hadn't been scratched.[28] Equipment that measured the vessel's speed, however, had been irreparably damaged by ice passing underneath the hull. For the remainder of the voyage the crew employed a decidedly low-tech solution, one called the Dutchman's log that dated back to the sixteenth century. Someone at the ship's forecastle would shout "Mark!" and toss a piece of scrap wood overboard, while another at the stern would yell the same when it passed by. Clocking the elapsed time and knowing the length of the ship made for an easy calculation of the vessel's speed. The crew who performed this duty took to calling themselves woodchucks.

On the morning of Friday, September 5, as the tanker weighed anchor and left Thule bound for the entrance to the Northwest Passage, the ice scientists from CRREL and the University of Alaska gathered to formalize their research program for the coming weeks. Most of the Alaskans were engineering graduate students who had lucked into the expedition. Humble had authorized the university to send ten scientists, and back when the *Manhattan* was scheduled for a summer sailing ten senior faculty had put their names on the roster. When the date of departure slipped into late August, just days before classes were to begin, the professors had to withdraw. This left several open slots for students who suddenly felt a semester off might do them some good. The lone exception was Dr. Elbert Rice, professor of civil engineering, who told the dean in Fairbanks he would quit if not granted a leave of absence to make the voyage. "There are not many chances to make history," he explained, "and this is one."[29] Another member of the Alaska contingent was Ed Clarke, a recent graduate in civil engineering who had spent his senior year studying how a buried pipeline would react to forces generated by polygonal cracking (geometric rifts on the surface of the land caused by underground ice wedges on Alaska's North Slope). Like so many other Alaskans, Clarke had emigrated from somewhere else—in his case Melrose, Massachusetts—and quickly fell in with the crowd of talented, self-reliant pioneers for which Alaska had long been known. He'd rebuilt the engine of a 1956 Ford and driven up the Alaska Highway, in his words, "just to see what was happening up there."[30] He now found himself with Dr. Rice and the other Alaskans on the history-making expedition.

The men now divided themselves into teams and assumed specific responsibilities so as to operate with utmost efficiency when their limited time on the ice finally came. The men intended to disembark each time Captain Steward determined it safe to stop the vessel, and take several cores from a spectrum of various ice layers.

The cores would be drilled and extracted by hand because the scientists feared that a motor-driven auger would create friction and heat that might spoil the samples. If the voyage to date was something of a pleasure cruise for the dozens of scientists onboard, the real work was about to begin. The *Manhattan* herself had received from the Coast Guard the official dual designation of commercial ship *and* scientific research vessel. Stan Haas called her a "floating laboratory."[31] The wood-chucking speedometer notwithstanding, the entire expedition was about to prove itself as one of absolute technological superiority.

TECHNOLOGY VERSUS THE ICE

The voyage of the *Manhattan* fit squarely with the oil industry's overall approach to development in the Arctic. Oil exploration, production, and transportation systems did not merely emphasize scientific innovation to solve every problem but relied on it repeatedly and exclusively. For every obstacle posed by the Arctic's daunting environment, some technological fix could be counted upon to either adapt to the environment or conquer it. So clear was the concept that it needn't even be explicitly stated by anyone either directly involved with industry efforts or just observing from the periphery: oil development at Prudhoe Bay depended on the application of science and technology on a massive scale.

At the Washington conference where Humble first pitched the Arctic Tanker Test to scientists, academics, and government officials, Haas explained that regular commercial tanker traffic in the Northwest Passage would likely require ships weighing a quarter of a million tons, an almost unimaginable proposal. He later described the reaction from the attendees:

> I literally saw their mouths open. Their enthusiasm was terrific. These men had dedicated their lives to a mission that they thought was very important but to which no one in a position of power would pay any attention. Here was a chance for them to turn the exotic into the practical; their frozen north into the frontier of the future. They had the potential of becoming prophets in their own time, and the support of all of them could not have been more wholehearted.[32]

The conferees' enthusiasm, not to mention the hyperbolic nature of Haas's comments, directly informed this science-driven mind-set. A marine transportation system that featured massive icebreaking tankers could only have been a dream for these individuals, something heretofore theoretical that would only exist in their imaginations so long as any practical application was lacking. Yet here was that very application. The promised windfall from Prudhoe Bay development—untold billions of dollars coupled with Humble's already deep pockets—would surely provide whatever financial resources the Arctic Marine Task Force required to best every challenge. The process was really quite simple: once Humble arrived at its objective of sending a tanker through the Northwest Passage and committed the necessary funding for the experiment, the project became a series of scientific problems that had to be solved, one after another. Outfitting the largest icebreaker in the history of the world was the most obvious example, yet this application of science and technology permeated every issue and became the lens through which each problem, including potential environmental impacts, would be viewed. Humble naturally pursued its industrial goals via research and technological innovation, but from a public policy standpoint the approach largely failed to incorporate a broader range of social values. Science and technology might indeed be capable of sending a ship through the Northwest Passage, but the question of how to identify and mitigate those social impacts would likely require something more than just throwing more science at the problem.

Lynton K. Caldwell, a professor of political science at Indiana University, attended the Alaska Science Conference in August 1969, where he provided public policy guidelines for the new state about to be thrust headlong into the rough-and-tumble oil business. He also cautioned against the science-as-panacea trap, believing that unbridled enthusiasm for rapid technological development put Alaska at risk of ignoring the full social and ecological costs of such industrialization. "We may have arrived at a point of technological overreach," stated Caldwell, describing a time when the sheer amount of scientific knowledge had outpaced the ability of public institutions to handle it wisely. Speaking of the state's rush for oil and the perils of science-driven policy making, he continued:

> What technology does is what man does with it. And what contemporary man has usually done with technology is to apply it from the perspective and with the assumptions of past time, when the earth was small and the "fit" between man and his environment was loose. He could then more easily afford to make environmental errors. He could afford to ruin an environment because all he had to do was pick up and move away. Now, however…a major reorientation of attitude and social effort is needed.[33]

Caldwell's remarks reflected the growing environmental consciousness of the time. Many came to believe that even in the seemingly limitless Arctic humankind had a responsibility to respect the natural world—even, or perhaps especially, when simply conquering it was made possible by technological advancements. No one seriously doubted that the oil industry's best engineers could find a way to snake a pipeline across eight hundred miles of wilderness or send giant ships crashing through icebound waters. But when even a single proposed scientific solution translated to unacceptable environmental risks, however that condition was to be defined, the question for many became not how to apply science but whether it should even be done. Science might identify the limits to growth posed by the environment, but many believed it required a separate value judgment to decide whether such limits should be respected or challenged.

Two decades after his warning call in Fairbanks, Caldwell would further articulate this ideological barrier to the appropriate application of science in environmental policy, something he called *scientism*:

> This belief, that science, in its several meanings, is inherently capable of solving almost all human problems, ought to be regarded as a science heresy. It is an unwarranted extrapolation from the unquestioned achievements of science, and reflects an oversimplification of the ways in which science relates to the social and political issues of human society.[34]

For Caldwell, technology could indeed have many wondrous applications and play an indispensable role in coping with environmental problems. It could also, however, lead to linear-track thinking and single-purpose applications that were wholly inappropriate when dealing with complex environmental interrelationships. Caldwell went on to state his disagreement with the idea that whatever nature has done, technological innovation can do better: "That science can sometimes improve on nature does not justify extending this potential to a general principle."[35] Speaking in the same panel at the 1969 science conference, Frank Fraser Darling and Robert F. Scott, both prominent and renowned ecologists, similarly noted the need for integrating social science research into what was commonly viewed only as technological problem solving.

As a private company engaged in its own capital investment project, Humble found itself under no real obligation to consider any questions other than those that had direct bearing on the *Manhattan*'s voyage. (Caldwell acknowledged as much when he placed the burden of socially responsible policy on the State of Alaska, not the oil industry.) Humble needed only to gather the required data that would assist in the development of the most efficient and economic marine transportation system in the Arctic. Whatever environmental policy implications could be gleaned from Humble's research were secondary to the stated mission. When the Arctic Marine Task Force first formed in August 1968, Stan Haas identified a comprehensive study of the arctic environment as one of its first priorities, yet again this study was placed only in the context of facilitating passage of an icebreaking tanker, not implementing a proactive policy of environmental protection. The many studies of ice composition and thickness helped ship builders reconfigure the *Manhattan*'s hull, for example, but any advance application of these data to understand oil spill scenarios in broken ice conditions appears not to have been done. Paul Heywood, a naval architect serving as one of British Petroleum's official observers on the *Manhattan*, noted as much in his post-expedition report: "No consideration has been given to anti-pollution designs such as double hulls or provision of a separate sea ballast capacity."[36] Whether the BP consultant had a freer hand than his Humble colleagues to raise such sensitive issues is unclear, but Heywood's comment was one of the only mentions of potential environmental impact to appear in the expedition's many volumes of data and analysis. Reporters sometimes erroneously called the *Manhattan* a "double-hulled vessel," which suggested she was uniquely qualified to carry hazardous cargo through environmentally sensitive waters. The tanker was not double-hulled, however. Engineers designed the ice belt to protect the ship more than the environment. Whether future tankers would require double hulls as environmental safeguards was a question to be answered later as a matter of policy, not technology. At the time of the tanker's voyage the general public was certainly aware of the environmental risks of marine oil transportation. The *Torrey Canyon* had grounded off the coast of England two years before, and just months before the *Manhattan* sailed, a blowout at a Union Oil drilling platform six miles offshore from Santa Barbara resulted in a release of two hundred thousand gallons of oil that despoiled beaches along the California coast. Should the *Manhattan* demonstrate the commercial viability of the Northwest Passage and lead to full-scale development of the transportation system, questions of environmental protection would no doubt require comprehensive analysis. Could consideration be put off until the experiment proved whether regular tanker traffic would even occur? From Humble's perspective, the proper role of science and technology was to advance the development of a marine transportation system in the Arctic, not determine whether the Arctic could environmentally sustain such a system.

Humble did not altogether ignore oil development's secondary effects, environmental or otherwise, and again demonstrated the belief that scientific solutions could be effectively applied to a host of social problems. In developing sewage disposal systems for its Prudhoe Bay camps, for example, Humble noted the "unbelievably primitive" nature of rural Alaska villages that lacked indoor plumbing. The company boldly asserted that by sharing its technological advances in that area it could help to solve long-standing problems of the Native population.[37] When it came to surface disturbance of the North Slope tundra, both Humble and ARCO emphasized that experimental seeding programs then under development could fully rehabilitate the damaged ground and result in higher-quality grasses that might actually be favored by the wildlife of the area. In short, the oil industry was quick to admit its affinity for technological solutions. As Humble's James Galloway noted at the very same science conference attended by Lynton Caldwell, if oil development on the North Slope was going to proceed anyway and some beautiful country would be disturbed in the process, then his company would be delinquent to withhold the very brand of scientific solutions it was best at devising.[38] Art Joens, Humble's chief environmental manager, known within the company as the "mission possible man" and the executive who would represent Humble the following year at the University of Alaska's Earth Day celebration, readily acknowledged that the misuse of technology was a significant problem. Joens believed the practice should not constitute an indictment of technological solutions altogether: "That's...my responsibility—to see that my company's technology is not misused."[39] Charles Behlke, an engineering professor at the University of Alaska who consulted for Humble on the *Manhattan* experiment, spoke for many development-minded Alaskans when he bluntly offered, "There isn't a damn thing up there [the North Slope] that can't be solved."[40]

The pipeline teams in Alaska operated by the same science-driven principle. When it became clear that a buried hot-oil pipeline would be untenable in the permafrost, for example, and that even elevating the line aboveground would result in significant heat transfer to the frozen ground, engineers designed an ammonia-based cooling system that siphoned heat from the line and radiated it to the atmosphere. The invention was one of many on the project that garnered numerous engineering awards for the oil companies that pioneered the research. The many impressive technological fixes the oil industry came up with did little to mollify critics who still questioned whether the oil should be produced at all.

This debate over Alaska oil brought into focus such questions concerning the "appropriate" use of science and technology in an ever-shrinking world where humankind's every action carried with it some kind of ecological impact. Only a few weeks after the *Manhattan* finally arrived in Alaska, John Lear penned an article, titled "Northwest Passage to What?," in which he discussed what the tanker's voyage and oil development in general might portend for the future of the people of the circumpolar North:

> Except in time of war or threat of war, science is seldom in the forefront of the confrontations that invention provokes between technology and humanity. An exception prevails in the current activity designed to shape the future of the North. So many scientific probes of the problem are now in motion that it is difficult to identify them all, let alone evaluate their relative import.[41]

Lear described several of these scientific probes, including those undertaken by the federal government and the State of Alaska, and noted a few admirable, if largely ineffective, attempts to incorporate social, economic, and political issues. The *Manhattan*'s voyage was really just another study that would add significantly to the growing mountains of data in several scientific fields, and Lear's observation points to the paradox that huge quantities of data have a way of actually obscuring knowledge of the whole. Humble could be excused for defining a scientific study of the arctic environment as "comprehensive" when it only facilitated passage of its icebreaking tanker, but public officials in state and federal government had no such license to ignore what those data might tell them about a proactive environmental policy.

The general public's affinity for machines often drives this myopia. Historians and anthropologists have long noted the tendency to refer to different eras throughout time by their respective artifacts, tools, and technological processes—the Stone Age, the Steam Age, the Computer Age, and so on. This linguistic habit gives rise to the apparently self-evident notion that material objects are the links in the chain of human progress, that the use of such artifacts takes place in a progressively linear fashion across millennia, and that all of human history can be characterized as a quest to discover, utilize, refine, and finally improve the tools that define who we are. Labeled "technological determinism" by historians, the approach can be comforting for its implication that we always exist at the very pinnacle of human civilization.[42] Defining a historical epoch by its dominant technology is an elusive prospect while the era is still developing, yet Alaskans in 1969 had no need for restraint. From the moment of the Prudhoe Bay discovery theirs was the Age of Oil. Development of the resource stood to enrich and improve their lives for decades to come. Because that development was so dependent on the technology Humble and its industry partners brought to the state, the artifacts themselves—drilling rigs, oil tankers, an eight-hundred-mile pipeline—became powerful symbols that represented the ineluctable march of progress. For historians, however, this is precisely the argument against technological determinism as a useful paradigm. It not only overemphasizes the role of technology as a singular force but mistakenly assumes it develops in some self-propelling manner in a vacuum where social, political, economic, and environmental factors do not apply. If technology drives history, the successful transit of the Northwest Passage by the SS *Manhattan* suggested that an entire fleet of icebreaking tankers would follow. That none did demonstrates the powerful influence of other forces on development decisions, in this case the political power of relevant states and stakeholder groups, economic considerations vis-à-vis not only the competing pipeline proposal but Humble's global corporate strategy and capital management, and, of course, the challenging arctic environment, which one could argue had the final say on the *Manhattan*'s chances.

Congress passed the National Environmental Policy Act (NEPA) in 1969, and President Richard M. Nixon signed it into law on January 1, 1970. In addition to creating the Environmental Protection Agency and the Council on Environmental Quality, NEPA provided for the first time a direct mechanism for evaluating environmental issues in the public policy-making process. Any project, whether public or private, that involved federal funds and/or the use of public lands fell under the act, and therefore was subject to a full governmental review of potential environmental impacts. NEPA also required the government to consider alternatives to the proposed action (which included the ubiquitous "no action" alternative, or the consequences of *not* allowing a particular project to proceed). Although NEPA was only a mechanism for government to *evaluate* and then *consider* a project's environmental consequences—nothing in the act required actually terminating a project even if studies revealed the impacts would be tremendous—the nascent environmental movement seized upon the act, as a way first to force deliberation of the diversity of viewpoints it believed had been ignored to date, and then to steer the policy-making process to courses of action that incorporated this broader range of social values.

On March 26, 1970, three environmental groups sued the Interior Department, claiming the agency violated Section 102(2)(D) of NEPA when it approved an oil industry permit to build a road north of Fairbanks intended for pipeline construction. This was the section of the act that required consideration of alternatives to the proposed action. The groups argued that since the road was essentially only a part of the larger pipeline project, the agency's approval of the road permit represented de facto approval of the pipeline—something that could not be done until Interior had considered alternatives to the entire project. Judge George L. Hart Jr. issued a preliminary injunction against not only construction of the road but the pipeline project itself. Interior was also in violation, according to Hart, of Section 102(2)(C) of NEPA, which required the preparation of a so-called impact statement, a study of the project's potential environmental effects. This would be the first Environmental Impact Statement (EIS) prepared under NEPA.

Judge Hart also issued a preliminary ruling on a lawsuit brought by five Native villages north of Fairbanks that claimed that TAPS had reneged on its promise to hire Native contractors and workers for the road-building project. Hart's order enjoined Interior from approving the road permit for some twenty miles of Native-owned land it was slated to cross. David P. Wolf, one of the attorneys for the plaintiffs, made sure to differentiate between his clients' interests and those of the environmentalists: "We are talking about property, not conservation."[43]

If the proposed Alaska pipeline proved a catalyst for the environmental movement it also galvanized the Alaska Native community behind the issue of land claims. For decades prior to the discovery of oil at Prudhoe Bay, Alaska Natives had unsuccessfully asserted aboriginal title to lands their ancestors had occupied for thousands of years. Any proposed settlement of these claims had long been resisted by public officials and private developers alike, but it soon became obvious to all that construction of an eight-hundred-mile pipeline across the patchwork of land ownership that was Alaska could not proceed until the issue was resolved. Alaska Natives suddenly found themselves in a position of unparalleled bargaining power. In December 1971, Congress passed the Alaska Native Claims Settlement Act (ANCSA), which set up a number of regional and village corporations and allocated to them some forty-four million acres of land and nearly $1 billion. The act, in addition to clearing the way for Prudhoe Bay oil development to proceed, also further demonstrated the overlap between a purely scientific industrial endeavor and the many social issues it engendered.

The voyage of the *Manhattan* itself similarly created societal ripple effects. In 1976, seven years after the tanker's voyage, Alaska Native leader Eben Hopson testified before a commission led by Canadian Supreme Court Justice Thomas Berger studying the likely impacts of oil development in the Canadian Arctic:

> It is clear now that the first symbol of circumpolar oil politics that have enbroiled [*sic*] our people was the Supertanker S.S. *Manhattan*. The voyage of this ship...confirmed our worse suspicions about the real ability of the oil industry to extract oil and gas from our Arctic homeland safely and responsibly. I was pleased that this voyage drew world attention to the environment of the Arctic Ocean and the Beaufort Sea. Until the voyage of the *Manhattan*, I had heard a lot of loose talk among the oil industry people about what could and could not happen in the Beaufort Sea.[44]

The following year in Barrow, Hopson hosted a gathering of Inuit from all over the Arctic to discuss their united future. In his welcome address, Hopson stated, "The defense of the world's Arctic environmental security must rest upon the strength of local home-rule government."[45] For several days, the attendees experienced both a cultural and political reunification as a single people, and the Inuit Circumpolar Conference (ICC) was born.

What started nearly a decade earlier as nothing more than a private oil company exploring ideas on how to bring its product to market had somehow launched international discussions of environmentalism, economics, politics, and even self-government for the indigenous peoples of the Circumpolar North. Stan Haas, in his 1969 paper to the Alaska Science Conference, characterized the Arctic Tanker Test as "perhaps the most interesting that American industry has undertaken."[46] The *Manhattan* experiment certainly stands as one of the remarkable scientific and engineering feats of the century. The voyage further demonstrated that when science is at the primary point of contact in human-environment relationships, a host of secondary social issues are brought into focus, issues that suggest there is no such thing as value-free science.

6

In the Passage

This part of the coast is the most sterile and inhospitable that can be imagined. One trap-cliff succeeds another with tiresome uniformity, and their debris cover the narrow valleys that intervene, to the exclusion of every kind of herbage. From the summit of these cliffs the ice appeared in every direction.
—Sir John Franklin, on the arctic coast
near the mouth of the Coppermine River (1821)[1]

The *Manhattan* officially entered the Northwest Passage late in the afternoon on Friday, September 5, 1969, when she rounded the southern shore of Devon Island and crossed into Lancaster Sound. Cartographers cite seven distinct marine routes through the Canadian Arctic, each of which technically qualifies as a "northwest passage."[2] If one were to count the minor variants to those routes—alternate paths around small islands or shallow inlets, for example—the available routes would number in the dozens. Of the seven primary routes, six use Lancaster Sound as the entrance (Hudson Strait to the south of Baffin Island being the exception). The most direct passage follows a straight east-west line through Lancaster Sound, Barrow Strait, Viscount Melville Sound, and McClure Strait. Collectively these waterways are known as Parry Channel. The route measures at least fifty miles wide for all but a fraction of its length and is deep enough to accommodate ships of any draft. The one significant impediment is McClure Strait, the last leg of the channel, whose narrow passage opens into the Beaufort Sea and the entire western Arctic Ocean beyond. Winds and ocean currents from this wide expanse force heavy pack ice into the bottleneck, creating massive pressure ridges and effectively choking off the exit from Parry Channel. At the time of the *Manhattan*'s voyage, no ship had ever transited westward through McClure (the U.S. Coast Guard icebreaker *Northwind* used prevailing winds and drifting pack ice to make an eastward crossing in 1959). Ships traveling west through Parry Channel must instead leave Viscount Melville Sound through an alternate route, an escape hatch of sorts—Prince of Wales Strait between Victoria and Banks Islands to Amundsen Gulf and the Beaufort Sea beyond. The officers on the *Manhattan* intended to take the vessel as far as Viscount Melville Sound, postponing until then the choice between McClure Strait and Prince of Wales Strait. Humble hoped to make an attempt at McClure, for not only did the strait contain the heaviest ice conditions the expedition could hope to encounter, but a successful transit of the treacherous channel would make history and only add to the prestige of the company's effort.[3]

But that decision was several days and hundreds of miles away. The vessel had many ice floes to break before she would arrive at McClure. Under foggy skies and at a rather balmy thirty-five degrees Fahrenheit, the *Manhattan* glided through open water into the Northwest Passage. A school of beluga whales followed the ship through the blue water. Loose ice packs began to appear, some up to twenty feet thick. The ship's officers, their confidence perhaps buoyed by the vessel's impressive performance thus far, decided to break a little more ice. They also desired to show off the tanker's abilities to a number of dignitaries from Washington who had boarded the ship the previous day in Thule. The retinue included special advisors to President Richard Nixon, officials from the Maritime Administration, and a few senior Humble executives. Most would disembark the very next day at Resolute. That these VIPs wandered the ship's decks with drinks in hand while the crew was officially prohibited from consuming alcohol caused hard feelings among the rank and file. Some on the crew, for whom the high seas had traditionally been and should always remain the exclusive domain of men, were further offended by the presence of the expedition's only female, Helen D. Bentley. Bentley had served as maritime editor for the *Baltimore Sun* and with a full two decades on that beat was widely regarded as an expert on commercial shipping matters. Like most mariners, she was a tell-it-like-it-is soul who wasn't afraid to do so in salty language. Now she had been nominated by President Nixon to chair the Federal Maritime Commission. Bentley would remain onboard for several days, right through the heart of the Northwest Passage, finally departing for her Senate confirmation hearings back in Washington.[4]

With the VIPs watching expectantly, Steward guided the *Manhattan* into a maze of multiyear floes at an incautious speed of fifteen knots. The ship cannoned into blue ice fifteen feet thick, not so much breaking it as exploding it to bits. It was too much for Pullen, who remonstrated with the master to reduce speed. All ships have limits, Pullen knew, and he feared the *Manhattan*'s officers were pushing hers too quickly. "I had been concerned at the outset with timidity," Pullen wrote in his personal journal, "but ended the day wondering whether there was too much recklessness."[5] The episode discomforted Pullen for another reason. Although designated as the Canadian government's official observer on the *Manhattan*, Pullen never had his role on the bridge clearly defined. Earlier that day he had requested that Steward reduce speed—but could he *order* him to do so? Surely not, for Steward was the ship's master. So what level of authority short of direct order *did* Pullen possess? Captain Goettel of the U.S. Coast Guard also wondered about his role, especially when Stan Haas, a man with no maritime experience whatsoever, often stood directly behind Steward giving directions. If Canada was to fulfill its stewardship role in the Arctic as then being proposed by Ottawa, Pullen recommended all future crossings have a clear chain of command that specified the authority of the Canadian observers.

The *Manhattan* reached Resolute, a weather station on Cornwallis Island, on September 6 in the midst of a thick fog and light rain. After a day's respite, during which several journalists were rotated off the tanker and replaced by new members of the press, the three ships—the *Manhattan* in the lead, followed by the *John A. MacDonald* and the *Northwind*—left for a large icefield that the air reconnaissance survey had identified some forty miles to the west in Viscount Melville Sound. Along the way, the first polar bear of the expedition was spotted hovering over a freshly killed seal. With nary a glance to the giant ship barely a hundred yards away, the bear turned his backside to every fascinated observer on the deck and promptly defecated.

One member of the crew in particular became entranced by the bear. Dan Guravich ran a camera store in Greenville, Mississippi, and had started his professional career taking pictures of agricultural equipment for catalogs and trade magazines. He eventually became interested in ships, and Humble hired him as the expedition's official photographer. But the sight of the polar bear was a life-changing experience for Guravich. He couldn't believe that such an animal thrived in what seemed like an empty, lifeless environment. He began lingering on the decks, shivering in the cold, hoping for another glimpse of the majestic creature. Guravich resolved at that moment to become a nature photographer. Over the next twenty-five years he established himself as the world's foremost expert on photographing polar bears, publishing numerous books and mentoring a whole generation of wildlife photographers in the process. Guravich also teamed up with scientists from the Canadian Wildlife Service and other research agencies. In doing so, he not only became an indispensable research hand but also changed the way polar bears were studied. It was not uncommon in those early days for scientists to spray paint identification numbers on the bears they had tranquilized. Guravich felt the practice was demeaning to the bears and convinced researchers to stop. He also spoke out for more humane methods of drawing blood samples and removing teeth (done to determine the age of the animal). The camera remained Guravich's most powerful tool, which he used to educate people. "The public thinks of [polar bears] as vicious, sneaky killers not worth protecting," he once complained. In 1992, Guravich founded Polar Bears Alive, a nonprofit organization dedicated to the worldwide conservation of the animals. "Save polar bears and you go a long way towards saving the entire habitat of the circumpolar North," he said.[6]

Near Bathurst Island the ship approached the magnetic north pole, sending compasses gyrating wildly. Regular radio communication on the ship was also affected in the high latitudes by solar storms that showered the upper atmosphere with subatomic particles. This phenomenon results in the brilliant aurora borealis (more commonly called the northern lights) but also wreaks havoc with conventional radio operations. Dr. Charles Baker, head of Humble's telecommunications division, managed all electronic and communications systems on the *Manhattan*. He installed all ship-to-shore, ship-to-ship, ship-to-helicopter, ship-to-ice, and intra-ship communication devices, as well as closed-circuit TVs, fax machines, and sonar navigation units. If it had a transmitter, it was Baker's. When informed that the nautical charts Humble would be using in the Northwest Passage were sometimes up to a mile in error, Baker decided to employ a then-experimental technique for fixing the position of the ship by tracking multiple satellite signals. Today this commonplace device is known as a global positioning system, or GPS. Baker first set foot on the *Manhattan* in early 1969, and immediately spied the first thing he wanted to fix. "They had acoustic tubes to talk between the wheelhouse and the engine room," Baker noted. "Acoustic tubes! I was shocked!"[7] The electronics expert immediately ordered dozens of UHF portable radios, another maritime first that is standard practice today. The Earth's magnetic vortex, however, posed a challenge Baker could not best, even with transmitters and antennas five hundred times as powerful as those typically found on merchant vessels.[8] Occasional radio blackouts proved to be a minor inconvenience, but news of what lay ahead foretold a potentially more serious hindrance.

Two and a half weeks earlier, two barges had become nipped by ice and sank in the very waters of Parry Channel the *Manhattan* was due to cross. A company called Panarctic Oils Limited operated an exploratory drilling site at Rea Point on Melville Island, and had loaded the barges *Learmonth* and *Johnny Nordberg* with thirty-five hundred tons of supplies for its upcoming winter season. With the Canadian Coast Guard icebreaker *Labrador* leading the way, the tug *Irving Birch* pushed one barge and towed the other. The convoy was just two thousand yards from open water and fifty miles from its destination, when an engine failure on the *Labrador* brought the vessel to a stop on an ice hummock. Floes soon closed in on the trailing vessels, ultimately tilting the lead barge at a precarious angle and forcing the tug's crew to cut both barges loose. The list to the *Learmonth* increased when racks of steel pipe on her deck broke free. The barge sank with astonishing speed. The *Nordberg*, her hull punctured and now drifting some three hundred yards astern of the tug, slipped beneath the surface a few days later. The dual sinking meant the loss of $6 million worth of goods and the complete undoing of Panarctic's winter plans. It also posed a direct problem for the *Manhattan*. Both vessels carried lighter-than-water fuel cargo that kept them from sinking to the ocean bottom. The two barges floated just thirty feet below the surface, suspended like submerged mines that effectively blocked passage for every deep-draft vessel.

The irony briefly thrilled some politicians in Ottawa, who had been offended by the American tanker's intrusion. What diplomacy and international law could not do, a couple of sunken steel barges just might. Canadian officials quickly realized, however, that a failure to rectify the potentially dangerous situation—in waters they vociferously argued were under their control—represented extreme negligence and stood to undermine their sovereignty claims. Leaving two oil-laden barges to endure the long arctic winter posed an environmental risk of the very sort Ottawa steadfastly opposed. Divers from the Canadian Navy subsequently secured the barges on the ocean floor, far below the migrating ice layers that might crumple them to pieces. The *Manhattan*, by this time just approaching the continuous icefield of Viscount Melville Sound, now had a channel clear at least of every manmade obstacle.[9]

ONE HUNDRED PERCENT ICE COVERAGE

The expedition to date had encountered only isolated pockets of ice. Some proved surprisingly solid this late in the summer, but for the most part the *Manhattan* encountered leads of open water. This would change by midafternoon on Sunday, September 7. "A strange luminous white and yellow haze appeared on the horizon," observed *New York Times* reporter William Smith. This was an iceblink, the result of the sun's rays reflecting off a large icefield in the distance. As the ship drew closer and the pack came into view, Smith described it as "a white barricade covering the whole horizon."[10] Open water was no more. Seven hundred miles of frozen seas now separated the *Manhattan* from the exit to the Northwest Passage.

Sea ice freezes much differently than lake or river ice. Freshwater becomes less dense as it freezes (the reason ice cubes float in a glass of water), which means the top layer of water remains at the surface and is in constant contact with the air whose temperature is at the freezing point. A smooth sheet of ice is the result. Sea ice behaves differently, however. Most of the salt in ocean water is pushed out of sea ice as it begins to form, creating a dense layer of salt-rich water directly below the surface. This heavy layer sinks, falling away from the freezing-point temperatures at the surface before it has a chance to become solid. Only when the surface temperature is two degrees Celsius colder than the freezing point will seawater begin to form a solid. The small amount of salt that remains in sea ice is trapped in brine droplets, which stay in a liquid state while the salt-free ice around them is solid. Over time, the brine drains from the ice by migrating downward through holes and fissures, leaving behind rock-hard ice of such low salinity it can be thawed for drinking water. The *Manhattan* was now approaching Viscount Melville Sound in the heart of the Canadian Arctic where she was sure to encounter such strong multiyear floes.

Humble had long been aware that the heaviest ice in the Northwest Passage would be found starting in Viscount Melville Sound. The currents and prevailing winds there typically induced a movement of ice floes from the north side of the channel to the south, an action that could be counted upon to produce east-west pressure ridges. At the western end of Viscount Melville Sound, however, just before the entrance to McClure Strait, active currents tended to produce rotational patterns of ice flow, which in turn created random ridges pointing in every direction and numbering fifteen to twenty per mile. Lookouts on the bridge would have to carefully note not just the position of every ridge but its surface characteristics as well. The action that produces ridges—two floes being pressed against one another, the compressive forces eventually thrusting a heap of fragments skyward—also creates an inverted ridge on the bottom of the floes. Where the height of the surface ridge depends on many factors, including gravity and the lateral pressure of the ice, the depth of the underwater ridge is a function of the buoyant forces required to support the upper pile of ice fragments. In other words, a ten-foot ridge on the surface could be assumed to have an underwater ridge sixty feet thick supporting the entire structure. For the watch officers on the *Manhattan*, noting the height and angles of the surface ridges was essential to estimating what lay underneath. Furthermore, a surface ridge with jagged peaks and sharp-cornered fragments was evidence of a recent collision between the floes and compressive forces likely still at work. Ridges with weathered, rounded tops, on the other hand, indicated the collision occurred some time ago. While the compression may have dissipated in the interim, such a formation suggested the two floes had frozen together, their interlocking fragments often twice as strong as the smooth sheets from which the ridge formed.

The *Manhattan* struck the Viscount Melville Sound icefield at a point estimated to be about six feet thick. The layer cleaved easily, yet the wedge-shaped pack grew thicker as the vessel progressed. Soon ice layers ten to twelve feet thick cracked, spun, and rolled in the ship's wake. Advance helicopter surveys revealed that ice twenty feet thick was not far off. By nightfall the crew erected two enormous floodlights on the bow. The beams benefited both the officers on the bridge and the enthralled crew members who remained on deck into the midnight hour. Merritt Helfferich, one of the University of Alaska ice scientists, described the spectacle:

> Day and night, people with free time congregated on the bow, watching the ice
> split and slip aside: summer-rotted floes as holed as Swiss cheese, new ice like
> sheets of obsidian, multiyear ice with pale-green surfaces, layered with blotches

of brown algae and differing greens. Occasionally a seal would pop up in a lead, take one disbelieving look, and disappear, but it was the moving ice itself that held us fascinated until we were shaking with cold.[11]

Helfferich and the other "ice-tronauts," as they called themselves, had hoped to hop off the ship and begin their ice testing program the previous day in Resolute, but thick afternoon fog kept them on the vessel. Despite the teams having all their equipment assembled on deck, this day also passed without the opportunity to disembark onto the ice. Guenther Frankenstein, the chief ice scientist who had been diligently training his teams for days to ensure maximum efficiency, was nearly apoplectic at the delay.

Throughout the evening both the *Manhattan* and the *Johnny Mac* easily maintained continuous motion through the ice. The same could not be said of the *Northwind*. Back in July, while under way for Thule, the Coast Guard cutter had experienced problems with one of her six engines. A damaged crankshaft rendered the engine inoperable. Repairs performed while at sea kept the *Northwind* going, and for the month the ship sat idle at Thule awaiting the *Manhattan* the crew carried out further engine maintenance.[12] Problems persisted, however, and now the Coast Guard ship lagged considerably behind her two counterparts. So long as Captain McCann could keep the *Northwind* a short distance behind the other vessels he could trail in their wake of broken ice and slushy water. But a failure to keep pace meant the intermediate channel would refreeze in a jumble of broken slabs that was harder to break than a clean sheet of virgin ice. More than once the *Northwind* found herself beset. Soon she would not be alone.

Coast Guard Lieutenant Virgil Keith awoke in his *Manhattan* cabin at 5:41 a.m., September 8, to what he called a "sudden silence" that enveloped the ship:

> The reassuring throb of the engine was stilled. I peered out the port into the Arctic twilight, and it appeared as though the *Manhattan* had been suddenly displaced onto a desolate range of small white mountains. There was no movement, and as far as I could see, there were 12-foot pressure ridges and snowy hummocks. I dressed hurriedly, grabbed my parka, and ran up one deck to the bridge.[13]

The ice of Viscount Melville Sound had the tanker firmly in its grasp. The previous evening the Humble team had decided to reduce the ship's speed gradually throughout the night in order to determine at what point the ice would hold fast and stop her forward momentum. That point was reached just before dawn as the vessel crawled along at only two knots. The offending barrier was an ice ridge that would have been no match for the icebreaker at a faster speed. But with so little momentum in one hundred percent ice coverage so pressurized that it bound to the hull and squeezed the ship like a vise, the *Manhattan* simply ground to a halt. Haas made perfectly clear in the Humble press release that day that the ice had not yet beaten the ship: "We stopped because we wanted to, not because we had to.... Unlike other ships which in the past have avoided ice up here, we're looking for it."[14] Captain Steward was content to let the tanker sit while the *Johnny Mac* turned back to help break the *Northwind* free. The delay gave the ice scientists the chance they had been waiting for. A crane lowered two snowmobiles and four bright orange sleds over the side. Five study teams zoomed off ahead of the tanker, each group peeling off at prearranged intervals. The last team found itself more than a mile from the ship. Each team carried a high-powered rifle in the event a polar bear took an interest in their work. The hand drills proved slightly problematic as the different models each team used did not have inter-changeable parts. Working in subfreezing temperatures with a brisk twenty-mile-per-hour wind was difficult enough, but the teams further discovered that cranking the augers by hand was exhausting. One team spent all morning extracting only four ice cores. Chief Steward Leo Oliveira attempted to soften the experience by sending out lunches—Cornish game hens, barbecued chicken, ham sandwiches, and, for a good laugh, several flavors of ice cream.

Many nonscientists also used the opportunity to step out onto the ice. William Smith, the *New York Times* reporter and avid rugby enthusiast, put into action a plan he had hatched months before. "I decided I wanted to kick a rugby ball farther in the Arctic than anyone had ever done before," he explained. Smith acknowledged the achievability of his goal since he would likely be the first man in history to pull such a stunt at all. "And then Ralph Maybourn [the BP representative] comes along," Smith continued, "and boots it twice as far as I did."[15]

While on the ice the men experienced one of the Arctic's disorienting visual tricks. Sunlight bounces around in odd ways in the uniformly white environment, while the complete lack of shadows erases the dimension of depth. *National Geographic* reporter Bern Keating discovered this the hard way while attempting to climb a ladder. His foot came down well short of the first rung and he collapsed in a heap, wrenching his shoulder badly in the process. Glaciologist and polar veteran Charles Swithinbank assured Keating he was not the first man to be fooled by arctic light—nor would he be the last on this very expedition. Sprained ankles and hyperextended knees were common among the crew by the end of voyage.[16]

At one p.m., the tanker's whistle and a yellow flag on the tower announced that it was time to return to the ship. Captain Steward subsequently backed the ship astern, though not without some difficulty, and reached a full six knots before smashing through the pressure ridge that had previously stopped the tanker.[17]

The same scenario repeated itself that night. Shortly after midnight, the *Northwind* again became stuck well astern of the other vessels, the *Johnny Mac* turned to lend a hand, and when the *Manhattan* slowed to wait she herself became locked in ice. At one point all three vessels sat motionless in Viscount Melville Sound. The substandard performance of the *Northwind* now seemed to be jeopardizing the entire mission. As Captain McCann of the crippled icebreaker put it, "The assister has become the assisted."[18] The *Northwind* had previously become icebound several times on her solo eastbound voyage in July. On those occasions the crew detonated explosive charges to break the ice that gripped the ship. One charge was successfully fired a mere thirty-five feet from the vessel. While such operations remained at McCann's disposal, setting the charges would still force the other two vessels to wait. That morning, McCann and Captain Fournier of the *Johnny Mac* traveled by helicopter to the *Manhattan* and joined the tanker's officer crew on the bridge to discuss the situation. McCann opened (and thus essentially closed) the meeting by announcing his intention to detach his vessel from the expedition and proceed to Prudhoe Bay via Coronation Gulf, a less difficult route along the coast. His priority cable to Coast Guard Commandant W. J. Smith recommending such action had been received and approved.[19] The *Johnny Mac* freed herself with a heeling system that literally rocked the vessel out of the ice on her beam, then proceeded back to the *Northwind*, where she sailed around the disabled ship and chewed up the offending ice. In the meantime, Captain Steward attempted to dislodge the *Manhattan* by again backing the tanker astern and making a run at the ice pack ahead. But the tanker wouldn't budge. The incident revealed one of the glaring weaknesses of the vessel. The *Manhattan*'s power astern was so limited—only fifteen thousand horsepower in reverse compared to forty-three thousand horsepower of forward thrust—that backing out of a tight channel proved next to impossible. While in constant forward motion the enormous bulk of the tanker usually sustained enough momentum to shatter extraordinary layers of ice, but should the vessel be forced to slow down for any reason the lateral pressure of the ice pack was perfectly capable of seizing the hull. Said Haas, "It was like parking your car in the garage and having the garage shrink around it."[20] In a report later prepared by Humble engineers Bram Mookhoek and W. J. Bielstein, the authors praised the tanker's main propulsion plant, which performed reliably and experienced virtually no problems for the entire voyage, but acknowledged that it simply did not have adequate horsepower when it came to backing the vessel astern. Any future development of an icebreaking tanker system, they explained, must correct this flaw.[21] Captain J. W. Moreau of the U.S. Coast Guard would further speculate that such tankers would require eighty thousand to two hundred thousand horsepower for arctic service.[22]

With the *Manhattan* unable to move in any direction, Steward turned to Captain Pullen and asked him to radio the *Johnny Mac* for help. Protocol required that only Pullen, Canada's official representative on the tanker, could request assistance from the *John A. MacDonald*. He complied with a quick appeal to Fournier: "Would you mind coming over to nibble about our quarters?"[23] The quip, once relayed in media accounts, again thrilled some Canadians who delighted in the notion of the American behemoth having to be rescued by the tiny, bright red Canadian ship. Even one junior officer on the *MacDonald* candidly expressed his glee: "It's not that we don't want the mission to succeed. We most certainly do. But the fact is that every one of us has been on his knees praying that your big bastard would get stuck just once."[24] That the *Manhattan* did get stuck—more than once, in fact—and had to be rescued by the *John A. MacDonald* actually bolstered Ottawa's claim of operational jurisdiction, which the Trudeau government was making at that very moment. The passage could only be made, it seemed, with assistance from the Canadian Coast Guard. Many arctic veterans on the *Manhattan*, even non-Humble personnel with no obligation to defend the tanker, disputed this conclusion. The *Manhattan*'s inadequate reverse thrust was a normal design limitation, as tankers on conventional routes require astern power only when docking or for emergencies. While in forward motion the *Manhattan* thoroughly outclassed not just the *John A. MacDonald* and *Northwind* but every other icebreaker in the world. The tanker's defenders noted that the next generation of icebreaking tankers, once beefed up with adequate astern thrust, would be virtually unstoppable.[25] Now, however, the *Manhattan* needed help. Fournier pulled his vessel to the stern of the tanker, breaking out the track that had frozen over in the intervening hours, then ran the length of the ship, up the port side and down the starboard, so close the crews could talk to each other from their respective decks. The maneuver eased the pressure on the tanker, allowing Steward to pull astern and ram forward through the mounds of ice.

Soon both vessels reached a lead of open water at Cape Clarendon. The *MacDonald* used the opportunity to pull alongside and top off her diesel tanks from the reserves on the *Manhattan*. In addition to her own store of 184,000 barrels of bunker oil—a record fuel order in commercial maritime history—the *Manhattan* carried thirty thousand barrels of special diesel oil for refueling the escort icebreakers and another five thousand barrels of jet fuel for the helicopters.[26] A gangplank was set up between the two ships allowing crew members to wander freely back and forth from one to the other. One Canadian official visiting the U.S. tanker compared her to an immense factory: "At any moment one expects to hear clanking and see flames as large ladles of molten steel go rushing past."[27] Those from the *Manhattan*, a starkly utilitarian ship whose color scheme consisted mostly of different shades of gray, marveled at the *MacDonald*'s mahogany paneling, its varnished wooden rails, and the fireplaces in every cabin. Even better, especially for those suffering under Humble's prohibition against alcohol, was the *Johnny Mac*'s lounge, which featured glasses of beer for fifteen cents and highballs for a quarter. Lieutenant Commander E. B. Stolee explained the importance of a comfortable lounge, especially on a long expedition: "The bar is a meeting place where the trials and tribulations of the day assume their rightful proportions and where old Joe doesn't seem quite the bastard he was during the forenoon watch." Noting the scruffy, wide-eyed crew taking over the lounge, Stolee likened it to "farmers at the vicar's tea party."[28] Before long, a number of impromptu parties broke out on the smaller vessel, one featuring a journalist bleating away on his bagpipes. The black tams worn by every member of the *MacDonald*'s crew became coveted items in the bartering that followed, for which the *Manhattan*-ites freely traded their Esso Tiger patches.[29] The two ships disengaged at 7:30 p.m. and continued around Dundas Peninsula on Melville Island, where they could peek into the ice-choked barrier of McClure Strait.

The expedition was now in its seventeenth day. The *Manhattan* had traversed Lancaster Sound, Barrow Strait, and Viscount Melville Sound. Only McClure remained in the quadripartite passage known as Parry Channel. Whether the tanker would attempt the previously impenetrable route or head southwest through the relatively ice-free Prince of Wales Strait was a matter to be decided by Stan Haas and the *Manhattan*'s officer crew. Every sailor relished the prospect of attacking the challenge head-on, but Haas was quick to point out that such abstract notions of glory did not compare to the tanker's more practical mission: "We would like to go through [McClure Strait], but the historical emphasis is secondary to our stated mission of acquiring data. If we can do both, fine. If we can do only one, then putting our name in the history books will have to take second place."[30] An aerial reconnaissance film drop that afternoon from the Coast Guard C-130 revealed that of the strait's one hundred percent ice coverage, an estimated fifty percent was rock-hard multiyear ice, forty percent was second-year ice, and a mere ten percent was the relatively fragile first-year ice.[31] The visible pressure ridges rose ten to thirty feet in the air, leading some ice experts to surmise that the subsurface layer might extend down a full one hundred feet in places. Despite these intimidating obstacles, the expedition's entire officer crew—Roger Steward, Arthur Smith, Don Graham, Tom Pullen, Fred Goettel, and Paul Fournier—all hoped for the chance to test both the vessel and their own nautical skills against the legendary passage. Humble's Bram Mookhoek threw his lot in with the others. Even regular crewmembers yelled out to Haas as he walked the decks, encouraging him to throw caution to the wind and give a try at McClure. The Humble executives back in Houston deferred to Haas, giving him the green light if he believed the vessel had a reasonable chance for success. As he deliberated that day, Haas instructed the Humble press office to prepare two news releases—one announcing the McClure attempt, the other explaining why the tanker was bypassing the strait—and be ready to transmit either one at his direction. The *Manhattan* had already made history as the largest icebreaker in the world. Her successful transit of the Northwest Passage, all but a given in the coming days via one route or another, would stand as the closing chapter to a five-century tale that featured some of the most famous names in polar exploration. Should the vessel cross McClure Strait it would represent a crowning achievement like no other. On the evening of Tuesday, September 9, the tanker rounded the southern cape of Melville Island, opposite the northeast corner of Banks Island. Prince of Wales Strait lay to the port side, McClure to the starboard. Haas announced to the crew that the *Manhattan* would make for McClure in the morning.

7

Through the Passage

Oh ye of little faith.

—Sign on the desk of Stanley B. Haas[1]

At the very moment the *Manhattan* was preparing to enter McClure Strait, another event of historical significance was about to unfold some twelve hundred miles away in the city of Anchorage, Alaska. A line of curious and hopeful Alaskans began forming outside the Sydney Laurence Auditorium in the predawn darkness of Wednesday, September 10. By the time the sun finally rose on that cool, clear morning, hundreds of people waited in a queue that ran the length of F Street, turned the corner, and extended down Sixth Avenue. Inside the auditorium, television and radio crews diligently wired their equipment for live broadcast, while over a hundred journalists from as far away as London and Tokyo staked claim to the best seats in the press section. Bank officials from New York, Dallas, and San Francisco milled about, their chartered jets parked at the airport. Dozens of Alaska State Troopers and local police officers stood by to provide security, most in uniform but some casually dressed to allow them to wander unnoticed through the crowd. Up on the stage, behind a long table, a few secretaries double-checked the phone connections and organized files, while behind the curtain a full team of office staff did the same.

The event was the innocuously named State of Alaska 23rd Oil and Gas Lease Sale, better known to locals as the Prudhoe Bay lease sale.[2] In fact, throughout that summer any Alaskan could have simply referred to "the sale" without causing confusion. On that autumn day, the state put up for competitive bid 450,858 acres, divided into 179 separate tracts, of the most promising oil-rich lands on the North Slope. Since the Prudhoe Bay discovery some eighteen months before, Alaskans generally believed that oil development would be their state's ticket to future economic prosperity, yet in specific terms one could hardly contemplate the true value of the oil or how much the state could receive for leasing the drilling rights on all that acreage. Three other North Slope lease sales in the previous five years had earned the state a modest $12 million, but this next sale would be the one to break the bank. Everyone knew this to be a watershed day for Alaska. In taking in an almost unimaginable amount of money, the state would step confidently and at the same time awkwardly into the age of oil. This single day would set a course for the state's development for the next several decades. The sale put on full display the power and influence of Humble, BP, ARCO, and the world's other major oil companies, for whom Alaska was just another stop in their international pursuit of oil and wealth. Just as importantly, this day would reveal the extent to which Alaskans were politically and economically astute enough to play such a high-stakes game.

That Prudhoe Bay even belonged to the Alaskans and was theirs to lease was due to the incredible foresight of a state geologist named Tom Marshall. With the passage of the Alaska Statehood Act of 1958, Congress authorized the state selection of just over one hundred million acres of unappropriated public land to be made in a twenty-five-year period. Marshall recognized the resource potential of the North Slope and within a few years of statehood convinced officials to select some two million acres sandwiched between the Arctic National Wildlife Range (now Refuge) to the east and the Naval Petroleum Reserve No. 4 to the west. That fortuitous selection now placed the most valuable real estate in the Arctic at the state's disposal.

The North Slope witnessed a flurry of activity in the spring and summer of 1969. Every oil company lucky enough to already hold leases drilled test wells and frantically gathered every scrap of data they could extract from the ground. Tom Kelly, Alaska's resource commissioner, recognized that the state would be wise to hold a lease sale as soon as possible. Every new well that was drilled on Prudhoe Bay acreage provided new information that could be used to map the entire reservoir. Yet a scarcity of data on the exact structure of Prudhoe Bay could actually help the state. The less information the oil companies had to work with, the more likely they would be to bid top dollar for every chunk of land in the area. If Kelly waited too long to offer new Prudhoe Bay leases, the many delineation wells and ongoing seismic work could tell the industry which tracts to avoid and the state might fail to maximize revenue.

But then Kelly himself faced the very same dilemma. The state possessed so little hard data on the Prudhoe Bay reservoir that it would be difficult, if not impossible, to determine what constituted an acceptable bid. The state reserved the right at every lease sale to reject bids it deemed too low; nothing would frustrate state officials more than to see valuable oil leases given away for pennies on the dollar because someone made a lowball bid that happened to come out on top. But without hard seismic data, making such a valuation was problematic, and the state found itself at a disadvantage to those companies that at least possessed a few well logs. Kelly met both publicly and privately with the major oil companies, hoping to learn something of their respective lease strategies, and his staff performed an acre-by-acre estimate of the field's value and oil potential. In the end, he did what any good poker player in a high-stakes game would do: he bluffed.

Kelly spent the summer of 1969 ratcheting up tension and excitement for the September lease sale. First, he cancelled another sale planned for the Gulf of Alaska in July, leaving no doubt that the state's full attention was on Prudhoe Bay. Kelly also systematically added new tracts to the sale, a few at a time, intimating to everyone that some new piece of information justified adding this valuable acreage. All summer long he and his staff scheduled highly visible meetings all over town, and Kelly consistently hinted to any industry executive he ran into that his competitors were poised to bid high. When Kelly heard a rumor that his brown leather briefcase contained reams of invaluable data on the Prudhoe Bay leases, he disabused no one of the notion and made certain to be seen in public with the case conspicuously on display. In fact, the briefcase carried only a single well log and some random seismic data. Kelly's entire game, he later admitted, was little more than a ruse designed to create excitement and uncertainty around the lease sale: "The more mystique we could put out, the better [our] chance of deriving maximum bids."[3]

Kelly did not have an exclusive hold on mystery, suspense, and secrecy. A handful of major oil companies and literally dozens of smaller ones each vied for a piece of the valuable Prudhoe Bay action, and the levels of secrecy they practiced to protect their interests often reached an almost absurd extreme. Some crews erected barbed-wire fences around the drill sites and hired guards to patrol the area day and night with dogs. When the crews pulled cores from the well itself, they often drew a curtain made of heavy canvas around the activity. Even in the remote reaches of Alaska's North Slope, the oil companies feared that spies with high-powered binoculars might be able to count the lengths of pipe being pulled from the hole and ascertain the depth of the well.[4] Some companies, fearing the indiscreet boasting sure to occur when off-shift laborers returned home, alternately forbade crews to leave the site or bribed them with hefty bonuses to remain. Even wells that did not strike oil still provided information on the subsurface geology that ostensibly hinted where the crude might lie. And the oilmen, a notoriously tight-lipped bunch to begin with, kept especially mum all summer long. ARCO would only state that its results "will not be announced for some time." BP kept its drilling rigs going round the clock, yet Eric Drake, the company's president, would offer only this frustratingly vague summation: "The results of the eight wells so far drilled have confirmed our earlier optimism regarding the Prudhoe Bay discovery." Jim Gillespie, the company's senior drilling supervisor, proved the most succinct when asked about the performance of one North Slope well: "No comment."[5]

As the summer of 1969 drew to a close, and the state's rendezvous with Prudhoe Bay riches approached, Alaskans collectively began to appreciate that the developments on the North Slope stood to alter their lives in ways they could scarcely imagine. At the Alaska Science Conference in Fairbanks, in between heated debates featuring environmentalists on one side and developers on the other, Alaskans also discussed the economic effects of oil. With the prospect of untold lease revenues just around the corner, the conference took on a sense of urgency concerning the extent to which the state would, in effect, be irrevocably aligning its future with that of the oil industry. Two conference speakers in particular—John S. Hedland, an Anchorage attorney, and Gregg Erickson, a resource economist with the University of Alaska—raised important questions concerning the upcoming lease sale. Hedland noted that Alaska's oil revenue mechanism utilized a combination of high leasing costs (the competitive bidding system to be used for Prudhoe Bay two weeks hence) and relatively low royalty rates and severance taxes. This system held that through competitive leasing the state would receive upfront and all at once the very same amount that it might have earned under another regime of low lease costs and higher production taxes. By keeping those taxes relatively low, it was hoped that the state would encourage development even of marginal fields. But, as Hedland noted, such a system was predicated on a few key assumptions. First, that sufficient competition existed within the industry so that the bidding process would indeed result in Alaska receiving the true value of the leases. Within only the last few years, however, Richfield had partnered with Humble, merged with Atlantic, and later acquired Sinclair, while BP entered into a complex merger with Standard Oil of Ohio. Hedland offered, "The inescapable conclusion is that most of the potential competition has been eliminated by these mergers and joint ventures."[6]

Hedland secondly noted that in the absence of such competition, the state must possess sufficient information about the value of the leases themselves to set an informed refusal price. The very paucity of such data caused Hedland to wonder whether the state could first recognize whether a bidder was failing to offer a fair price and then muster the courage to refuse that offer. He went on to state that by accepting high lease revenue now, rather than future profits as the oil was actually developed, the state would essentially be borrowing money from the oil industry at an indeterminate rate of interest, but one that almost surely would not work in the state's favor over the long term. "Sufficient doubt exists with respect to North Slope leasing to cause considerable concern," he warned.[7]

Gregg Erickson went Hedland one better and advocated that the state postpone the lease sale altogether. Noting the state was "very likely" to receive less for the Prudhoe Bay leases than what they were actually worth, Erickson suggested pushing the sale back at least six months to give the state more time to determine an effective leasing and taxation policy. He estimated the true value of the acreage in question to be between $2 and $4 billion, and noted that the companies were unlikely to put up that kind of cash. "Such a price tag is unprecedented, to say the least, and it is doubtful that the bidders will have either the ability or the will to raise this much money in today's tight capital markets."[8] Erickson also lamented what he called the state's "inefficient" severance tax, which treated all producers the same, whether profitable or break-even, and all oil fields alike, whether large or small. Assuming a twenty-year period and a severance tax at the current four percent, he calculated producers at Prudhoe Bay stood to realize an astonishing forty-three percent return on their investment. His calculations, which he noted an oil industry analyst would neither confirm nor deny, demonstrated that the state could conceivably raise its severance tax to a whopping ninety percent— and the oil industry would still turn a profit at Prudhoe Bay. "If we wish to maximize our revenue without regard to other long-range goals," he cautioned, "then we must overhaul our leasing policy to eliminate or at least reduce the impact of tax uncertainty, and we must do it before we lease much more land."[9]

The arguments of Hedland and Erickson made the front page of the local newspaper and became fodder for intense debate at the conference. In the end, however, the tantalizing prospect of the all-but-guaranteed revenues made the average Alaskan unwilling to consider the proposals. Hedland admitted as much in his lecture, noting that the social value of immediate revenue—building hospitals and schools, for example—would always take primary importance over any theoretical abstractions of interest rates and severance taxes. The political will to march boldly toward a lease sale only weeks away proved too strong for anyone to resist.

On September 9, the night before the sale, Governor Keith Miller addressed Alaskans in a statewide radio broadcast from Anchorage and understandably lapsed into hyperbolic rhetoric: "Tomorrow we will reach out to claim our birthright; we will rendezvous with our dreams." But Miller also advised caution and restraint. Hundreds of millions of dollars, perhaps even a cool billion, would be in state coffers within twenty-four hours, and Miller wanted to inform Alaskans that no spending spree would result. "There should be no mistaken impressions that all of Alaska's financial difficulties will disappear immediately after tomorrow's sale. As we anticipated, this fiscal year has been and will continue to be a tight one. We cannot spend money just because we have it."[10] Miller went on to advise a prudent use of the pending revenues to stimulate every sector of Alaska's economy in a way that would continue to accrue benefits long after the immediate rush of oil wealth had been spent.

Early the next morning a beaming Miller arrived at the Sydney Laurence Auditorium, where Kelly and his staff were preparing to receive the many bids from the oil companies. When the doors opened to the public at seven a.m., the 656-seat hall quickly filled with executives, bankers, curious members of the public, and, of course, a steady procession of stone-faced oil men. The official representatives from each company signed the registry and, usually accompanied by armed guards, handed to state officials the envelopes containing their bids. A few bids had been submitted in advance, some as early as the week before, but most companies withheld theirs, again under constant surveillance by armed guards, until the eight a.m. deadline the morning of the sale. Every executive feared the amount of his bid would somehow become known, leaving him to watch in horror as a rival company topped each one by some token amount.

Oil companies rented entire hotel floors to preclude competitors from eavesdropping through the walls, floors, or ceilings. One paranoid executive admitted to sleeping with his briefcase at the Captain Cook Hotel. On the day of the sale, some companies wrapped their sealed envelopes in aluminum foil to thwart any hidden X-ray devices. Perhaps the most curious episode was one newspaper reporters dubbed the "Canadian Mystery Train." A group of industry executives chartered a train at a cost of $10,000 per day and spent the better part of a week negotiating bids while shuttling between Calgary and Edmonton. No one, including the train's porters and engineers, could disembark until deliberations had been completed. The executives then chartered two airplanes to each carry identical copies of the bids to Anchorage, a precaution taken in the event one airplane was somehow delayed.[11]

As the crowd filed through the doors to the auditorium, they passed a dozen Alaska Natives protesting the sale. With signs that read "Bad Deal at Tom Kelly's Trading Post," "Eskimos Own North Slope," and "$2,000,000,000 Native Land Robbery," the group marched up and down the sidewalk. Charlie "Etok" Edwardsen Jr., an Eskimo from Barrow whose outspoken nature and fanatical support of Native rights often put him at odds with the more conservative, established Native groups, led the march in front of the auditorium and did not mince words: "Today's lease sale is perpetration of economic genocide on a Native minority."[12]

Edwardsen and his followers gave voice to the Native land-claims movement by questioning the true "ownership" of the North Slope. The indigenous people of Alaska, they argued, could claim aboriginal title to lands their people had inhabited for thousands of years. The United States government, by contrast, could only produce a receipt from 1867, when the territory was purchased from Russia. And the state's claim to the North Slope proved even more tenuous, the lands having only been "selected" a few years before. "How can the white man sell our land when they do not own it?" asked Edwardsen.[13]

Another Native leader, Eben Hopson, also of Barrow, proved less militant than Edwardsen, but reflected the same sentiment in an interview earlier in the year:

The oil companies, the able few, and all awe-struck would-be millionaires are fighting over the very lands that we have claimed, and to which we are legally entitled. Are we to assume that the attitude of the non-Native is such that so long as their pockets are full of green stuff derived, incidentally, from a piece of property claimed and owned by the Natives, that everything is fine? What manner of conscience is this?[14]

Despite the fact that Alaska Natives were virtually united in favor of some kind of land-claims settlement, Edwardsen could get only a dozen followers to join him in the sidewalk protest. Don Wright, the chairman of the Alaska Federation of Natives, believed the group should work within the system, not attack it from the outside, and noted that official Native organizations did not support the protest.[15]

The environmental community remained largely silent regarding the lease sale. Edgar Wayburn of the Sierra Club traveled to Prudhoe Bay that summer and reaffirmed his group's stance on wilderness and wildlife protection. In a phone interview from San Francisco two days before the sale, Wayburn stated, "We think it's unfortunate they [the State of Alaska] have decided to open up so much land so quickly, but we understand they feel the need for the funds."[16] The Sierra Club and other environmental organizations planned no legal action against the sale, though only six months later they would file suit against the planned construction of the eight-hundred-mile trans-Alaska pipeline.

Tom Kelly officially opened the State of Alaska 23rd Oil and Gas Lease Sale at 8:13 a.m. on Wednesday, September 10, 1969. He had chosen the date to coincide with the birthday of Ermalee Hickel, wife of former governor Walter Hickel. Hickel, who famously arrived in Alaska as a young man with only a few cents in his pocket and proceeded to build a real estate empire worth millions, had been elected governor in 1966. Three years later he left Juneau to become President Nixon's secretary of the interior. Hickel epitomized the pro-development attitude in Alaska that welcomed oil development as the state's ticket to prosperity. The lease sale's folksy opening ceremony got under way with Governor Miller leading the crowd in a decidedly off-key rendition of the Alaska Flag Song. Miller then scrapped his planned hour-long speech and instead spoke off the cuff about the day's importance, summing it up quite simply: "Alaska will never be the same." A ten-minute film on the state's natural beauty followed. In the ceremony's only unscripted performance, a practical joker dressed as what newspapers called an "Arabian sheik" got chuckles from the crowd when he marched onstage and melodramatically handed over his bid. Larry Beck, a showman who billed himself as the Bard of Alaska, then stepped onstage in a fur parka and mukluks and recited all thirty stanzas of his ode "Black Gold." The spectacle caused one impatient executive to quip, "It's getting more like the *Ed Sullivan Show* all the time."[17]

The interminable ceremony proved necessary, however, as it gave the secretaries behind the stage curtain ample time to tear open the outer envelopes on each of over one thousand separate submissions, certify the enclosed paperwork, and file the bids according to tract number. By 10:31 a.m., this work had been completed, and Kelly nodded to his staff to open the envelopes starting with Tract No. 1. F. J. Keenan, Kelly's deputy in the Division of Lands, methodically documented each company's bid taken in random order, then announced that a consortium led by the Gulf Oil Corporation had taken the first tract with a winning bid of $15,528,960. The capacity crowd in the auditorium went silent for a few moments until someone let out a low whistle. The State of Alaska had just taken in more money for a single tract than it had at every other North Slope lease sale combined. And there were still 178 tracts to go.

Keenan was just getting warmed up. The same Gulf Oil consortium that took the first tract also took the second, this time for over $20 million. Tract 3 also went to Gulf, for $31 million. The fourth, fifth, and sixth in rapid succession all went to the group led by Gulf Oil. A running scorecard on the stage now displayed the total take thus far: $97 million. The crowd had overcome its initial shock, and now cheered wildly as Keenan announced each bid.[18] Newspaper reporters rushed to the lobby to phone in the first stories that would appear in special editions, some published before noon.[19]

Most in the crowd found the first six bids all the more spectacular because they knew that the prime acreage, that in the immediate vicinity of the discovery well, had yet to come up. Kelly would later admit that the numbering of the tracts had not been accidental. Those first six represented a block of acreage on the Colville River Delta, an area that had not been thoroughly explored but that many believed held deposits of oil. "We put out a nibble in that area to see if the bidders would bite," said Kelly. "We wanted to whet their appetites."[20]

By the time the leases immediately adjacent to Prudhoe Bay came on the block, no one doubted that the oil industry was hooked. Tract 37 fetched a winning bid of $41.2 million, the highest so far. Tract 56, in the same general area, topped that figure when two giants of the industry, J. Paul Getty and H. L. Hunt, put down $43.6 million for it.

The high point of the day came in the bidding for Tract 57. Keenan drew the bids in random order and first announced ARCO's offer of $26 million. Next came the partnership of Gulf and BP—$47.1 million. Two other bids in the range of a mere $36 million followed, and the Gulf-BP offer looked promising. Keenan next revealed an astonishing bid of $72.11 million from the partnership of Standard-Mobil-Phillips. While the crowd cheered this seemingly unbeatable number, Keenan pulled the last envelope and announced that a consortium led by Amerada Hess had won the tract with a bid of $72.28 million. Amerada Hess had topped the next highest bid by the slimmest of margins, a mere $164,133. Gasps went up from the crowd and almost immediately some began to speculate that the razor-thin margin was no coincidence but that some form of industrial espionage had taken place. The second-place bidder, the Standard-Mobil-Phillips consortium, would later conduct its own investigation of the bidding process, but found no evidence of tampering. One executive at the sale wrote the matter off as "mathematical coincidence" caused by different parties using essentially the same data in calculating their bids.[21]

When the lease sale finally ended at 5:14 p.m., the scorecard on stage said it all: $900,220,590 (and 21 cents to be precise). The winners of each bid were required to immediately put up twenty percent of the total amount owed, with the remainder due within fifteen days. Just minutes after the close of the sale Alaska State Troopers escorted officials from Bank of America and a satchel containing $180 million worth of checks to the airport. The state had spent $23,000 to charter a United Airlines DC-8—what the press dubbed a "flying armored car"—to deliver the checks to banks in San Francisco and New York, where they could be deposited and immediately begin earning interest. Had Alaskan officials deposited the checks in local banks, a delay of even one or two days in the actual transfer of funds would have cost the state up to $90,000 in interest.

The state had offered 179 parcels of nearly half a million acres of land and had received bids on every single one. Kelly would later reject fifteen winning bids for not matching the state's minimum set value, including a handful of joke bids of one dollar that actually won the tract when no other bids were submitted. The final take exceeded the entire state budget that year by a factor of six. At a party that evening held at—where else—the Petroleum Club on the top floor of the Anchorage West-ward Hotel, Kelly expressed unbounded glee. "[The sale began] with a tremendous bang," he enthused. "The lease sale total is great! There's no disappointment!"[22] Drinks were on the house all night long, and as starry-eyed Alaskans mingled with Texans and Londoners, it seemed everyone had ideas on how to spend the money. Divide it equally among every Alaska resident! (It worked out to roughly $3,000 per person.) Free college tuition for our kids! Build a brand-new city across the inlet from Anchorage and connect the two with a huge aerial tramway! Though the gov-ernor and the legislature ultimately had more reasonable proposals in mind, that evening the possibilities seemed endless. The party lasted well into the early morn-ing hours on the top floor of Anchorage's tallest building, while far below the city's residents went to bed nearly $1 billion richer than the day before. Bartenders at the Petroleum Club later commented that the evening's glass breakage exceeded any New Year's Eve in recent memory.

Jack Roderick, an independent oil broker and future mayor of Anchorage, believed it was only after the Prudhoe Bay lease sale that Alaskans really began to grasp how much their lives were about to change.[23] The lease sale was really the first actual *event*, as opposed to the plans, proposals, and feasibility studies that comprised the sum total of the oil industry's efforts thus far. The pipeline hadn't fully sunk in, perhaps because it was hard to conceptualize when the companies themselves didn't quite know what it was going to look like or the exact route it would follow. The National Environmental Policy Act would pass Congress the following year, but at the time there were only vague notions of the heated environmental debates that would later occur in crowded hearing rooms and on newspaper opinion pages. The *Manhattan*, for its part, seemed almost too outlandish to be real, according to Roderick. John Havelock, the state's attorney general, agreed: "The whole thing actually seemed rather preposterous."[24] But $900 million landing in the state's bank account in a single day has a way of getting people to take notice.

The Humble Oil and Refining Company, its icebreaking tanker entering McClure Strait that very day, was conspicuous for its absence from the intense bidding at the sale. The company secured only three tracts for a relatively paltry $4 million. When queried about the apparent disinterest a company spokesman explained, "The sale covered an extensive area within which it was relatively difficult to find a number of tracts worthy of sizable bids." Humble had always been only the bankroll behind ARCO's exploration campaign. The company possessed little geological data in advance of the sale that would have enabled it to compete with those outfits engaged in more aggressive exploration. An executive of one such rival company speculated that with more than a million acres already under lease, Humble had "such fabulous Alaskan reserves already that they won't get all the oil out in 50 years."[25]

For the first three weeks of her history-making voyage, the *Manhattan* had been forced to share the front pages of Alaska's newspapers with the Prudhoe Bay lease sale. Only when the sale concluded did news of the *Manhattan* receive any significant attention from the Alaska print media, and by that time it was word of her being repeatedly stuck that received prominent coverage. Humble executives had to be disappointed when they saw the front-page headline of the *Anchorage Daily News* on Saturday, September 13: "Polar Ice Stops the Tanker *Manhattan*." An article farther down the page noted that townspeople in Valdez were ready "to commemorate the arrival...of the first shipload of line pipe for the Trans Alaska Pipeline System." That spring, the oil industry had contracted with three Japanese companies to produce eight hundred miles of forty-eight-inch-diameter steel pipe. The Valdez shipment was the first of some half a million tons of pipe that would shortly arrive and subsequently be staged in Valdez, Fairbanks, and Prudhoe Bay. The recent deposit of $900 million into state coffers was widely viewed in Alaska as the nest egg that would keep the state solvent until the pipeline could be completed. The Humble media department must have wondered exactly how, in the very week the *Manhattan* was poised to make history, first Alaska's richest day and now the competing pipeline proposal conspired to steal the headlines.

MCCLURE STRAIT

Sir Robert McClure commanded the *Investigator*, which, while searching for the lost expedition of Sir John Franklin in 1850, entered the Northwest Passage from the Pacific side and ventured nearly the length of Prince of Wales Strait before becoming beset in the ice. Reaching the northeast cape of Banks Island on a clear day, McClure was able to look across the sound to Melville Island some sixty miles away. With that he set his eyes upon the final link of the Northwest Passage. Though the ice remained fast and ultimately prevented McClure from actually transiting the channel, he now had conclusive proof of a waterway connecting the Atlantic and Pacific Oceans. During the short summer of 1851, the ice pack relaxed its grip just enough to allow the *Investigator* to sail back out of Prince of Wales Strait, sneak up the unprotected west coast of Banks Island, and find a shallow inlet on the island's north side, where McClure anchored just in advance of the encroaching winter ice. The grateful captain named this shelter Mercy Bay, but it would prove to be an ice prison from which his ship would never escape. McClure wrote in a letter to his former commander Sir George Back:

> No idea can be formed unless witnessed of the stupendous masses of ice with which this terrible polar sea is entirely filled. We were actually squeezed through it and frequently so close to the cliffs that the vessel had to be listed over to prevent the boats being carried away at the davits by projecting rocks.[26]

When the summer of 1852 came and went with no relief from the ice, McClure was forced to cut his men's rations. By the spring of 1853, at least two of the crew had gone insane, the rest uniformly afflicted with scurvy and starvation. Only days before launching a desperate plan that would send two-thirds of the crew on an overland trek in search of rescue, the men of the *Investigator* experienced salvation in the form of a lone individual walking toward them across the ice. Lieutenant Bedford Pim announced the presence of the *Resolute* near Dealy Island. McClure returned to England a hero, where he claimed a £10,000 prize for discovering the Northwest Passage. (That McClure began the passage in one vessel, which he later abandoned, and then accomplished the feat in a second ship not under his command were facts excused by the Crown.) McClure never again returned to the Arctic, though the ice-choked strait that kept him icebound for three consecutive winters now bears his name.[27]

The *Manhattan* entered McClure Strait in the predawn hours of September 10, 1969, nosing her way at between two and six knots through ice ridges six to eight feet thick. The *MacDonald* recorded the heaviest ice conditions to date—"10/10 multi-year ice under pressure"—yet both vessels proceeded without much difficulty.[28] The *Manhattan* called her escort for assistance twice that morning, though in neither instance was she firmly beset. The *MacDonald* dutifully responded by quickly easing the pressure on the tanker's starboard side. The ice teams had hoped to go out and test the conditions on McClure that afternoon, and when a broken hydraulic line in the tanker's steering gear necessitated a stop for repairs they took full advantage of the opportunity. This would be an ill-fated mission, however. With two teams disembarked from the *Manhattan* and a third from the *MacDonald*, a helicopter arrived on the ice to ferry the men back to their respective ships. The pilot inadvertently set the helicopter down near a melt pond, and almost immediately the right front pontoon broke through the thin ice. The chopper tilted precariously for a moment, just long enough to allow the pilot to jump out unharmed, then tipped over on its side, crushing the rotor blades. The *MacDonald* had an on-deck crane that could lift the downed aircraft, yet Fournier had to position the ship close enough to effect the boom operation without breaking the ice layer and sending the aircraft to the bottom of the sea. The *MacDonald* backed carefully into position and, using a lifting lug in the center of the helicopter's rotor blades designed for just such an operation, successfully hoisted it on deck. To cap the unfortunate escapade, the *MacDonald* pulled alongside the *Manhattan* (in order to transfer the helicopter from deck to deck), struck a heavy ice floe, and promptly lurched heavily against the tanker's hull. Damage to both vessels was thankfully minimal.[29]

It might have been the cold, or the challenges of working in the Arctic, or perhaps just the stress of having more than one hundred people crammed onto a steel ship for over two weeks, but nerves on the *Manhattan* were becoming a bit frayed. A meeting was called for nine o'clock that evening to allow everyone a chance to air their gripes. The helicopter pilots expressed frustration at the questionable condition of the choppers, conflicting flight schedules, and an uncertain chain of command that left them wondering from whom exactly they were taking orders. It was not uncommon for one of the visiting bigwigs to request a quick flight just to have a look around, and when the pilots refused, the request sometimes turned into an order they were unsure whether they had to obey. Dr. Frankenstein relayed the day's events on the ice, noting that not only did his men lack handheld radios or any means of communication with the ship, but the chopper accident left them a full mile away in fog that obscured all visibility. Crew members regularly disembarked to walk around on the ice, and with no one keeping track of names it left open the terrifying possibility that someone could be left behind. Probably the most vociferous complaints that week came from a group not even invited to the meeting—the onboard press

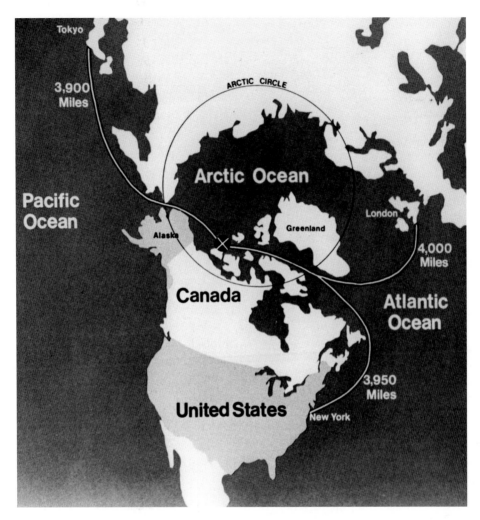

Map produced by Humble Oil in 1969 showing marine shipping routes from a point in the Canadian Arctic that is roughly equidistant from New York, London, and Tokyo.
EXXON MOBIL CORPORATION

The *Manhattan* as originally constructed in 1962. Note the conventional shape of the bow.
EXXON MOBIL CORPORATION

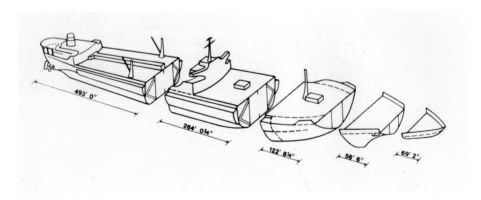

493' 0"

264' 0¾"

122' 8¼"

56' 6"

69' 2"

Graphic showing Humble's plans for cutting the tanker into pieces during its conversion to an icebreaker. EXXON MOBIL CORPORATION

The *Manhattan*'s original bow is removed at Sun Shipyard. EXXON MOBIL CORPORATION

The afterbow section being towed to Newport News Shipbuilding for ice strengthening.
EXXON MOBIL CORPORATION

Shipyard workers install a protective "ice belt" around the tanker's hull. EXXON MOBIL CORPORATION

The *Manhattan*'s icebreaking bow was constructed of steel capable of withstanding up to 900 pounds of pressure per square inch. CHARLA BAUER

Installation of the icebreaking bow. CHARLA BAUER

Shipyard workers preparing to install one of the *Manhattan*'s propellers. The specially designed screws were constructed of a bronze-nickel alloy with tips five times thicker than those on a conventional propeller. DAN GURAVICH/POLAR BEARS INTERNATIONAL

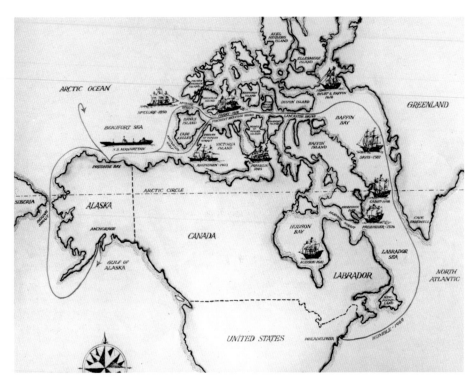

Produced by Humble Oil, this historical map of the Northwest Passage traced the route of the *Manhattan* and noted other vessels throughout history that attempted to find the fabled crossing. EXXON MOBIL CORPORATION

Official insignia of the *Manhattan* expedition. PERSONAL COLLECTION OF AUTHOR

Board game produced by Humble Oil showing the *Manhattan* smashing her way through towering icebergs. PERSONAL COLLECTION OF AUTHOR

The reality of the tanker's voyage through the Northwest Passage was certainly dramatic, but involved only the breaking of flat, stationary pack ice. MERRITT HELFFERICH

Crew members could be found at all hours watching the spectacle of the *Manhattan* breaking ice. DAN GURAVICH/POLAR BEARS INTERNATIONAL

Scientists drill through the ice pack in order to insert temperature probes. The U.S. Coast Guard gave the *Manhattan* the official dual designation of commercial ship and scientific research vessel. DAN GURAVICH/POLAR BEARS INTERNATIONAL

The initiation of all crew members into the "Royal Order of the Polar Bear" is an arctic maritime tradition with a long and whimsical history. From left to right: Boreas Rex (Don Graham), Queen Amphitrite (Guenther Frankenstein), and the Royal Baby (Frederick Goettel). MERRITT HELFFERICH

Paul Fournier, captain of the *John A. MacDonald*. EARLE GRAY

The *John A. MacDonald*. EARLE GRAY

The *Manhattan* and *John A. MacDonald*, with the *Northwind* astern. DAN GURAVICH/POLAR
BEARS INTERNATIONAL

Stan Haas (center right, at head of table) confers with technicians on infrared imagery of ice conditions in the daily ice meeting aboard the *Manhattan*. CHARLA BAUER

The *Manhattan* icebound at Pond Inlet, Baffin Island, on her second arctic voyage in spring 1970. CHARLA BAUER

Captain Arthur Smith and Master Roger Steward. Both men are wearing tam o' shanters obtained from sailors on the *John A. MacDonald*. DAN GURAVICH/POLAR BEARS INTERNATIONAL

Alaska Governor Keith Miller (holding microphone) and resource commissioner Tom Kelly (far right) at the state's triumphant Prudhoe Bay Lease Sale, September 10, 1969. WARD WELLS, WARD WELLS COLLECTION, ANCHORAGE MUSEUM, B83.91.S4794.6

Governor Keith Miller and Humble project manager Stan Haas. CHARLA BAUER

The golden barrel ceremony aboard the *Manhattan*, September 19, 1969. From left to right: Tom Kelly, Alaska resource commissioner; James Galloway, Humble Oil vice president; Governor Keith Miller, and Stan Haas. MERRITT HELFFERICH

The *Manhattan* enters New York harbor on November 12, 1969, the official end of the historic expedition. DAN GURAVICH/POLAR BEARS INTERNATIONAL

MERRITT HELFFERICH

crew. Several months earlier, back in Houston, the Humble PR department had formulated its Media Operations Plan, which contained procedures for maintaining the "continuous flow of information" to all reporters.[30] Humble's own staff photographer would provide still and motion pictures to the media every day, and the ship's radio and teletype machines would be available for filing stories. The plan made sense on paper, but once in the Arctic it proved completely unworkable. The promised photographs rarely materialized from a darkroom reserved and prioritized for developing ice photos. Official Humble business usually monopolized the radio, leaving dozens of reporters to share a single teletype machine. During the frequent radio blackouts even this became a hit-or-miss proposition. A correspondent for *Life* magazine visited the tanker and wrote an eight-thousand-word feature that never appeared in print because his deadline came and went with no means for getting the copy off the ship. Hank Rosenthal, the onboard Humble media liaison, worked eighteen-hour days in a heroic, if often unsuccessful, effort to satisfy every media demand. Rosenthal's plans for putting out a daily newspaper, the *Manhattan Times*, quickly fell by the wayside because he simply didn't have the time. For their part, Stan Haas and the tanker's officer crew also felt the stress of dealing with the press. Captain Steward found himself yelling almost daily at reporters who had no reservations about wandering onto the bridge to snoop around. He finally tacked up a handwritten sign: "ALL UNAUTHORIZED PERSONNEL KEEP OFF BRIDGE. THIS MEANS YOU." He had to be persuaded not to add, "VIOLATORS WILL BE SHOT."[31] (This was in direct contrast to the *John A. MacDonald*, where Captain Fournier gave the handful of reporters on that vessel open access to the bridge and even showed them navigational charts and transcripts of radio transmissions.) Haas, though ever the polite and professional company man in his dealings with reporters, vented in a letter to his family:

> [T]he balance of the day is devoted to...satisfying the unending demands of news media people who have the view that the ship is a platform which we have brought up here for their use in obtaining Arctic pictures. Some of them will feel the trip has been wasted if some terrible event does not occur.[32]

Reporters on the *Manhattan* were further incensed at what they believed were misleading statements if not outright lies coming from Humble personnel. While conversing with reporters who were boarded on the *John A. MacDonald*, the *Manhattan* press learned the tanker had been icebound numerous times as far back as Viscount Melville Sound, unable to move under her own power. They had been told every stop so far was intentional in order to conduct ice studies and that the vessel had freed herself each time. It was a small point that could have been chalked up to simple miscommunication, but it further eroded the journalists' confidence in Humble just the same.

The tense relationship between Humble and the media reached its nadir in the middle of Viscount Melville Sound, when Haas announced that the Federal Communications Commission (FCC) had immediately forbidden all radio transmissions of news copy. Helen Bentley, the Maritime Commissioner-designate—though on this voyage still working as a reporter for the *Baltimore Sun*—had apparently let slip an expletive in filing a story by radio. The rewrite man in Baltimore kept asking Bentley to repeat herself, to which she had responded, "Shit, Ralph, take the wax out of your ears."[33] The FCC picked up the profane transmission and, according to Haas, promptly clamped down on all radio transmissions not essential to the mission itself. Though a few reporters directed their anger and frustration at Bentley—even though most were probably guilty of a little colorful language themselves from time to time—most reserved their hostility for the nameless FCC bureaucrat in Washington who had no idea of the challenges the reporters already faced in delivering stories from the Arctic. Within a few days, however, the real story came out. One reporter, while urging his editor in New York to somehow fix the problem with the FCC, was informed there was no such problem at all. The agency had placed no restrictions on the *Manhattan*, and in fact, the radio-silence order appeared to have originated with Humble headquarters in Houston for reasons that were never made clear. Bentley was furious at what she saw as a ham-handed attempt to embarrass her. She demanded retractions from every reporter who had filed stories mentioning her role in the affair. Joe LaRocca, an indefatigable and outspoken reporter from Alaska, would later rip into what he called Humble's "inept communications aides, grossly inadequate transmission facilities and a monitoring of copy which was tantamount to censorship."[34]

The cloak of secrecy also fell on the crew. Navigators on the bridge knew the tanker's position at all times, but were under strict instructions not to inform the engine room. At one point divers took to the water to investigate a strange noise coming from near the stern. Roger Steward—as Master, the man ostensibly in command of the ship—was subsequently prohibited from viewing the photographs. Haas seemed to anger people daily by denying them open seats on the helicopter or attempting to prevent them from visiting the *John A. MacDonald*. The stranglehold Humble kept on virtually all information meant that even peeking in the wrong open door could result in a harsh rebuke, yet by this point in the voyage it had become as much a point of ridicule as anything. When asked the time of a polar bear sighting, Ralph Maybourn, the tart-tongued BP representative, replied, "It was 1520 hours exactly by my watch. This is not proprietary information for British Petroleum although it might very well be for Humble."[35]

The *Manhattan* recorded slow but steady progress farther into McClure Strait throughout the foggy night. Between eight p.m. on the tenth and eight a.m. on the eleventh, the tanker stopped only once for about twenty minutes and did not require the *MacDonald*'s assistance to start under way again. The *Manhattan*'s officers were becoming more experienced by the hour and by McClure had obtained a degree of familiarity with the giant ship and how she handled in different ice conditions. Captain Fournier of the *MacDonald*, a true arctic veteran who began his career as third officer aboard the icebreaker *Saurel* nearly three decades before, knew full well the steep learning curve these men found themselves up against. He dutifully indulged their every request for assistance as they felt their way through the Arctic, even when he believed the present conditions posed no real problem for the tanker. Fournier would write in his post-expedition report that the *Manhattan*'s officers "would surprise us by asking for assistance in conditions we know for a fact she had no problems with previously."[36] Roger Steward acknowledged to a reporter his habit of calling for help too soon.[37] Stan Haas, in a memo to his personal file, expressed frustration with the master's timidity: "Steward does not communicate enough with others on plans of action. Lacks aggressiveness. Too cautious which gets him in trouble in ice. Needs an external spur to get him going." At one point in Lancaster Sound, Haas observed Steward carefully maneuvering the tanker around an ice floe and encouraged him instead to attack it head-on. "For God's sake," exclaimed Haas, "that's what we're here for."[38] (Of the other two captains on the bridge, Haas wrote that Graham "displays good judgement [*sic*]" and that Smith was "undoubtedly the strongest of the three men.")[39] In time, the *Manhattan*'s officers picked up on the many navigational tricks of icebreakers. They learned to back out of tight channels before their forward motion was entirely stopped, and that letting the ship "drift" ever so slightly in heavy ice allowed her to steer herself toward weak spots in the ice pack.[40]

Throughout the morning of Thursday, September 11, the *Manhattan* pounded her way through heavy, multiyear floes between twelve and fifteen feet thick. At one point Ralph Maybourn and Charles Swithinbank climbed down through a hatch on the forecastle into the icebreaking bow (a move Stan Haas surely would have stopped had he seen them do it). They clambered through the maze of steel I-beams and descended to the level at which the hull was striking the ice. The sound was deafening. Swithinbank later commented it was more intense than the cordite explosions he'd felt as a turret gunner on a cruiser in World War II.[41] The ice floes in McClure were under so much pressure that the broken pieces did not slough cleanly off to the sides, but turned to the vertical until they lay flat against the hull and exerted friction for its entire length. The afterbow's shoulders managed to shatter some of these trapped fragments, but doing so resulted in random buckling of the surrounding ice sheet, an action that absorbed a tremendous amount of energy and noticeably impeded the ship's forward progress.[42] The practical effect of one hundred percent ice coverage was that even when the tanker could break through the ice layer there was simply nowhere for the shattered pieces to go. Every time the tanker backed astern, an immense regurgitation of broken ice occurred in the forward track, a clear indication that ice was being forced and trapped directly under the bow. The masters of both ships then worried about damage to the rudders and propellers from large chunks of ice sliding down their keels. Indeed, those looking back off the stern observed huge slabs with sawtooth gouges showing where the propellers had made contact. Crew in the engine room watching the tailshaft tachometers saw clear evidence of ice contacting the propellers. Revolutions per minute would drop suddenly from seventy to sixty-six, then to sixty-two, and quickly rebound back to seventy. One report indicated a reduction in rpm from seventy to forty in a matter of seconds.[43] The men kept a supply of shear pins close at hand, knowing that such heavy impacts placed enormous strain on the shaft-gear mechanism and that failed pins in the shear coupling would have to be replaced quickly.

Despite being close in line astern of the *Manhattan*, the *MacDonald* found that the tanker's track closed up and froze over so quickly that as the trailing vessel she was effectively breaking her own ice. As though such challenges were not enough for the captains of both ships, the nature of McClure's ice layer itself proved taxing. Ice that forms as a solid, continuous sheet tends to split cleanly if subjected to enough downward pressure. McClure Strait, on the other hand, featured windblown and tide-driven layers that continually shifted and collided with one another. This action formed pressure ridges and generally resulted in an uneven, irregular jumble of ice that behaved much differently under pressure than the flat, uniform sheets the ships had previously encountered.

By midafternoon, the *Manhattan* found herself firmly trapped in one such pressure ridge composed entirely of rock-hard second-year and multiyear ice. The vessel lay motionless just miles from Mercy Bay, where more than a hundred years earlier Sir Robert McClure and the *Investigator* endured the winter that did not end. The *MacDonald* relieved pressure on the tanker's port side, yet the ice refused to release the ship. The *Manhattan* still foundered for lack of power astern, yet Colos Bennett, the tanker's chief engineer, had figured out that by shutting down all generators and auxiliary power (including the ship's heat) he could deliver an extra three to five percent power to the turbines. The maneuver provided just enough power to allow the ship to back off the ridge that held her.[44] Rear Admiral A. H. G. Storrs, a Canadian official on board the *MacDonald*, described what happened next:

[The] *Manhattan* backed off as far as she could go and really had a go at it with everything opened up wide. The difference in that ship was the highlight of the trip for me—it was an astonishing performance. She was a different vessel entirely.... She went charging through this very heavy ice, ice up to 20 feet in thickness, and maintained a speed of four knots or so, these huge masses of ice being thrust aside by the bow, tilted up on edge, pushed down and shoved aside, as this great ship just kept going.[45]

The victory would be the *Manhattan*'s last in McClure Strait. With barely a moment of breathing room past the recently conquered pressure ridge, the tanker rammed headlong into the next. At one point the *Manhattan* managed only five hundred feet of progress in one agonizing hour. During a single four-hour watch, the engine room responded to a full sixty-two bells—orders for a change of speed and/or direction—or about one every four minutes. At times like this the din on the bridge was nearly unbearable. Telegraphs and telephones would be buzzing constantly, radios ablaze with communications from the *MacDonald* and the helicopters, and all the while general shouting went on between the captain, watch officer, conning officer, quartermaster, and anyone else with an opinion who happened to be on the bridge. While locked in a massive floe later estimated to be four miles across, the *Manhattan* spent twelve fruitless hours alternately backing up and ramming forward, a technique Steward dubbed the "yo-yo system."[46] Captain Fournier of the *John A. MacDonald* offered probably the most accurate description of the effort: "It's as though she were sailing through a granite quarry."[47]

Stan Haas assembled the crew and media that evening to give them the bad news. The officer crew had decided to abandon the attempt at McClure Strait. Responding to groans from those in the room not yet ready to give up the fight, Haas stated, "We would like to have been the first to make the Northwest Passage the hard way, of course, but we are on a test voyage, and our first duties are to the experiment."[48] Haas went on to explain that the propellers on both ships were taking a real beating from the broken ice, much of which was being forced directly underneath the vessels for want of room to the sides. For a ship like the *MacDonald*, with a draft much less than that of the *Manhattan*, this posed a real danger. A broken propeller on the *MacDonald* might not only jeopardize the mission itself but leave the *Manhattan*, like countless other vessels in the history of polar exploration, trapped for the duration of the winter—a public relations debacle Humble could ill afford.[49]

The simple, insurmountable fact Humble came to acknowledge was that McClure Strait just could not be crossed at that time. The *Manhattan* had not yet reached the halfway point of the channel, and additional film drops from the aerial photography operation showed that even worse ice conditions lay ahead. Humble maintained that the next generation of icebreaking tankers, specifically designed and constructed for the Northwest Passage/Alaska route, would be at least twice the size of the *Manhattan* with vastly more engine power. Such ships might indeed be able to fight their way through McClure Strait. But in September 1969, the puny *Manhattan* simply wasn't up to the task.[50]

Now that the decision had been made to back out of the channel and make for Prince of Wales Strait, the captains held another conference to discuss exactly how that could be done. The tanker sat in the very center of the four-mile-wide floe, a colossus of ice determined to have arrived in McClure after migrating for years from near the North Pole. When morning came on September 12, the strong winds and ever-shifting ice pack had brought the tanker a full three miles closer to Banks Island. Heavy fog and snow flurries prevented any helicopter flights that morning, but by noon the weather had cleared enough so that Haas, Steward, Pullen, and Fournier could take to the air for a bird's-eye view. They visually inspected an area to the north and east of the tanker's present position where infrared film the day before indicated the presence of reduced ridging and, incredibly, small leads of open water. The team had been considering attaching a line from the *MacDonald* to the *Manhattan* and having the smaller ship tow the tanker astern. This new information revealed that the tanker, if she could manage to thrust forward just enough to break the ridge holding her fast, could turn sharply to the starboard and likely reach the lead.[51]

The *MacDonald* moved into position at 4:49 p.m., working on the tanker's starboard side. Steward ordered full power astern. The *Manhattan*'s heeling system went into full operation, and by backing the vessel while simultaneously rocking her laterally a full six degrees, the ship's masters finally managed to snap free of the ice. The tanker backed down half her length, then plunged forward against the ridge, making another two hundred feet before grinding to a halt. Colos Bennett again temporarily shut down all auxiliary services on the ship and directed every trace of available power to the propellers. After four more cycles of backing astern and pushing ahead, the *MacDonald* all the while chipping away at the ridges clinging to the tanker's hull, the *Manhattan* finally achieved some measure of forward momentum. Steward then ordered a fifteen-degree turn to the starboard, a maneuver that while necessary still exposed the rudders to possible damage from chunks of ice being forced under the ship. The rudders fortunately emerged from the operation unscathed, and the *Manhattan* executed what one observer called the "toughest U-turn in the history of the Arctic."[52] The *Manhattan* had reached a western longitude of 117 degrees 24 minutes, farther into McClure Strait than any other vessel in history. Though disappointment ran high among the crew for failing to traverse the entire strait, few onboard, especially the beleaguered officer crew, would deny feeling relief that the ship was now pointed east back toward the ice-free Prince of Wales Strait.[53] Haas speculated that from that point forward the voyage would "look like a summer cruise down Chesapeake Bay."[54]

THE FIRST COMMERCIAL TRANSIT

Noon on the thirteenth found the *Manhattan* crossing back into Viscount Melville Sound, with Banks Island now on her starboard. The tanker was in exactly the position she had been in only three days before—only seventy-two hours by the clock, but, if the weary faces on the bridge and in the engine room were any indication, a length of time that must have seemed eternal. And now the ice-free Prince of Wales Strait proved to be anything but. The same winds and tides that swirled through McClure had pushed a plug of ice thirty-five miles across into the narrow entrance between Passage Point on Banks Island and Peel Point on Victoria Island, a channel that had been open just a few days before. The massive ice floe buckled as the wind continued to push it into the channel, forming heavy pressure ridges across its breadth. That the ice was under extreme lateral pressure was never more apparent than when the two ships achieved forward motion and their tracks closed up almost immediately behind them.

Early the next morning, William Gray of Esso Marine stood on the bridge of the *MacDonald* with Martti Saarikangas as the vessel fought her way through the barrier. "Look at your watch," Saarikangas suddenly said to Gray.

"Seven forty-five a.m. Why?"

"We just lost a blade on the starboard prop."

Gray stared incredulously at the Finn. He hadn't felt a thing. Divers later determined the blade had snapped two feet from the hub. They also found jagged edges along the tips of the other blades. The injury had little effect on the ship's performance in the relatively mild ice of Prince of Wales Strait, though the asymmetric propeller did result in heavy vibrations in open water.[55]

Once the vessels had punched through the ice floe blocking the entrance to the channel, they found more ridges but none under such pressure that they presented any notable challenge. Now the physical geography of Prince of Wales Strait posed the greatest threat. The 150-mile-long channel measured only twelve miles wide in most places, with depths as shallow as ten fathoms. The presence of uncharted shoals presented a real concern for the *Manhattan*, a vessel that drew a full fifty-five feet. Near the Princess Royal Islands, two small rocks in the very center of the channel that divide it into two even narrower waterways, the ship's fathometer recorded shoals only seventeen feet below the keel. Virg Keith of the U.S. Coast Guard subtly noted the need for a detailed hydrographic survey of the channel before any future sailings.[56]

Tom Pullen and Fred Goettel, men with a combined eight decades of naval experience between them, gazed across the tanker's bow on the afternoon of September 14 and pointed out dark streaks in the clouds on the far horizon. This was water sky, the phenomenon generated by sunlight reflecting off dark water, a sure indicator of open sea ahead.[57] At 5:13 p.m., both the *Manhattan* and the *MacDonald* tasted open water for the first time in exactly a week.[58] Amundsen Gulf, whose waters marked the end of the Northwest Passage, lay less than one hundred miles away through the fog and approaching darkness. That evening the stewards broke out champagne for a celebratory dinner. Stan Haas and T. J. Fuson, head of Esso/Humble's marine division, presented each crew member with a handsome certificate from Boreas Rex.

The documents proclaimed the bearer "has displayed the fortitude and endurance to cope with freezing winds, prolonged days and nights, permafrost, polar bears, walruses, icebergs, and longhandles at locations North of the Arctic Circle, while maintaining a dignity which is a credit to our Brotherhood."[59] Blue noses no more, each man was now an arctic veteran. Fuson, a garrulous man whose obvious joy at being a part of the expedition made him a popular figure among the crew, rambled off the cuff for several minutes about the incredible voyage, then raised his glass to the mess hall and stated, "All I really wanted to say, gentlemen, is that I am just thrilled as hell to be here." Stan Haas followed, "Here's to the men and the ship."[60] All hands cheered.

The *John A. MacDonald* steamed one mile back of the *Manhattan* through the thick evening fog. Several times both ships had to drastically reduce their speed due to the poor visibility and their location in poorly charted waters. In the early morning hours of September 15, Captain Fournier noted his ship's position as 71.15'N Long 120.42"W. In the deliberately dry language of naval captains everywhere, he wrote in his logbook, "Both vessels...cleared Prince of Wales Strait."[61] Over on the *Manhattan*, watch officer Albert M. Scara wrote in his deck log, "Fog cleared—Full ahead. Clear Prince of Wales Channel."[62] Both were understatements. The *Manhattan* and *John A. MacDonald* had just completed the Northwest Passage.

The Humble press release that morning heralded the achievement in words not nearly so modest: "The most talked about ship in the world today, the SS *Manhattan*, slipped quietly into the frigid waters of the Amundsen Gulf late last night and became the first commercial vessel in history ever to traverse the formidable Northwest Passage." Calling the ship "the world's best icebreaker," Haas noted, "The *Manhattan* is performing in excess of our expectations and we have a superb crew."[63]

Nothing but blue water now separated the *Manhattan* from Prudhoe Bay. At noon, the tanker dropped anchor at Sachs Harbor, a small village on the southwest shore of Banks Island. School was called off that day so every child could come see the giant tanker. It seemed to the *Manhattan*'s crew that the entire population of 120 people showed for the event. The shallow seabed kept the tanker a full ten miles from shore. Villagers maneuvered skiffs and canoes (some with outboard motors, some without) right up to the vessel. Others received an aerial tour via helicopter. Hank Rosenthal, ever the public relations man, took the chopper to shore and began handing out expedition patches and chocolate bars to the kids. When those ran out, he found a stash of pencils and ballpoint pens that were just as well received. Moses Raddi, the mayor of Sachs Harbor, arrived via canoe with his eight-year-old son to inform the ship's officers that they needn't have kept such distance but were welcome to use the town harbor any time they wished.

The airstrip at Sachs Harbor provided the first opportunity since Resolute over a week before to transfer personnel to and from the ship. Helen Bentley departed for her Senate confirmation hearings in Washington, but not before threatening to sue everyone in sight for the FCC debacle she believed had sullied her reputation. Two prominent Alaskans boarded the *Manhattan*—Congressman Howard Pollock, Alaska's lone member of the U.S. House of Representatives, and Robert Atwood, the editor and publisher of the state's largest newspaper, the *Anchorage Daily Times*. Pollock cited the *Northwind*'s unfortunate demise in announcing his intention to seek a buildup of the U.S. Coast Guard's icebreaker fleet. "It is unacceptable to our national pride to discover that the U.S. icebreaker could not keep up to a commercial tanker and had to let the Canadians do the job alone," he stated.[64] Pollock envisioned a fleet of three new icebreaking ships and four C-130 support aircraft patrolling the American Arctic. Two weeks later, upon his return to Washington, Rep. Pollock wrote to Transportation Secretary John Volpe to express his concern that an increasingly commercialized Arctic presented the United States with political and economic responsibilities for which it was not prepared. "It is my considered opinion," the Alaska congressman wrote, "that the prestige and power of the United States in marine affairs of the North are seriously challenged and the future is at stake."[65] Pollock also brought his case directly to President Nixon by presenting him with a gift from the *Manhattan*'s crew: a silver paperweight, a Zippo lighter with the tanker's insignia, and one of the Esso Tiger expedition patches. (Whether by Pollock's efforts or not, the Coast Guard would commission its next icebreaking cutter, the *Polar Star*, in 1976. The *Polar Sea* followed the next year. Pollock's dream of three new ships would not come to fruition until 1999, when the Coast Guard launched the *Healy*.)

While anchored at Sachs Harbor, the *Manhattan* again received the *MacDonald* along her port side. The smaller ship needed to top off her diesel tanks from the tanker's reserves. Once again, fuel was not the only thing crossing from one ship to the other. A procession of the tanker's crew celebrated the Northwest Passage success by taking over the bar on the *MacDonald* where, in the words of one Alaskan, "Much was consumed by few."[66] The bar closed at ten p.m., whereupon the revelry shifted back over to the *Manhattan*. Within minutes, two dozen people had crammed into the helicopter pilots' tiny stateroom and were being entertained by a three-man band that featured bagpipes, an accordion, and a harmonica. Finally, at the stroke of midnight, the fateful hour of the ships' disengagement arrived. Merritt Helfferich described the scene:

> We lined the rails of both ships and swore eternal friendship, cheered the *Manhattan*, the *John A.*, the Queen, the President, the people of Sachs Harbor, our captains, the ice of Melville Sound, and the whole list all over again. The

bagpipes screamed and the pilot almost swallowed his harmonica and had to be led away coughing. We sang "Auld Lang Syne" twice in three different keys and then retired for the night.[67]

Dr. Guenther Frankenstein had scheduled a meeting for the ice scientists at 8:30 the next morning. Almost no one made it.

8

What Did the *Manhattan* Prove?

It has been shown that vessels can not reach [the north coast of Alaska] until after the first of August and should be out of that region early in September and that even during this short period they run the hazard of being caught in the ice and lost. Furthermore, there are no harbors for ocean-going vessels for several hundred miles.... Under these conditions it seems extremely unlikely that any considerable quantity of petroleum can be moved by vessels.

—From a 1924 report by the U.S. Geological Survey
on the resource potential of the Alaska North Slope[1]

Captain Joseph Bernard, a legend in polar exploration who at the time of the *Manhattan*'s voyage probably had more firsthand experience in the Arctic than any person alive, was retired and living quietly in Cordova, Alaska, when a reporter called on the telephone and asked him about the tanker's chances for success in the Northwest Passage. "I have doubts about this big ship getting through," the ninety-one-year-old Bernard replied. "They can probably get through once in a while.... But I don't think they'll ever be able to make it a regular route for steamer traffic."[2]

Bernard first came to Alaska as a young man at the turn of the century and spent two decades traveling around the Arctic in his schooner, *Teddy Bear*. Bernard downplayed the threat posed by the ice-blocked channels of the Canadian Archipelago, pointing instead to the wide-open Beaufort Sea as the most problematic for tankers:

Out there the sea is shallower and the floes get bigger and thicker. I remember the season of 1913 out there when we had practically one solid floe that was 20 feet from the surface of the sea to the top of the ice sheet. That means there was either 150 or more feet under the surface or it was anchored fast to the bottom. Nothing that man can make can break ice like that![3]

Fortunately for the *Manhattan*, the 1969 season in the Beaufort Sea featured only intermittent layers of rotten ice that had been degraded by the continual summer sunlight. Humble recognized that any year-round tanker traffic would be forced to battle the solid, migrating pack ice on that open expanse and had originally planned to send the *Manhattan* due north from Prudhoe Bay into the thickest floes on a data-gathering mission. (Actually, the *original* plan, hatched many months before back in Houston, called for the *Manhattan* to continue past Prudhoe Bay, sail through the Bering Strait to the North Pacific, and drop anchor at Anchorage, thus connecting the Atlantic and Pacific Oceans in a single sailing. The many delays at every stage of the project caused that plan, which was mostly for public relations anyway, to be scrapped.)

Now Stan Haas announced a change in the polar ice plans. "We have decided not to do any extensive testing in the Beaufort Sea," he told reporters just two days shy of Prudhoe Bay. The vessel would instead call at three Alaska ports—Barter Island, Prudhoe Bay, and Point Barrow—and then return to Viscount Melville Sound for several weeks of testing where, according to Haas, ice conditions closely resembled those of the Beaufort Sea. Haas also noted that operations in Viscount Melville Sound retained "a greater escape capability."[4] He elaborated no further on this point in the day's press briefing but privately acknowledged a number of factors that led to the decision. Though it was still only September, the arctic winter was not far away, and the ship's officers feared Prince of Wales Strait might freeze over while they dallied about in the Beaufort Sea, effectively blocking their only route back to New York. The captains further worried that the damaged propeller on the *John A. MacDonald* might compromise its ability to rescue the tanker. The experience in McClure Strait convinced Haas he did not want to challenge the polar ice pack without a fully operational *Johnny Mac* running escort.[5]

The decision to turn around at Point Barrow introduced an element of ambiguity, if not for Humble at least for geographers and maritime experts who took such things seriously, as to whether the *Manhattan* had actually completed the Northwest Passage. Tom Pullen and Charles Swithinbank believed that the tanker's voyage through the Canadian Archipelago qualified as a transit of the passage, while others held to a more technical definition that required a vessel sail from the Atlantic Ocean all the way to the Pacific or vice versa.[6] "A consequence of this definition," wrote R. K. Headland of the Scott Polar Research Institute, "is that some major voyages within, but not through, the Northwest Passage are excluded for they are incomplete or partial transits."[7] Headland specifically cited the *Manhattan* as an example of one such incomplete crossing. Indeed, future listings of Northwest Passage transits compiled by polar geographers often gave the *Manhattan* an asterisk or neglected to mention the tanker altogether. Humble obviously had no interest in such technical distinctions when it trumpeted its tanker's success. From a layperson's perspective, that the powerful icebreaker reached Alaska, its intended destination, was quite enough.

The *Manhattan* received several additional visitors while anchored at Barter Island on Thursday, September 18. The first was Alaska Governor Keith Miller, fresh off the state's triumphant lease sale one week before. Elected to the office of secretary of state (a position now called lieutenant governor) in 1966, Miller assumed the governorship three years later when Walter Hickel resigned to become President Nixon's interior secretary. Joining Miller on the tanker at Barter Island were Tom Kelly, the state's resource commissioner; Brad Phillips, president of the Alaska State Senate; and Jalmar Kerttula, speaker of the State House of Representatives. All remained on the *Manhattan* overnight and accompanied her to Prudhoe Bay the following day.[8]

The final "visitor" to meet the vessel at Barter Island was the *Northwind*. After having separated from the expedition in Viscount Melville Sound the week before, the damaged Coast Guard icebreaker backtracked to Barrow Strait, then proceeded via a relatively ice-free passage through Peel Sound to Coronation Gulf and finally into the Beaufort Sea. The *Northwind* arrived at Barter Island a day ahead of the *Manhattan*. The hoopla surrounding the *Manhattan*'s historic transit largely overshadowed a doubly impressive feat by the *Northwind*. By making the eastward crossing to Thule in July, followed by the round-trip back to Alaska in September, the Coast Guard ship became the first in history to complete the Northwest Passage in both directions in a single season.[9] Over the next two days the icebreaker would rejoin the convoy as far as Point Barrow, where she was relieved by one of her fellow Wind-class vessels, the *Staten Island*. The *Northwind* then made for her home port of Seattle, which she reached on October 3.[10]

At exactly noon on the clear but cold and windy day of Friday, September 19, the *Manhattan* reached Prudhoe Bay, site of the largest oil reservoir on the continent and the destination to which the entire Humble effort had been directed. This would be a day of celebration and ceremony for both Humble and the State of Alaska. The event signified yet another incremental step toward the eventual development of Alaska North Slope crude oil. The formal celebration got under way with a luncheon onboard the *John A. MacDonald*, where Captain Fournier entertained such dignitaries as Governor Miller, U.S. Coast Guard Commandant W. J. Smith, and Humble vice president James Galloway.[11] Following lunch, the entourage proceeded by helicopter back to the *Manhattan* where at two p.m. the golden barrel ceremony was scheduled to begin.

Some months before, the public relations team at Humble had decided that upon the *Manhattan*'s arrival at Prudhoe Bay a single symbolic barrel of crude oil would be loaded onto the tanker for the return trip to New York. The word went out to field workers to pull an empty barrel from one of the warehouses, fill it with crude, and have it ready to go. The barrel they selected was not technically a "barrel" of crude—that term is only a unit of measure equaling forty-two gallons, not a physical object—but rather a standard fifty-five-gallon drum. The distinction was certain to elicit no complaints. Every available drum the roughnecks could locate, however, came from Chevron and featured that company's distinctive logo painted on the side. This simply would not do for a Humble celebration. The problem was easily solved by painting the entire barrel gold, the perfect color for the ceremonial occasion.

While the assembled VIPs waited onboard the *Manhattan*, helicopter pilot Kenny Blurton, for whom this would be his last flight before retirement, took off for shore to collect the golden barrel and bring it to the ship. No sooner did he arrive at the oil field than a thick fog rolled in, making his immediate return to the tanker impossible. The dignitaries waited, then waited some more. The officials, several of whom wore coats and ties, marked a sharp contrast with the scruffy crew, whose personal grooming habits had regressed as the expedition wore on. Nearly all the able-bodied seamen had stopped shaving the day they set foot on the vessel. Knowing the University of Alaska scientists never passed up a chance to mock Humble for its unfamiliarity with the Arctic, Haas ushered them to the back row. He grabbed the arm of Dave Schafer, the most outspoken of the bunch, and with a clenched jaw whispered, "No wisecracks." Moments later Jay Kerttula, the Alaska House Speaker, spotted his friend in the back row and called out, "Schafer, you son-of-a-gun! Get down here and get your picture taken!" Haas turned red, but had to be relieved when Schafer only smiled for the camera and kept his mouth shut.[12]

Finally, at six p.m., the chopper returned with the golden barrel. Tom Brennan, the ARCO public relations officer who had arranged the ceremony, took his first look at the barrel and recoiled from what he called "the ghastly thing." Its surface was pockmarked with numerous dents and dings (though in fairness to the workers who selected it, probably every single drum on the North Slope was riddled with such blemishes). The gold paint accentuated every flaw "like a Broadway floodlight," according to Brennan, making it look like a "giant bad girl's piggy bank."[13] No one at the ceremony seemed to mind. Governor Miller had no sooner hopped onboard the chopper to make the presentation than someone yelled out a question: Had Humble paid a royalty on this first barrel? "No," the governor jokingly replied while placing both hands firmly on the barrel, "that's why I'm hanging on to it."[14] Finally, James Galloway pulled a single dollar from his wallet and handed it over to Tom Kelly—certainly the least complicated financial transaction between the private and public sectors in the history of oil development—and the ceremony was complete.[15]

THE OFFSHORE TERMINAL PROBLEM

The tanker again had to anchor several miles offshore due to the shallow coastal shelf surrounding Prudhoe Bay. This feature of Alaska's northern coast posed a significant obstacle to Humble's plans for regular tanker traffic. The enormous icebreakers the company had in mind for the trade would draw anywhere from sixty to eighty-five feet of water, meaning their closest approach to shore would measure a full thirty miles. Humble first tapped the Esso engineering technology department to study how crude oil might be loaded from onshore fields into tankers, and later contracted with Van Houten Associates on an arctic harbor research program.[16] Several ideas emerged.

The first proposal under consideration called for the dredging of both a deep-water harbor at the coastline and wide shipping channels that would extend into the Beaufort Sea. With billions of barrels of oil right at its disposal, Humble theorized that a system of large diesel-powered heating devices could keep the harbor and shipping lanes free of ice year-round. Tankers could simply steam down the channel to loading docks located safely within a manmade breakwater. The Esso marine department also suggested that an air bubbler system could control ice formation within the harbor. A simple network of subsea pipes fed by an air compressor would release bubbles at the ocean floor. The motion of the bubbles toward the surface would agitate the water layers just enough to retard ice growth. The system need not keep the surface ice-free; a layer even two feet thick was deemed acceptable by Esso. Plans were modeled on the air bubbling system at Thule Air Base in Greenland, which had operated successfully for several years.[17] Engineers briefly considered a fully enclosed, climate-controlled harbor—what they called "the garage"—with a movable entrance gate and lightweight yet durable roof.[18] The dredging operation would move untold quantities of earth, by some estimates up to ten million yards of material per mile depending on ocean depth. "Although dredging in Arctic regions is within the realm of present day technology, the costs would be substantial," one Humble subcontractor dryly noted.[19] Edward Teller, the pioneering physicist and father of the hydrogen bomb, helpfully suggested that an underground nuclear blast could quite effectively excavate such a harbor.[20]

An alternative to the dredging operation was to locate the terminal offshore at sufficient ocean depth and run subsea pipelines out from a land-based pumping station. This could be done directly off the Prudhoe Bay coast at a distance of thirty miles. Seventy miles east of Prudhoe was Brownlow Point, a site that afforded eighty feet of ocean depth just twelve miles offshore. Such a facility, wherever placed, would undergo constant battering from wind-driven ice floes dozens of feet thick. Bechtel Corporation, retained by Humble to investigate the different methods for laying subsea pipelines, reported two options as technically feasible. In the lay-barge method, lengths of pipe would be successively welded together in an assembly-line manner on the barge deck, then lowered off the stern into the water as the barge moved slowly away from shore. Floating stringers would support the pipe as it was lowered to the seafloor. The bottom-pull method used the same basic concept, except that the pipeline assembly occurred onshore and a large winch on an anchored barge pulled the entire string out to sea. Despite the significant cost and Bechtel's belief that climate and ocean conditions would be suitable for pipe-laying operations for a maximum of sixty days in each of the two years allotted for offshore terminal construction, the company declared that either method could be employed successfully.[21] (Indeed, it appears that of the dozens of contract-hungry companies with whom Humble contracted for feasibility studies, not a single one returned with a negative response.)

Esso also identified Herschel Island as a possible terminal location.[22] Located just off the Canadian coast about 250 miles east of Prudhoe Bay, the windblown knob measured nine miles wide by seven miles long and featured a protected deep-water basin on its southern side, a cove in which historical records showed nineteenth-century whaling ships often sought shelter during the winter months. A submarine canyon between one hundred and three hundred feet deep came to within just a few miles of Herschel Island, thus only a short stretch of the seabed would have to be dredged to allow passage of deep-draft tankers. Despite these favorable geographic advantages, Esso cited two distinct drawbacks to the Herschel Island location. First, a comprehensive analysis of the subsurface geology revealed that the island's bedrock lay under thick layers of silty soil, gravel, and soft clay—substances that would make for unstable foundations for terminal facilities and oil storage tanks. Esso speculated that most of the infrastructure would have to be located on the mainland, with only pipelines and the oil loading arms themselves situated on the island. The other disadvantage was that an onshore pipeline connecting Prudhoe Bay and Herschel Island would have to cross the Arctic National Wildlife Range, a federally protected wilderness area established a decade earlier by President Eisenhower. Obtaining right-of-way permits in the environmentally sensitive refuge would be next to impossible absent a presidential directive or an act of Congress. Humble could always run the pipeline offshore, but doing so would be logistically difficult and wildly expensive.

In October 1968, just as Humble was gearing up for the Arctic Tanker Test, A. Ronald McKay, a professor of arctic environmental engineering at the University of Alaska, observed a belt of several hundred ice islands stretched along the contour of the Beaufort Sea coast from Barrow to Prudhoe Bay. These were fragments of multiyear floes that had broken apart in the summer melt season and were now grounded in the shallow waters just off the coast. Most were small, barely the size of a single-car garage, but a handful measured up to 480,000 square feet in surface area. McKay noticed that many of the stationary islands showed a wake behind them caused by the movement of the relatively thin sea past them. Different wake formations behind islands of varying sizes suggested some had grounded while others remained just buoyant enough to allow themselves to be pushed ever so slightly by surface forces, their bottom edges skipping and scouring the ocean floor. McKay suspected the islands could act as research platforms to study the pressure and frictional effects of ice island and sea ice interaction. He selected two large, flat-topped specimens grounded adjacent to one another in eighty-five feet of water for his study. He named them UNAK 1 and UNAK 2. When Humble Oil learned of McKay's plans, the company quickly signed the professor to a research contract. The behavior of stationary structures in the midst of an ever-shifting ice pack was of particular interest to Humble in the context of its offshore terminal study.

McKay first brought pumps and water cannons to the location and sprayed tons of seawater atop UNAK 1 and 2. He needed to make sure the islands did not budge an inch until the study was completed, and by surcharging them with another fifteen feet of ice he added more than enough weight to keep them stationary (at least until the summer melt of the following year). During the winter of 1968–1969, he noticed that the formation of sea ice between the two islands and on their coastal side exerted lateral pressures not to the point of ridging failure but in such a way that the entire system became anchored with the islands as strong points. The coastal ice now acted as a backstop that would resist whatever action the seaward ice pack brought to bear. The motion of the sea ice soon created pressure ridges in front of the islands. One ridge connected UNAK 1 and 2 with other islands in the chain, effectively bonding the entire system together and increasing its overall strength. Additional ridging and buckling occurred farther out on the ice pack, but McKay found that the action exerted almost no force on the islands that were now protected by the adjacent barrier ridge. According to McKay, "The system now had sufficient strength that further pressure from the north did not deform or ridge the inshore ice but resulted in the formation of a mild pressure ridge parallel to and along the northern edge of the ice island chain."[23] So long as the system remained frozen, it seemed the islands could withstand the pressure and motion of the frozen Beaufort Sea. The summer melt season, however, resulted in a mosaic of degraded floes that moved against UNAK 1 and 2 at speeds up to two feet per second. The barrier ridge that had acted as a buffer while frozen and stationary now swelled vertically against the sides of the islands. Forces were slow to develop and dispersed over a wide area, McKay noted, and little major damage to the islands occurred as a result. Like all scientists, McKay was quick with a caveat—the observed experience was unique to this exact location at this precise time and should not be taken as evidence of the nonhostility of the Beaufort Sea ice pack in general. UNAK 1 eventually did begin to fragment, with certain pieces being thrust several feet higher than the main body of the structure. The study basically told Humble what it already knew: arctic ice is simultaneously predictable in its general seasonal character and unpredictable in time- and site-specific behavior. Probably the most important takeaway for Humble was McKay's finding that the use of a seaward structure, such as a barrier wall or chain of grounded ice fragments, could create conditions for the growth of pressure ridges that might provide protection for an offshore terminal.[24]

With this in mind, Humble and Esso Marine designed a square, island-type offshore loading terminal that would be anchored with huge conical pylons at each corner and oriented in a diamond formation with one corner pointing to the shore and the opposite corner pointing out to the open sea. With two tanker berths on each of the island's four-thousand-foot sides, the terminal could load eight icebreaking tankers simultaneously if necessary, but most loadings would take place on the two protected, leeward sides nearest the coast. Stationary ice wedges would be encouraged to form along an outer barrier wall, leaving the island protected in the same manner observed at UNAK 1 and 2. Esso took a more minimalist approach in a later island design that featured a single circular mooring module 286 feet in diameter just below the waterline with sides that tapered to a conical top where the loading arm was located. Constructed of reinforced concrete and armor plate covering, the hitching-post module would be further protected by a semicircular barrier wall over two miles in length.

Preliminary cost estimates for each of the offshore terminal designs ranged as high as half a billion dollars—and if the oil industry had learned just one thing in the months since the Prudhoe Bay strike it was that so-called preliminary estimates nearly always had to be revised upward, often to an almost exponential degree. In August 1969, while the unfinished *Manhattan* still occupied her berth at Sun Shipyard, E. F. Broderick of Esso's civil and industrial engineering division informed Stan Haas that the design of a test module for the arctic marine terminal would not be completed that year pending the results of the tanker's maiden voyage. "Deferral of this design means the first installation cannot take place before 1971, resulting in a very tight schedule for an operational facility in 1973," Broderick wrote.[25] At the time of the tanker's sailing Humble could not be certain whether development of such a terminal would even be needed. The astronomical cost estimates associated with every possible terminal design convinced the company to postpone such a decision for the immediate future.

AN INTENSELY COMPETITIVE INDUSTRY

The feasibility of the loading terminal notwithstanding, Humble believed the *Manhattan* had clearly proven the tanker concept. The company made the announcement even before the vessel arrived at Prudhoe Bay. On September 11, while the tanker still battled the ice of McClure Strait, Humble issued a press release announcing she had "sailed far enough through Parry Channel…to know that ships easily could head southwestward from this point through Prince of Wales Strait south of Banks Island without difficulty." All future tankers would use this route, which, according to Haas, "is why scientists and shipping experts aboard this floating laboratory now can express confidence that such traffic through the Northwest Passage is feasible."[26] The mountains of data collected by the scientists and the ship's onboard sensing equipment still had to be processed, a task that would last many months back in Houston, but on the basis of the straight tanker-in-ice test the *Manhattan* led many to believe the idea might work. One newspaper reporter found at least a few industry sources (albeit those with an acknowledged bias toward the Humble tanker) willing to suggest that the proposed Alaska pipeline be scrapped before the oil companies wasted any more resources on it.[27]

The apparent success of the Humble test did not quell all skepticism. On the morning of the *Manhattan*'s arrival at Prudhoe Bay, the editors of the *Anchorage Daily News* celebrated the remarkable achievement but speculated as to what the voyage might, or might not, have proven: "Numerous questions, however, remain to be answered—questions of economic practicability, questions of how a supertanker will perform under winter ice pack conditions."[28] For many, the tanker's arrival at Prudhoe Bay was not the end of a voyage at all but the start of the more difficult process of figuring out what exactly had been accomplished. Roger Benedict, a staff reporter with the *Wall Street Journal* who had been on the tanker from the very beginning, noted the powerful "psychological" nature of the successful transit and believed that the emphasis on this goal detracted from the expedition's stated mission of gathering scientific data. The *Manhattan* still faced lengthy testing, wrote Benedict, before any conclusions could be drawn one way or another. "Up to now, we've spent about 80 percent of our time learning how to handle the ship in the ice and only about 20 percent in scientific testing," Haas admitted.[29] He hoped to reverse that ratio on the return voyage, a desire doubtlessly shared tenfold by Guenther Frankenstein, who complained regularly about his lack of time on the ice. Like others on the expedition, Frankenstein had come to believe that the voyage was as much a publicity stunt as anything.[30]

Within the oil industry, a group made up of serious men not given to hyperbolic platitudes, skepticism ran even deeper. One unnamed executive made his doubts known to the trade publication *Alaska Industry*:

> What did the *Manhattan* voyage prove? It proved that using a specially-built ship and sparing no expense (and with a lot of free government-furnished assistance) the Northwest Passage could be negotiated in September 1969. It did not prove that it could be done at any other time of the year (or in any other September). Most important, it did not prove it could be done at a reasonable cost.[31]

The criticism that ran so high in some quarters probably proved as premature as the rosy optimism and congratulatory rhetoric in others. Both camps aired their respective views before the *Manhattan* broke through the last ice of the Northwest Passage (in some cases before she'd even left the dock in Pennsylvania). Humble still had to sort through the collected data, which would inform the specifications of future ships and which, in turn, would determine the economic viability of the marine transportation method. Haas himself admitted that much testing remained before any firm conclusions could be drawn. Humble already planned another arctic voyage in the spring of 1970.

One must consider the *Manhattan*—not to mention every industry effort to develop Prudhoe Bay, including the Alaska pipeline—in terms of the field's unique joint ownership structure where different companies alternately cooperated and competed with one another. The voyage of the *Manhattan* can be viewed both on its face as a simple transportation experiment but also in this larger context regarding the strategic maneuverings of ultra-competitive companies in a cutthroat industry. Many both inside and outside the industry suspected that Humble intentionally hindered development of Prudhoe Bay for a number of self-interested reasons. Under such a scenario, the *Manhattan* might have served as little more than a clever ruse—the proverbial "slow boat"—that allowed Humble to defer its overall commitment.

Sir Eric Drake, the chairman of British Petroleum, believed Humble sponsored the *Manhattan* test as a delaying tactic to put off construction of the Alaska pipeline and generally postpone oil production at Prudhoe Bay for the immediate future. It was no secret that at the time of the North Slope discovery, the Humble-Esso-Jersey conglomerate held ample crude reserves elsewhere in the world, particularly in the Middle East, that could be developed at a much lower cost than those in Alaska. "One thing is certain, [Alaska oil] won't be cheap," Jersey chairman Michael J. Haider explained shortly after the Prudhoe Bay discovery. "It is very unlikely that it will be able to compete with Mideastern oil on world markets."[32] This fact might explain Humble's failure to bid aggressively for additional North Slope acreage at the Prudhoe Bay lease sale on September 10, 1969. Humble would happily sit on those leases it already owned, but Jersey, the parent company with a more international focus, saw no need to sink more capital into an oil reservoir whose immediate development was not essential to its worldwide operation. In fact, bringing Prudhoe Bay online immediately might actually have disadvantaged Jersey's worldwide position by allowing the newly aggrandized ARCO and BP to introduce new oil into existing markets. Humble was simply in no hurry to allow any Alaska oil to enter the world market. Although his company invested $2 million in the *Manhattan* experiment, BP's Drake privately threatened to bring antitrust litigation against Humble for its allegedly obstructionist tactics.[33] (BP's representative on the tanker, Ralph Maybourn, certainly took the effort seriously, as evidenced by his official report, in which he wrote, "While the performance of the *Manhattan* has not demonstrated conclusively that an icebreaking tanker can…operate effectively through the Northwest Passage, the results of the voyage are regarded as sufficiently encouraging to justify further study."[34])

Regardless of Humble's true motivations behind the *Manhattan* test, that the company did indeed move slowly when it came to development at Prudhoe Bay is beyond dispute. In 1988, Bennett H. Wall, a professor of history at Tulane University, authored *Growth in a Changing Environment*, a history of Exxon in the years 1950–1975. (Standard Oil of New Jersey officially changed its name to Exxon in 1973.) Wall, who was funded by a grant from Exxon itself, was given access to company archives and personnel, and his book may be considered an official record of the company's history. Wall's account of the Alaska oil situation in the postdiscovery years is worth quoting at length:

> Quite early it became evident that ARCO wanted the pipeline more than did Humble. Before 1974 and the assertion of power by the Organization of Petroleum Exporting Countries (OPEC), Humble seemed less enthusiastic about the immediate construction of a pipeline. A much smaller company than the other two, ARCO needed to get oil to its markets, in order to recoup its tremendous investments in Alaska. As for BP, the merger contract with Standard Oil Company (Ohio) provided stock incentives; so BP's share in Standard of Ohio would automatically increase as Prudhoe Bay oil came on stream. With clear self-interest in view, both partners accused Humble of "dragging its feet" on the pipeline. When asked to explain, Humble Chairman [Michael] Wright responded, "We aren't as eager as they."[35]

As Wall points out, both BP and ARCO proved eager to bring Prudhoe Bay crude oil to market as quickly as possible. BP had long sought an entry into the lucrative American market, and its success at Prudhoe Bay placed the company in a position to secure such a footing. BP first acquired refineries and filling stations in the Northeast from Sinclair, its former partner in Alaska and the company whose early withdrawal from the North Slope ultimately spelled its own demise. A complicated merger agreement with Standard of Ohio (Sohio) soon followed under which BP's share of ownership in Sohio was tied directly to production levels at Prudhoe Bay. The agreement further stipulated penalties against BP, including loss of both profit and majority control in Sohio, if these levels were not achieved by certain deadlines. Although some deadlines were as far off as 1984, BP clearly had incentive to push ahead. The company's aggressive pursuit of the Sinclair and Sohio mergers attracted the attention of the U.S. Justice Department, and although both deals ultimately received government approval, the antitrust scrutiny might have encouraged BP's ostensible cooperation in the *Manhattan* test.[36] Anthony Sampson, whose book *The Seven Sisters* took a critical look at the power wielded by the world's major oil companies, wrote that BP's not insignificant financial investment in the *Manhattan* was merely a good-faith gesture to demonstrate to Justice that they could be "good Americans" too.[37] The investment also allowed BP (as well as ARCO) to place its own representative onboard the *Manhattan*. In this respect, $2 million was probably a bargain for the chance to keep a close eye on Humble. By the end of 1969, BP had secured its much-desired network of refining and retail outlets. Now they were waiting to be fed by Alaska crude.

For its part, ARCO also depended on the immediate delivery of Alaska oil. The company's share of the projected daily production at Prudhoe Bay would adequately supply its refining and marketing capacity on the West Coast. A steady, dependable supply of domestic crude is what every oilman dreams about, and the Alaska windfall stood to facilitate ARCO's pursuit of other energy-related business opportunities and its expansion into the diversified, integrated company its chairman, Robert O. Anderson, hoped to build.[38] Almost from the very moment of the Prudhoe Bay strike, ARCO became the driving force behind the design and construction of the Trans-Alaska Pipeline. The company also wasted no time in announcing plans to build a refinery at Cherry Point, Washington, as well as several tankers specifically designed to ferry crude from Alaska to the West Coast. Within TAPS, the industry consortium formed to design, build, and operate the pipeline, ARCO proved the most eager to proceed. When the dysfunctional TAPS was reorganized as the Alyeska Pipeline Service Company in 1970, ARCO again took the lead and found itself battling the other companies, Humble foremost among them, to move ahead. Time and again in regular meetings of the TAPS Owners Committee (composed of the eight companies with a pipeline interest), Humble voted against motions to allocate funding and resources for the pipeline effort.[39]

This brand of resistance, whether by Humble within the pipeline consortium or other industry players in various forums, often functioned as political gamesmanship by which the industry sought to appear ambivalent toward Alaska in the hopes of securing favorable concessions from the state and federal governments. Calls for increased taxes on oil production invariably met with such a response. When it became clear that environmental controls would be written into state and federal permits for Prudhoe Bay development—regulations that to the industry seemed always to be intensifying in number and degree—Humble and the other oil companies appeared to have no real compunction about threatening to leave the oil in the ground.[40] According to Alaska legislator Chancy Croft, the oil companies "answered all questions by saying, 'If there isn't a healthy atmosphere in Alaska, we're just going to leave.'"[41] John M. Blair, an economist with the Federal Trade Commission who authored a study of competition within the oil industry titled *The Control of Oil*, reached a similar conclusion: "Confronted with a government action which they [major oil companies] opposed, a few large owners would be in a position to keep the oil in the ground, secure in the knowledge that over a long-term inflationary period time would be on their side."[42] If any oil company had the size and influence to employ such a hardball tactic, it was Humble. The company could easily absorb any delay, even one lasting many years, if it kept alive some possibility of a better deal or a more advantageous political position down the road. In Alaska in the late 1960s, BP and ARCO were in no such position.

This point engendered some of the more conspiratorial theories regarding the industry's behavior in Alaska. Noam Chomsky has argued that the entire oil industry intentionally delayed Prudhoe Bay production. He theorized that the high costs of development in Alaska precluded production until the OPEC embargo of 1973 caused oil prices to skyrocket. Environmentalist David Brower also believed that the oil shortage was "contrived" to obtain congressional approval for the Alaska pipeline. Such theories remain difficult to support. That at least one company (Humble) did not act with precise haste in Alaska, and that the industry as a whole did indeed benefit from high oil prices caused by world events, does not prove any causal relationship between the two. Believing in such theories requires one to ignore the voluminous record of industry-wide efforts to push ahead from the very day of discovery at Prudhoe Bay and also accept that eight major oil companies, who can rarely agree on anything, conspired for years on end to forgo a return on their investments.[43]

Those in Alaska with an up-close view of the industry had no trouble identifying Humble's reticence when it came to Prudhoe Bay. Wally Hickel, Alaska's governor at the time of the Prudhoe Bay strike, believed Humble had little interest in developing the field because it conflicted with its interests elsewhere in the world. He further suspected that the *Manhattan* doubled as a smokescreen that enabled Humble to put off any firm commitments to the pipeline favored by Alaskans. In his role as Interior Secretary, Hickel observed how the oil industry viewed government oversight and environmental regulation as little more than impediments to development, yet he believed Humble itself was as much to blame for the delays.[44] In his 1971 book, *Who Owns America?*, Hickel describes a meeting held in his office the year before where representatives from BP, ARCO, and Humble gathered to discuss permit requirements for the Alaska pipeline. Just when Hickel was prepared to discuss the timeframe for approving the permits, the Humble man got up and walked out of the room. His company was simply not ready to commit to Alaska development. Tales of Humble's aggressiveness in the Alaska political arena abound. Referring to the company's penchant for heavy-handed negotiations with overmatched local landowners, former Attorney General John Havelock recalled, "Alaska was no different to [Humble] than another county in west Texas."[45] Victor Fischer, another longtime Alaskan with an impressive résumé of public service, summed his view of the company in stark terms: "They came over and didn't give a crap about what anybody in Alaska thought about anything. They did what they wanted, and nobody could stand in their path."[46] Journalist Joe LaRocca described the company as "the corporate simulacrum of a control freak. Because of its size and dominance of the industry, it arrogates unto itself the role of undisputed master in its dealings with everyone, including government, and usually prevails."[47]

Such harsh assessments of Jersey/Humble were generally tempered by an acknowledgment that the company remained unmatched within the industry in terms of technical expertise and the ability to solve complex engineering problems.[48] Jersey was known for hiring the top candidates in every scientific and engineering field, then rotating personnel through its various divisions (including management) until the right person landed in the right place. The company's decentralized management structure, implemented in the 1920s by legendary Standard chairman Walter Teagle, purposefully granted a large degree of autonomy to company divisions and affiliates in order to encourage unique and cooperative problem-solving. "It stands to reason," one Jersey executive explained in 1950, "that if you get five men together and one man is wrong, the mistake is going to be picked up. Or if one man has a good idea, the others will contribute to it and develop it."[49] (The philosophy explains how Stan Haas was able to begin studying arctic transportation methods more or less on his own initiative in 1960.) Outfitting the largest tanker in the world with icebreaking capabilities for a Northwest Passage expedition, a task that at first glance proved easy to dismiss as foolhardy, was therefore exactly the sort of colossal technical challenge a company like Humble would accept. It would simply leave no possible solution unexplored. As Jersey CEO Mike Haider explained to a newspaper reporter, "Drilling and developing will be relatively simple despite the harsh Arctic conditions, but transporting the oil will be the problem."[50] That single sentence is a pretty good assessment of Humble's attitude toward Alaska in 1968—the best engineers in the world had already figured out the drilling part and were now hard at work on the transportation method, which, naturally, would be solved in due course.

This longstanding practice by Jersey undercuts the "slow boat" theory regarding the *Manhattan*. Stan Haas and the marine division had contemplated the future need for icebreaking tankers for at least four years prior to the Prudhoe Bay strike, at a time well before the politics of the jointly owned North Slope oil fields had even been established. That the idea was born in a laboratory and not at a meeting of the Jersey board of directors suggests it was the product not of politics but of a well-established research and development program where technical expertise and lots of money were eagerly thrown at complex problems. To suggest that Humble merely latched on to the tanker idea as a clever way to forestall commitments to more feasible transportation methods ignores the tanker's potential market-based benefits and, more importantly, misunderstands the nature of Jersey's decision-making processes where comprehensive study of a whole range of alternatives (even seemingly outlandish ones) was the norm. That such a tanker system might take several years to develop was of no real consequence to Humble. Its ample worldwide reserves afforded the luxury of a more steadied approach. The slow boat theory also shortchanges the efforts of Humble and Esso personnel. No one could ever suggest that Stan Haas and his team did not take their mission seriously. Nothing about Humble's competitive machinations undermines the earnestness with which those individuals undertook the effort.

In sum, it appears the most straightforward explanation behind the *Manhattan* test is likely the most accurate: Humble wanted to see if it would work.

The company's deep pockets, international reserves of crude, and standing as the world's dominant oil company enabled it to take a cautious, methodical approach to development. Where ARCO and BP found themselves in a dramatic rush to recoup their sizable investments and begin feeding Alaska crude oil into their respective and highly profitable refining and marketing networks, Humble proved content to take its time. The final irony of the entire *Manhattan* test was that such a bold, daring enterprise actually fit squarely within the cautious, conservative, plodding approach of a monolithic oil company not automatically given to tremendous risk.

9

Round-trip

The night is neither bright nor short,
The singing breeze is cold,—
The ice is not so strong as hope,
The heart of man is bold!

Bright summer goes, dark winter comes,—
We cannot rule the year;
But long ere summer's sun goes down,
On yonder sea we'll steer.

—Excerpt from George Henry Boker, "A Ballad of Sir John
Franklin," deposited by the crew of the *Manhattan*
in the Beechey Island cairn, October 27, 1969[1]

The *Manhattan* approached Beechey Island on a cold, dreary day at the end of October. For more than a month since leaving Alaska, the tanker had sailed back and forth in Viscount Melville Sound, all the while testing ice conditions and collecting voluminous amounts of data. For many on the crew, this segment of the expedition proved as tedious as the outbound voyage had been thrilling. The sense of history slowly faded as the ship stopped exploring new territory; the feeling of wonder began to vanish when the mighty tanker no longer conquered ice but instead stopped only to study it. Those who made their lives on the sea knew the feeling well. It was the isolation that results when one's entire realm of existence is reduced to the space of a ship's hull. Port to starboard, bow to stern—every sailor's finite reality paradoxically lost in the seemingly infinite expanse of the world's oceans. Whether by the lonely days, mundane routines, or perhaps the encroaching arctic winter, Merritt Helfferich found occasion somewhere in Viscount Melville Sound to record in his diary a contemplation of the Arctic and the ship's place in it:

One loses a sense of the difficulties which past explorers had or even the sense of any contact with a real environment. We work and live mostly inside our limited universe, the ship and the adjacent ice breaking around the hull, broken here and there by leads whose relationship to deep waters is easily lost. We sail effortlessly through black waters on a plane surface—no contact with hills or shore to provide reference. Back and forth from floe to floe.[2]

For a full month the men of the *Manhattan* lived by this routine. And before departing the Arctic once and for all they would stop at Beechey Island and pay homage to those sailors who themselves had endured the long winters of the isolated North.

The ill-fated Sir John Franklin and his ships, *Erebus* and *Terror*, wintered at Beechey Island in 1845–1846. Three of the crew died that winter. Some would later call them the lucky ones, as they received a proper burial and escaped the world before starvation and insanity claimed the rest. Those three graves and a stone cairn erected by Franklin's men (which, curiously, was later found to contain nothing at all) were discovered by later expeditions sent to search for the missing Franklin. These parties used stones and the mast from the *Mary*, Sir John Ross's abandoned yacht, to erect another cairn on the island. In the century that followed, Beechey Island became something of a meeting place for arctic explorers, its cairn a repository for the history of each expedition that passed.[3] Now the crew of the *Manhattan* arrived to leave its own record. Captain Tom Pullen prepared a certificate with the particulars of the expedition. With most of the crew shivering in a ten-knot wind, he and Don Graham removed a few stones and placed within the cairn a brass pipe containing the record of the first commercial vessel to complete the Northwest Passage.[4]

The *Manhattan* continued to linger in Viscount Melville Sound. The captains had no schedules that had to be obeyed. Dignitaries no longer visited the ship. Most of the reporters had gone, and their departure meant no more bothersome demands for electrifying copy. Now the ship's officers remained free to stop the vessel as often as they wished. They could also shut down the engines and secure the vessel each night, a respite that proved healthy for the crew. The constant noise and unpredictable shuddering on the outbound voyage, where the vessel remained in motion more or less round the clock, had taken a psychological toll that was only noticeable now that the tanker was stopped and silent for extended periods. The scientists disembarked daily onto the ice, now a dense pack with a dusting of new snow as opposed to the patchwork of melt ponds and open leads they encountered on the voyage in. After the cores had been pulled and the ice thickness recorded, the scientists placed bamboo stakes in the ice. Once the men were safely back on the ship, the captains followed the line of bamboo stakes and drove the *Manhattan* through the just-measured floes. Personnel on the ship's forecastle armed with stopwatches and clipboards made note of the tanker's exact position in order to establish the relationship between the physical characteristics of the ice and the operation of the ship in breaking through it.[5] Though the efforts of the ice teams were commendable, almost everyone onboard, including the scientists themselves, recognized the program's many shortcomings. Data were sporadic. One test might result in the drilling of dozens of four-foot ice cores, the next only a handful half as long, leaving gaps in the data record that made comparisons next to useless. By necessity ice thickness was measured from the surface, yet the ice floes were never perfectly horizontal, and without a datum line (such as sea level) it was impossible to create an accurate depth profile, especially with cores taken at such widely spaced intervals. Finally, the cores themselves measured only the ice at those exact locations. Just a few feet to the right or left and the ice composition and topography might be considerably different. And for a ship whose beam measured a full 150 feet, a single core four inches across was a negligible quantity, no matter how dead center the captain managed to steer the tanker over the bamboo stakes.

The experience in Viscount Melville Sound revealed another logistical challenge for the naval architects who would design the next generation of arctic icebreakers. The ice pack was now covered with a light dusting of snow, a substance so abrasive it increased the frictional resistance on the hull to an astonishing degree. The snow also conformed to the shape of the hull, coating the steel and exerting its drag over a much greater surface area than ice fragments, whose point of contact was usually limited to a single irregular edge. (Humble scientists later determined that the coefficient of friction for snow was up to seven times greater than that for slab ice.) Some months before, in thinking ahead to precisely this problem, the Humble team researched various materials that might be bonded, painted, or mechanically secured to the ship's hull to reduce frictional resistance. Several plastics companies contacted by Humble suggested a high-density polyethylene coating similar to that used on ski bottoms. The U.S. Coast Guard was then experimenting with a four-millimeter-thick inorganic zinc coating on the *Westwind*, yet its effect on friction was unknown because the ice pack quickly scraped the material completely off the hull. Humble also considered Teflon, stainless steel, various synthetic flooring materials, and even something called "flake glass," a plastic-epoxy composite that contained platelets of glass smaller than the width of a human hair. Humble finally elected to test none of these materials on the *Manhattan*, deciding instead to conduct model tests at a later date.[6]

The tanker also encountered an unusual and unexpected ice formation in Viscount Melville Sound. Pancake ice, so named for its circular shape and spongy, sticky consistency, presented a challenge to a tanker more accustomed to ice in the form of rock-hard sheets. The gelatinous slush clung to the sides of the vessel and piled up in front of her in great mounds until the tanker simply couldn't push any more. Both the *Staten Island* and the *John A. MacDonald* also became temporarily bogged down. Sheer engine power saved the ships this time, but Pullen suggested that some sort of hull-washing mechanism might be required for future sailings. Heating the steel of the bow in order to produce a thin film of water might also solve both the pancake ice and the snow problems.[7]

The icebreaker convoy gained another member in October when the *Louis St. Laurent*, a brand-new Canadian Coast Guard icebreaker under the command of Captain Wilfred Dufour, joined the expedition. Named for a former prime minister, the *Louis St. Laurent* measured 392 feet in length and eighty feet in beam, and weighed more than fifteen thousand tons. She was the newest icebreaker in the world and the pride of the Canadian fleet. The vessel came north as part of her sea trials and would accompany the *Manhattan* back to Halifax. The sight of two bright red ships flying the Canadian flag and dashing about in the Arctic filled a beaming Tom Pullen with glee.[8]

THE LAST ICE

The approaching winter signaled very clearly to the crews that the time had come to go home. According to Pullen:

> Winter was clamping her iron grip on the Arctic. The hours of daylight dwindled rapidly until there was only light enough to work from 10 a.m. to 2 p.m. A wan sun lifted just a few degrees above the horizon before dropping back out of sight heralding the time when night would be continuous. Temperatures dropped toward the zero mark and northwest winds howled through the rigging with a rising note of urgency. Nowhere could we see open water, and new ice was now cementing the spaces between the hard old floes.[9]

After two long months on this steel island in the midst of a colorless sea all were ready to turn south. The rookies were learning what the maritime veterans knew well—time never lags so much as when a ship finally turns for home. Stan Haas wrote to his family of his growing dislike for the tanker and eagerness to "terminate this damned thing" and return home. "People's nerves are getting a bit on edge," he wrote. "We shout sooner now."[10]

The tanker and her escorts steered for Lancaster Sound, Baffin Bay, and the North Atlantic beyond. The Arctic had one last surprise for the *Manhattan* before letting her go. Just east of Resolute the tanker encountered massive icebergs and even larger ice islands that had been snared by and then cemented to wind-driven ice floes, all moving inexorably in the ship's path. This was a mosaic of twisted, brutal ice that caused one crew member to note, "If we had seen this on the way in, we would have turned back then and there."[11] The four ships fell in a line, the largest in the lead, and picked their way through the jumble. At the far end of the sound, just before the eastern exit to the Northwest Passage, the *Manhattan* came upon an iceberg on the port side and an aged ice floe to the starboard. Don Graham, the captain on watch, ordered a gentle five-degree turn to the starboard, hoping to slice through the outer rim of the floe and skate by the berg. Tom Pullen, who stood next to Graham on the bridge, described what happened next:

> Unfortunately for him [Graham], he misjudged the angle of attack and instead of entering the floe the ship caromed off it and was inexorably committed to hit the berg while moving at eight knots.... Initial contact produced an explosion of ice fragments which showered onto the bow of the *Manhattan*. As contact continued this ice continued to cascade onto the ship. I fully expected to see the icebreaking bow severely damaged, even crushed, but instead the ship merely rebounded to the right. For 155,000 tons to bounce like that is no mean feat.[12]

Most of the crew were in the galley having lunch at the time, and the shock of the impact sent dishes and coffee cups crashing to the floor. Although it was barely noon, a few festive and enterprising individuals brought glasses of Scotch onto the deck of the supposedly dry ship and dropped shards of ice into their glasses. This inspired the stewards to collect hundreds of pounds of the ice and store it in the deep freeze. Onboard celebrations were being planned for the tanker's imminent arrival in New York and visitors to the historic ship would no doubt thrill at having their drinks chilled by genuine arctic ice. The crew discovered that the ice, when dropped into a beverage, caused it to fizz like soda water. Everyone looked to Tom Pullen, the acknowledged expert on all things Arctic, for an explanation. He had no idea. William Smith guessed that the phenomenon was due to the sudden release of air bubbles that had been trapped for years in the ice.[13]

Later that night the tanker again became sandwiched between two enormous floes, first bouncing off one to her port side and then careening heavily into the other. The officer at the wheel immediately felt a slight pull in the tanker's motion, a clear indication that the ship had been wounded by the impact. Three tanks on the starboard side of the ship began losing ballast water, indicating some sort of puncture in each, though no one would know the full extent of the damage until the ship reached port and could undergo a full examination. In any case the tanker was in no danger of sinking as bulkheads sealed off the breached tanks from the rest of the hull.[14] (Interestingly, Humble had previously identified exactly this scenario as one of the voyage's most dangerous risks. Where a smaller ship like the *John A. MacDonald* could turn on a dime and zigzag through narrow leads, the *Manhattan*, with its considerably larger turning radius, had little choice but to barrel straight ahead. In the pre-expedition model tests, engineers had studied the nature of side-impact collisions resulting from a ship caroming off one floe and into another. Although it was difficult to simulate such a collision in a laboratory in a way that generated useful data, the end result was quite clear. "In this case the stem does not come into contact with the ice and all of the impact energy is absorbed in the shoulders or cheeks," the test technicians wrote.[15] Like a swing of a hammer that is just a few degrees off to one side and catches the head of the nail not in line with its length but at an angle, such an oblique collision with ice would almost certainly injure the vessel.)

On the fog-shrouded morning of November 8, the *John A. MacDonald* and the *Louis St. Laurent* took their respective places ahead of the *Manhattan* and sailed triumphantly into the harbor at Halifax (the *Staten Island* had separated from the others earlier that day and was proceeding independently to New York). At 1:17 p.m., the *John A. MacDonald* berthed at Pier 20 in Halifax harbor, her assignment complete.[16] Canadian transport minister Don Jamieson and an assemblage of federal and provincial officials welcomed the vessels and later hosted the men at a reception at Dalhousie University. "What we have learned from your exploits and from your considerable skills," Jamieson told the crews of all three ships, "will help us advance by a great many years our competence and our ability to operate in this great northern territory of ours."[17] Jamieson noted the sense of national pride in the men and ships of the Canadian Coast Guard who patrolled the country's three oceans. He diplomatically avoided thorny questions of national sovereignty. This was a night of celebration, not politics.

Stan Haas took the stage in the banquet hall to thank the crew of the *John A. MacDonald*. He spoke officially on behalf of Humble, but made it clear his thanks were personal as well:

> When we encountered the heavier ice in Melville Sound…we Texans had not yet learned all the lessons…. But all during the voyage to Prudhoe Bay and Point Barrow, Alaska, the *John A. MacDonald* steamed along at our stern waiting for a call for assistance from us and then answering that call as required with a vigor and enthusiasm typical of the character of the ship and her master.[18]

Haas then called Paul Fournier to the stage, the standing ovation in full roar before he could even finish saying Fournier's name, and presented to the captain a brass plaque commemorating the historic voyage. (One month later, in recognition of both his prestigious maritime career and his leadership during the recently ended voyage,

Fournier was honored with the Order of Canada, one of the country's highest civilian honors.) Most of the crew, for whom the only shore leave in the last three months had come in the not-quite-bustling ports of Thule Air Base, Sachs Harbor, and Point Barrow, left for a raucous night on the town. The next day Humble opened the ship for tours to some eight thousand locals.[19]

Once in port at Halifax the officers of the *Manhattan* lightened her by discharging ballast and, with the ship sitting higher in the water, were able to inspect the hull for damage incurred the week before. The ship's heavy fall against the rock-hard ice floe in Lancaster Sound had driven a hole "big enough to drive a truck through" in the No. 4 starboard tank.[20] Two other hull plates showed cracks from the violent encounter. The only thing to leak from the breach was ballast water that had been taken on back in August from Chesapeake Bay, yet the incident sounded an alarm for environmentalists. Photographs of the jagged, gaping maw in the side of the ship starkly illustrated the environmental risks of shipping oil in tankers. Edgar Wayburn of the Sierra Club had long expressed his group's general opposition to oil development in Alaska on grounds of wilderness preservation. When asked about the *Manhattan*, he steadfastly opposed the idea of tankers in the Arctic: "The method of using the giant tanker runs considerable risk of another *Torrey Canyon* disaster which in the Arctic area would be of much greater magnitude because up there the mess would stay for years."[21] Wayburn referred to an incident two years earlier where a supertanker sailing off the southwest coast of England struck a well-charted shoal and spilled the entire cargo of thirty-one million gallons of crude oil. Wayburn's Sierra Club would soon publish *Oil on Ice*, an environmental "battlebook" (the group's term) that questioned the rush to development taking place in Alaska. In characterizing the *Manhattan* experiment as corporate hubris in the face of natural forces humankind could neither fully understand nor control, the environmental group spoke its mind: "Some men dream of supertankers plying the Northwest Passage. Others have nightmares—of crude catastrophes that could make the *Torrey Canyon* disaster seem like so much spilt milk."[22] The book was not all slogans and hyperbole. The Sierra Club made the very reasonable point that should the *Manhattan* lead to a full transport system, the presence of thirty supertankers in the arctic shipping lanes all but guaranteed an accident somewhere, someday. The law of averages demanded it. "Oil congeals at frigid temperatures," the book noted, "and a single spill could visit incalculable mischief on the Arctic ecosystem."[23]

Tom Pullen believed the breach in the *Manhattan*'s hull warranted no such wild extrapolations. He emphasized that the split occurred in the old plating of her original hull located under the waterline, well beneath the high-tensile steel ice belt. That belt, along with the other reinforced sections of the ship, emerged from the eleven-thousand-mile journey practically unscathed. Pullen also pointed out that any future oil tankers would be strengthened to the highest icebreaking standards, making them impervious to ice damage.[24] Pullen's Coast Guard colleague, Lieutenant Commander E. B. Stolee, had a more pragmatic view, however. "There is no doubt that the opening of the Northwest Passage to tanker trade will introduce oil pollution into the Arctic," he wrote.[25] Like Pullen, Stolee strongly believed appropriate shipbuilding standards and operational safeguards would minimize the risk of accidents—but he also recognized that some oil spillage was bound to occur wherever tankers operated.

The incident became one of the first things reporters asked about now that the tanker was back in port. Though obviously not pleased to be discussing a failure in the ship's hull, Stan Haas turned the story around by saying he was actually gratified that it occurred in the original steel. The heavily instrumented hull recorded every pressure event and Humble had identified the time of the breach down to the minute. The tensile failure was now another important data point for Humble to analyze.

"I think it's fair to say that the *Manhattan* did all she was supposed to do," Haas told reporters. "She performed as well as we expected, or better, and we've tested under some rather severe conditions."[26]

NEW YORK

On November 12, 1969, exactly eleven weeks and two days after departing the East Coast bound for the high Arctic, the *Manhattan* sailed up the Hudson River to New York harbor. Under a gray and cloudy sky, the tanker had an appearance to match. Her hull sported rust and abrasions where the ice had scraped away layers of paint. The ship "didn't look too pretty,"[27] according to one observer, but she received a triumphant welcome nonetheless. Tugs blew their whistles and fireboats sent up plumes of water in celebration. The *Manhattan*, led by the *Staten Island* and flanked on either side by Coast Guard helicopters, answered with her deep, bellowing horn. Humble had arranged travel to New York for the families of every crew member aboard, and now they waited eagerly on Pier 84 as the ship drew near.

For Stan Haas and the entire Humble contingent, the tanker's arrival in New York signified an end to the voyage, but definitely not the project. Much work, albeit of the office variety far from any ice floes or polar bears, lay ahead for these men. For those on the crew, from the ship's master down to the deckhands, the homecoming represented simply another welcome respite from the sea. Although none would deny that this expedition presented something special to their lives and careers, or refute the sense of camaraderie that united the men behind their historic undertaking, the voyage was, in the end, just another job that kept them away from their families for months on end. The men of the *Manhattan* were now home, until the next calling back to the sea.

As the crew disembarked from the ship and began to go their separate ways, one wistful Humble official called out, "When is the first reunion?" Jim Barrett, an able-bodied seaman, shouted back, "This is the merchant marine. We're just sailors. We don't have reunions."[28]

Two weeks later the *Manhattan* sailed for Pakistan with a cargo of several tons of grain in her hull.

Epilogue

Since we live on land, and are usually beyond sight of the sea, it is easy to forget that our world is an ocean world, and to ignore what in practice that means. Some shores have been tamed, however temporarily, but beyond the horizon lies a place that refuses to submit. It is the wave maker, an anarchic expanse, the open ocean of the high seas. Under its many names, and with variations in color and mood, this single ocean spreads across three-fourths of the globe. Geographically, it is not the exception to our planet, but by far its greatest defining feature. By political and social measures it is important too—not merely as a wilderness that has always existed or as a reminder of the world as it was before, but also quite possibly as a harbinger of a larger chaos to come.

—William Langewiesche, *The Outlaw Sea* (2004)[1]

On April 3, 1970, the *Manhattan* sailed from Newport News, Virginia, for a return voyage to the Arctic. Seatrain Lines, the tanker's owner, had reclaimed the ship from Humble in the intervening months for more orthodox commercial transits around the globe. Her icebreaking bow and steel-strengthened hull remained in place during this period, no doubt making her the only icebreaker to ply the waters of the Mediterranean. After spending the winter sorting through the first voyage's data, Humble chartered the tanker again for a second trip. Under the command of Captain Arthur Smith, and with Stan Haas again on the bridge overseeing the entire expedition, the *Manhattan* left to collect additional data on the viability of commercial marine traffic in the Northwest Passage.

The return trip proved necessary in order to test the vessel in more harsh winter ice conditions, as opposed to the previous arctic voyage, which encountered primarily sun-battered summer ice. By April, the long winter had forged a solid ice pack that held the entire Northwest Passage in its iron grip. This would provide the ideal conditions for more testing. Humble had no intention of sending the *Manhattan* through the entire passage, for the tanker's maiden arctic voyage had already made history. This would be only a routine research expedition.[2]

The *Manhattan*, accompanied this time by the *Louis St. Laurent* under the command of Captain George Burdoch,[3] encountered heavy pack ice in Baffin Bay. For two brutal weeks the ships made barely three hundred miles of progress as they fought their way through ice floes up to ten miles in diameter with pressure ridges that rose forty feet in the air. The tanker's limited astern power again proved detrimental to her overall performance, and she became stuck in the ice on several occasions. A cover of snow on the ice pack further increased friction on the tanker's hull. By the end of the month the ships had traversed Baffin Bay, something no other vessel had ever done so early in the year, and reached the entrance to Lancaster Sound. The *Manhattan* spent the next four weeks in the vicinity of Bylot Island, where W. F. Weeks of the U.S. Army Cold Regions Research and Engineering Laboratory led a team of scientists on a rigorous program of ice testing. While the scientists measured the temperature of the pack ice, compression and tensile strength of the ice, and salinity of the cores, the ship's officers kept corresponding records of the vessel's velocity and engine performance. Scientists discovered that excellent results could be gained by a technique they called the "ram test." The vessel would enter an ice sheet at high speed and subsequently decelerate to either a slower speed or a full stop. The maneuver not only resulted in resistance measurements over a measurable range of velocities, but did so in a relatively short run. Where the coring tests of the previous year's voyage took place over a stretch of ice sometimes two miles in length, and consequently took the tanker through ice regimes of wildly varying composition, the shorter ram tests measured as little as fifty feet and thus were limited to constant ice, from which a more accurate depth profile could be drawn.

By the last week of May, the *Manhattan* turned south again. Just before leaving the Arctic, the tanker called at the tiny village of Pond Inlet, where a poor hunting season had left residents with a shortage of meat. The *Manhattan*'s stewards pulled four thousand pounds of food—including beef, pork, and chicken, as well as fresh fruits and vegetables—and gave the lot to the village.[4]

The *Manhattan* again sustained hull damage from the arctic ice. On two separate occasions while backing astern, the tanker rammed into heavy floes that tore gashes in unprotected sections of the hull. One breach occurred below the waterline at the double-hulled engine room, but only to the outer skin. Exactly as designed, the inner hull kept the rushing water from flooding the engine room. The other hull puncture was in the afterpeak, a small compartment used to store fresh water. Neither injury inhibited the overall handling of the vessel. On May 25, just as the expedition prepared to return home, the *Louis St. Laurent* also suffered minor hull damage. While working alongside the *Manhattan* to free the trapped tanker, the Canadian ship found herself quickly beset and subsequently pressed hard against the ice belt of the larger ship. Both vessels remained trapped in the ice, side by side, for a full week before breaking free. The second arctic voyage of the *Manhattan* ended at Chester, Pennsylvania, on June 13, 1970.[5]

Humble chairman Mike Wright praised the tanker and her crew. "The two Arctic voyages were highly successful in providing valuable data for our studies concerning the various transportation alternatives for moving Alaskan crude oil to U.S. refineries," he stated.[6] Stan Haas believed the *Manhattan* was still on pace with the trans-Alaska pipeline. Environmental lawsuits and the Alaska Native land-claims issue had brought that effort to an almost complete standstill. In addition, cost estimates for the pipeline continued to creep steadily higher, leading Haas to believe the all-marine route still made economic sense. The data from the *Manhattan*'s second voyage would now help prove the point, Haas confidently informed colleagues.[7]

Following the second voyage, Wärtsilä Shipyard of Finland launched a comprehensive model testing program based on the real-world experience of the *Manhattan*.[8] The company produced numerous 1:50-scale models of the tanker, each made of wood, which it now planned to test in a basin constructed in a belowground bomb shelter in downtown Helsinki. The basin measured 128 feet long, sixteen feet wide, and four feet deep, and featured one side made of clear plastic to allow visual observation and filming of the tests at and below the waterline. A constant indoor temperature of minus eighteen degrees Celsius kept the pool frozen over. An elevated monorail over the basin's centerline featured a rigging that could tow the model ships at constant velocities. Wärtsilä used data from the *Manhattan*'s two voyages to calculate a baseline coefficient of friction for full-size tankers in arctic ice. It now sought to validate the test procedures by achieving the same level of performance in a twenty-foot wooden model. Basically Wärtsilä needed the models to experience exactly what the full-size ship did in the Arctic. At that point the engineers could make alterations to the parent model—different bow angles or a wider beam, for example—and evaluate how the changes either improved or worsened ship performance.

Wärtsilä quickly discovered that a wooden model with smooth, lacquered sides approximated the performance of the *Manhattan* on its first voyage, when it encountered mostly deteriorating summer ice, but that its resistance predictions were only one-half the measured values for the recent winter expedition. (Geophysicists theorized that the physical characteristics of winter ice varied in such a way as to display greater properties of resistance, an effect exacerbated by the non-uniform snow cover. Stan Haas himself noticed that the performance of the ship in winter ice just seemed different somehow from the summer before.) By roughing the sides of the model with 150-grit sandpaper technicians came close to replicating the vessel's performance at low speed in winter ice five feet thick. The resistance-to-speed ratio for this sandpapered model began to deviate sharply as speed and/or ice thickness changed—a problem Wärtsilä noted would have to be solved with additional correlation tests—but for the time being it would suffice for testing.

One of the first altered models to be tested featured a beam thirteen percent narrower than the *Manhattan*'s. Constant velocity tests through uniform ice showed a marked reduction in resistance over the parent, suggesting that an important relationship existed between vessel width, vessel length, and ice resistance. (Shipbuilders had long known this, although the *Manhattan* was the first test of the principle on such a large scale.) Although different bow configurations proved inconclusive, the sum total of these tests showed that approximately eighty-five percent of ice resistance occurs in the ship's forebody. Later models whose only modifications were to the vessel's sides (e.g., a tapered hull at the waterline) resulted in negligible frictional differences, further demonstrating that an icebreaker's forebody bore the greatest share of ice resistance, and therefore bow, afterbow, and beam design were paramount to efficient operations. In the interest of being thorough, Wärtsilä also tested a model with the Alexbow, the upward-thrusting snowplow design Humble engineers had briefly considered for the *Manhattan*. Tests revealed that Humble had made the correct decision. The conventional downbreaking bow proved vastly superior, able to maintain continuous forward motion through ice layers forty percent thicker than what the Alexbow could handle.

For steering tests, the monorail towed the models into the ice layer at a speed of three knots, whereupon the rigging was disconnected and the model, its rudder set at a predetermined angle, was free to turn. These tests showed that although a wider beam resulted in greater friction from the ice, it also increased maneuverability. The result led Wärtsilä to make just one definite conclusion: lots of additional testing was required to find the most efficient beam-to-length ratio, one that minimized ice resistance while maximizing steering ability.[9]

Based in large part on data from the *Manhattan*'s two voyages but also on the admittedly inconclusive Wärtsilä tests, Humble next contracted with Newport News Shipbuilding to design the next generation of icebreaking tankers—vessels twice as heavy as the *Manhattan* with engine rooms nearly five times as powerful. This was just the step the oil company had been working towards for the past two years. In its quest to understand the Arctic, Humble had to this point cast as wide a net as possible, contracting with every company, testing facility, university, weather bureau, and government agency it could find that possessed information that might prove useful. That all changed with the signing of the Newport News contract. Humble stipulated the shipyard not discuss its tanker design work with any regulatory body, such as the U.S. Coast Guard or American Bureau of Shipping, and further demanded that conversations regarding machinery components take place only with approved vendors. The project seemed to be moving from the experimental to the development stage, and Humble intended to keep its plans a secret.

Newport News started with a basic ship design 1,247 feet in length, 198 feet at its widest point, and weighing 289,733 deadweight tons. The angles of the downbreaking bow had been modified slightly from the *Manhattan*, but the general appearance was the same. The proposed tanker could accommodate 2.173 million barrels of crude oil in its nineteen cargo tanks. The most dramatic alteration would be found in the engine room—a steam turbine, triple-screw propulsion system capable of 200,000 shaft horsepower of forward thrust and 140,000 in reverse. So massive was the propulsion machinery that the naval architects initially believed it wouldn't fit within the vessel's trim limitations. They had to completely revise the engine room location and layout to accommodate the necessary equipment, sacrificing a not-insignificant amount of cargo space in the process.

Starting with this template the shipyard then worked through numerous design iterations. Double hull, single hull, wide beam, narrow beam, parallel sides, flared sides, tapered waterline, two-boiler steam plant, three-boiler steam plant, gas turbine propulsion plant—all variables could be interchanged on the basic ship arrangement to achieve the required operational parameters. Newport News identified four distinct vessel designs it deemed worthy of additional consideration. "Design and construction of an icebreaking tanker…is feasible," the shipyard reported. "No insurmountable problems have been identified, although there are a number of areas which will require development."[10] Newport News then listed those areas for further study and suggested to Humble that weekly meetings of company personnel should commence to hammer out final designs.

The Newport News study apparently led many within Humble to believe orders for the massive tankers would be submitted in due course. Bram Mookhoek, one of the original members of the tanker task force, expressed such enthusiasm that one overzealous reporter quoted him confirming the entire project was a go.[11] Stan Haas made his views clear: "Based on the experience during the testing period of thickest ice [the *Manhattan*'s winter voyage] it is believed that it is technically and operationally feasible to operate an icebreaking tanker in the areas tested on a year-round basis."[12]

TANKERS POSSIBLE, PIPELINES CHEAPER

Despite this apparent profusion of optimism, Humble announced on Wednesday, October 21, 1970, that it was suspending its icebreaking tanker project. The company stated its belief that the *Manhattan* had proven the feasibility of using such tankers in the Arctic yet the Alaska pipeline now appeared to have an economic edge. From this point forward Humble would focus its efforts only on the design and construction of the Trans-Alaska Pipeline.[13] Seatrain Lines took back the *Manhattan* for good, releasing Humble six months early from its two-year charter commitment and also freeing the company from the contractual obligation of removing the tanker's icebreaking bow, ice belt, and other steel hull plating. All but the bow were, in fact, later removed, bringing the tanker back down to a positively svelte 114,000 deadweight tons.[14] (The ship's original bow, the one that had been sliced off and replaced with the icebreaking model eighteen months before, still sat in a storage container at Sun Shipyard. Dubbed the "*Manhattan* monument" by shipyard workers, the relic would eventually be scrapped.)

Humble's public statements on the termination of the tanker program cited only economic reasons behind the move. Internal reports, however, acknowledged other factors. Marine transport of oil requires rigid schedules. Production facilities and refineries have to know exactly how much oil is arriving and on what date. Humble calculated that each ship in its icebreaking fleet would have to make the Prudhoe Bay–to–New York round-trip in thirty-five days, forty at the outset. Anything longer than that would create surplus product at the loading terminal and/or bottlenecks at the unloading terminal at the other end of the route. Costs would skyrocket. Holding tanks at both ends of the line could provide a buffer of a week or two, yet timely and predictable passage for a single ship in the Northwest Passage, not to mention an entire fleet, was an elusive prospect to be sure. Humble knew it could not afford to assign an escort icebreaker to each of the tankers—one *John A. MacDonald* for every *Manhattan*, as it were—so the tanker task force had proposed a "picket line" of six ships along the route to lend assistance and pass off the tankers down the line. But just a single tanker falling off schedule would tie up these escorts and create ripple effects throughout the entire organization. The unpredictability of the system presented a challenge that had no satisfactory solution.[15]

The final price tag also doomed the arctic tankers. The Jones Act of 1920 stipulated that any ships engaged in domestic commerce had to be constructed by American shipyards and operated by American crews, which Humble figured would roughly double the cost over ships registered in more tax-friendly nations and crewed by lower-wage foreign workers. In addition, the cost estimates of the offshore loading terminal at Prudhoe Bay went as high as $1 billion—and still Humble had no studies definitively proving such a facility could even be built.[16] Finally, Humble's number crunchers discovered the expected cost savings over pipelines would not be as great as anticipated. At the start of the tanker test in 1968, the company estimated that shipping crude oil to the East Coast via icebreaking tankers would cost roughly sixty cents a barrel. The following year, however, Humble announced at a meeting of the National Petroleum Refiners Association that this figure had risen to $1. By late summer, following the *Manhattan*'s 1970 voyage, projected per barrel costs stood at

$1.21. This amount still compared favorably to East Coast delivery via transcontinental pipeline, which Humble believed would run in the range of $1.35–$1.45 per barrel, yet the ever-shrinking margin might very well have given Jersey executives pause.[17]

In March 1970, just before the *Manhattan*'s second voyage, Stan Haas received the latest cost estimates for a full tanker system. The Prudhoe Bay terminal came in at $745 million, and the offloading terminal in the ice-free Eastern Seaboard carried a price tag of $405 million. Throw in a fleet of twenty-five icebreaking tankers at $90 million each, and Humble pegged its upfront capital investment at $3.4 billion. Humble had recently reported to stockholders that its share of trans-Alaska pipeline costs would amount to less than $400 million. While the costs for the pipeline project had also climbed considerably of late, it may have appeared to Humble that the wiser course was to partner with other companies and share the cost of a pipeline rather than pay the tab for icebreakers all on its own. What no one knew at the time was that the total cost of the Alaska pipeline would eventually balloon to an astonishing $8 billion. In an interview years later, Mike Wright of Humble looked back on the saga of Prudhoe Bay:

> We concluded that the pipeline would be cheaper, but the interesting thing was when we ran the Esso *Manhattan* up there and back, we thought we were talking about tankers that would cost about $30 million a piece [*sic*] and by the time we ran this ship up there and back, we found out we would have had to have double hulls, and we would have had to have more power and so forth, why the price at that point jumped up to $100 million at least. Therefore it didn't look like it was economic. But in the meantime, we were using $1,003 million [i.e. $1.03 billion] for the cost of the [Alaska] pipeline and that escalated up to $8 billion. So we might have done better if we'd gone to [icebreaking] tankers.[18]

In announcing the cancellation of the Arctic Tanker Test, Humble stated that the icebreaking tanker studies could be resumed on short notice if the economic factors changed. Despite the runaway costs of the Trans-Alaska Pipeline throughout the early to mid-1970s, Humble never revived those studies.

The voyages of the *Manhattan* were planned and executed by men with a firm resolve to see the resources of the Arctic developed for both the profit of private industry and the betterment of humankind. But it would be a mistake to characterize all onboard the tanker so uniformly. Merritt Helfferich, an Alaskan with a strong environmental ethic and an affinity for the Arctic's mysterious and untouched nature, looked out over the white expanse of Viscount Melville Sound on the tanker's first voyage and wrote in his diary a lament of sorts for what he saw as the industrialized future of the North:

I thought of the implication of this massive store of wealth [Prudhoe Bay], what it will do to Alaska and the world. It is easier to block all of this off in your mind as happening elsewhere without any contact on your life. But bringing it into focus, I look at it with a fair amount of horror as the indication of advancing civilization and the accompanying pressure of people—Arrgh! These non-inhabited islands hopefully ice-locked and thus protected from the encroachments of noisy, dirty people are perhaps soon to be removed from their protective layer and adorned with communities. The North Slope will be covered with people and in time there will be nowhere else.[19]

Helfferich's words echo the sentiments of John Muir, the founder of the Sierra Club, who at the turn of the twentieth century believed that the great wilderness called Alaska would remain largely protected from the crush of civilization by virtue of the winter, snow, and ice that kept interlopers at bay. Indeed, the frigid Northwest Passage kept its secrets from legions of explorers for hundreds of years. The *Manhattan* represented a revolutionary era far removed from that of other explorers in the five-hundred-year quest for the Northwest Passage—men in wooden ships, fending off cold, starvation, and the specter of death all the while. Very little mystery or suspense shrouded the Humble experiment, for this was not a voyage of exploration so much as one of conquest. The route was well known and the stores contained ample supplies of food. This massive ship made of the strongest steel bulled her way through the North, and, in the words of one crew member, "kicked the door wide open" to the Arctic.[20] By the time Helfferich sailed the waters of Viscount Melville Sound, the prospect that ice alone would repel the reach of humankind seemed altogether antiquated. Civilization was on the march.

Yet the arctic door had not been kicked wide open by the *Manhattan*—only cracked slightly, with a single foot in the threshold perhaps. Humble abandoned the project in 1970, and icebreaking tankers have yet to sail the Northwest Passage. But they are coming. Hundreds, perhaps thousands of vessels, everything from cargo ships to supply barges to pleasure craft, ply the waters of the Canadian Arctic today. And the prospect of resource development in the region remains very much alive. A recent U.S. Geological Survey report estimates that 130 billion barrels of crude oil—roughly seven times the amount at Prudhoe Bay—remain to be discovered in arctic regions.[21] No less than half a dozen mining companies have explored the islands of Nunavut in search of iron ore, uranium, gold, diamonds, and other minerals. Any developed finds must be shipped by barge. There will be no competing pipeline proposal this time. If we accept that the Arctic may one day experience the industrialization of the sort portended by the *Manhattan*, then it is worth considering why the Humble effort did not succeed and what has to happen for a similar project to do so in the future. Which of the variables that doomed the Humble project have to change if tankers are to sail the Arctic? Those variables include the obvious engineering challenges, as well as the socioeconomic, environmental, and geopolitical issues—all of which are viewed differently by the region's stakeholders now than at the time of the *Manhattan*'s voyage. Indigenous peoples in Alaska, Canada, and throughout the Arctic, for example, though largely absent from the *Manhattan* debates, are more politically engaged today through groups such as the Inuit Circumpolar Council and home-rule governments in Greenland and Nunavut. Environmental concerns today are debated on a global stage.

And then there is the ice.

Humble cited economics as the primary reason for canceling the Arctic Tanker Test—yet the company did not believe the tankers were *uneconomic*, only that the trans-Alaska pipeline appeared to have an economic advantage. It was the polar environment that had the greatest bearing on the marine route's projected costs. The economics of tanker traffic, if only marginally favorable in 1969–1970 for Humble, might improve in the face of changes to the ice of the Arctic. The present effects of global climate change are not to be underestimated.

In 2004, the Arctic Council, an intergovernmental forum composed of the eight circumpolar nations, commissioned a report designed to make scientific findings accessible to policy makers and the general public.[22] Authored by dozens of scientists from around the world, the largely nontechnical report, *Impacts of a Warming Arctic: Arctic Climate Impact Assessment*, notes temperature increases of three to four degrees Celsius over the past fifty years in Alaska and western Canada. Its forecast of future trends is no less alarming, noting that increasing global concentrations of carbon dioxide and other greenhouse gases due to human activities, primarily fossil fuel burning, are projected to contribute to additional arctic warming of up to seven degrees Celsius over the next century.[23] The ACIA authors name sea ice as a key indicator of the effects of this warming trend:

Just as miners once had canaries to warn of rising concentrations of noxious gases, researchers working on climate change rely on Arctic sea ice as an early warning system. The sea ice presently covering the Arctic Ocean and neighboring seas is highly sensitive to temperature changes in the air above and the ocean below. Over recent decades, Arctic watchers detected a slow shrinkage of the ice pack, suggestive of the initial influences of global warming. In recent years, the rate of retreat has accelerated, indicating that the "canary" is in trouble.[24]

Three years after the ACIA report, scientists at the National Snow and Ice Data Center (NSIDC) in Boulder, Colorado, announced that not only was arctic sea ice melting, it was doing so faster than anyone had previously predicted. NSIDC compared computer model simulations of late-twentieth-century climate with observed measurements of sea ice in the Arctic. Every available model had, on average, simulated a loss of September ice cover of 2.5 percent per decade from 1953 to 2006 (September marking the yearly ice minimum). Running the models with newly available data sets, however, revealed the actual September loss over that time span to be closer to 7.8 percent per decade. "The shrinking of summertime ice is about thirty years ahead of the climate model projections," stated Ted Scambos of NSIDC, a finding that suggested a seasonally ice-free Arctic might happen sooner rather than later.[25]

On October 1, 2007, just five months after that announcement, NSIDC followed with one even more stunning: "Arctic sea ice during the 2007 melt season plummeted to the lowest levels since satellite measurements began in 1979."[26] Scientists in Boulder reported that the average September ice cover measured 4.28 million square kilometers, a record-shattering twenty-three percent smaller than the previous summer minimum. Based on ship and aircraft records from before the satellite era, NSIDC estimated sea ice cover may have decreased by as much as fifty percent from the 1950s. What happened in the Arctic in 2007 shocked everyone. The loss of sea ice far outpaced even the most extreme computer model projections. For the first time in human memory, the Northwest Passage was free of ice. Where a 105,000-deadweight-ton icebreaker fought through the ice pack in September 1969, a fiberglass sailboat could have made the transit in September 2007. Even the formidable McClure Strait was open. "The effects of greenhouse warming are now coming through loud and clear," said Mark Serreze, senior scientist at NSIDC.[27] Earlier that year the Intergovernmental Panel on Climate Change (IPCC) had announced that some model scenarios showed an ice-free Arctic by the latter half of the twenty-first century—a prediction that seemed almost outdated the moment it was published. Serreze put the date closer to 2030, others even sooner than that.

The health of the arctic ice pack is about more than just its number of square kilometers. The disappearance of the ice exposes more dark water, which absorbs solar radiation as opposed to the white ice that reflects it back to the atmosphere, resulting in an increased heat budget that not only melts existing ice but hinders the formation of multiyear ice. According to Serreze, "The sea ice cover is in a downward spiral and may have passed the point of no return. As the years go by, we are losing more and more ice in summer, and growing back less and less ice in winter."[28] By September 2010, the arctic ice pack averaged 4.9 million square kilometers in area—the third lowest on record after 2007 and 2008—of which less than sixty thousand square kilometers was five years or older. When that multiyear ice is gone, the greatest obstacle to marine traffic will be permanently removed. According to Michael Byers, Canada Research Chair in Global Politics and International Law at the University of

British Columbia, "From that point onward, the Northwest Passage and the Arctic Ocean will resemble the Gulf of St. Lawrence or the Baltic Sea, where ice-strengthened ships and icebreaker-escorted convoys can safely operate in winter."[29] Under nearly every climate and transportation modeling scenario, Greenland, Canada, and Alaska all stand to experience sizable increases in maritime access over the next fifty years. For Canada, an additional 1.2 million square kilometers of ocean area within its extended exclusive economic zone (EEZ) could be accessible to light icebreaking vessels by midcentury.[30]

The thinning ice pack could paradoxically make shipping in the Northwest Passage more difficult, at least initially. While overall ice coverage has decreased since the *Manhattan*'s voyages in 1969–1970, the nature and extent of the migratory ice that drifts into the Canadian Archipelago appears to be in even greater flux. As ice bridges that block the narrow straits between islands recede, they open pathways for migrating floes and more hazardous icebergs to drift into shipping lanes—exactly the sort of obstacles that punctured the *Manhattan*'s hull on her maiden voyage. From an environmental perspective, then, the prospect of increased traffic in the Northwest Passage remains a concern. Another Exxon tanker, the *Valdez*, demonstrated the devastating effects of oil spills when she ran aground in Prince William Sound in 1989 and spilled eleven million gallons of crude oil. Ongoing monitoring of the region since then has revealed that the oil has lingered longer than anyone initially believed it would and that its detrimental effects to fish and wildlife continue.[31] The impact of such a spill in the Arctic would likely be just as severe and possibly last longer in the colder, less dynamic environment. Response would almost certainly be hindered by the remote location, lack of infrastructure, and enormous difficulty in transporting personnel and clean-up equipment to the incident location. Even then, testing, training, and drills have shown that mechanical recovery of oil in ice and broken ice conditions is extremely difficult, while the efficacy of in situ burning and chemical dispersants is often limited in the harsh environment. "There is nothing up there [the Arctic] to operate from at present and we're really starting from ground zero," Admiral Robert Papp Jr., commandant of the U.S. Coast Guard, told a conference of polar experts in Girdwood, Alaska, in June 2011. Although the state of oil spill response technology is ever improving, the basic challenges of operating in the Arctic remain the foremost concern. "No way could we deploy several thousand people [in the Arctic] as we did in the Deepwater Horizon spill," said Papp in reference to the April 2010 oil spill in the Gulf of Mexico, which, for its comparatively mild climate and environmental conditions, still proved taxing for responders.[32]

Of equal if not greater importance to the potential industrial uses of the Northwest Passage are the social impacts to the people who live in the Arctic.[33] The environment provides residents with fish, birds, seals, berries, and other traditional foods.

Reduced sea ice may negatively impact their ability to harvest such game, and in this sense climate change represents an appreciable impact to the culture itself. The environment serves as a marker of social identity and traditional values for the people of the circumpolar North. Increases in industrial activity and marine transportation will naturally be evaluated on global and national scales by corporate entities and participating states—yet impacts of those activities, both positive and negative, will be felt most acutely on regional and local levels. The need for a comprehensive view of climate change and its far-reaching effects, one that encompasses scientific knowledge, traditional knowledge, and social awareness, is widely agreed upon.[34] A 2009 report of the Arctic Council, *Arctic Offshore Oil and Gas Guidelines*, contains a suite of recommendations for protecting living resources, cultural values, and human activities in the region.[35] By the same token, the authors of the ACIA report acknowledge that theirs is an attempt at such a wide-ranging collection of data, and one that should lead to further explorations of the issue. Mary Simon, Canada's former Ambassador for Circumpolar Affairs, puts it this way:

> Protecting the Arctic and its people from the effects of climate change continues to occupy centre stage in the minds of many northerners and governments. Sound knowledge is an essential foundation for the integrated decision-making and risk management that will be necessary for the Arctic, where the sensitive environment and societal vulnerability are insufficiently understood.[36]

If such sentiments were few during the Prudhoe Bay debates of the late 1960s and early 1970s, or at least regularly dismissed as ramblings from the very fringe of acceptable discourse, that they are commonplace and wholly unremarkable today is a marker of both how far the conversation has progressed and the distance it still needs to go.

THE TANKER'S END

Stan Haas left Humble a few years after the company terminated the *Manhattan* test. Believing that the two arctic voyages had successfully proven the concept—not to mention validated the years of work he'd put into the effort—a slightly embittered Haas could only cite boardroom politics as the reason why Humble abandoned the project. He kept himself apprised of the ongoing construction of the Alaska pipeline, noting with skepticism and even incredulity the many engineering foibles and skyrocketing costs of the effort. Haas worked for a small oil exploration company for a time and kept in contact with his Humble associates and fellow tanker enthusiasts.

The men traded letters about the Arctic and speculated about when tankers might again be called upon to sail the Northwest Passage.[37]

On November 13, 1973, Congress passed the Trans-Alaska Pipeline Authorization Act, which barred further judicial review over the project's compliance with environmental statutes. Coming on the heels of the OPEC oil embargo, the act effectively cleared the way for long-delayed pipeline construction to begin.[38] The following spring, the industry began work on what came to be known as the haul road, a supply line connecting Fairbanks with Prudhoe Bay, enabling full-scale pipeline construction across all of Alaska. Three years later, the largest privately financed construction project in history went into operation with the long-awaited arrival of crude oil at Valdez. The ARCO *Juneau* sailed a few days later with her cargo of the first barrels of crude oil bound for the Lower 48.

The very first barrel of Prudhoe Bay crude was, of course, the golden barrel ferried to New York onboard the *Manhattan* in 1969. Humble shipped the barrel to its Houston headquarters, where it remained on display in the lobby for many years. The company produced numerous small, ceremonial vials that featured the official *Manhattan* logo and contained a small amount of oil from the golden barrel. The vials were handed out to VIPs. The golden barrel itself ended up at the Smithsonian Institution, where today it is stored in a wooden crate in a nondescript brick warehouse in Newington, Virginia.

❖ ❖ ❖

On July 7, 1987, the Joint Typhoon Warning Center (JTWC), a task force of the U.S. Navy and Air Force based in Pearl Harbor, Hawaii, observed strong surface winds in the South Pacific roughly five hundred miles southeast of Guam. The area is a prolific spawning ground for tropical storms, especially in the spring and summer. It gives rise to up to a couple dozen each year, a handful of which grow with such intensity they become super typhoons, storms that achieve sustained surface winds of 130 knots (about sixty-five meters per second) and are comparable to a category 5 hurricane. This particular system, if one could even call it that, was developing much more slowly than those meteorologists at JTWC usually observed. They called it "poorly organized" in the official log. A cyclonic circulation pattern began to develop, however, and the JTWC tagged the event a tropical disturbance.[39]

Just eight hours later wind speeds reached twenty knots and the JTWC issued an official cyclone formation alert. The system soon crossed a low pressure ridge that kicked its wind speeds even higher. It was now a tropical depression. Twelve hours later winds hit a sustained fifty knots and JTWC upgraded the system to a tropical storm. Before long aerial reconnaissance flights measured winds in excess of eighty knots and detected a banding eye besides. Winds would soon top out at 130 knots.

It was now a typhoon. Thelma was her name.

Typhoon Thelma moved due west toward the Philippines, turning sharply to the north on July 9. Although the storm's eye came no closer to Luzon than 350 miles, heavy rains and stormy seas resulted in at least twelve deaths there. Thelma was already losing intensity by this point—her reign as a super typhoon lasted only a few hours before meteorologists downgraded her again—but she remained a dangerous weather system as she moved north between Taiwan and Okinawa, Japan.

Thelma slammed into Pusan, South Korea, on July 15. Torrential rains resulted in massive flooding and mudslides that buried entire neighborhoods. The Kumgang River overflowed its banks and destroyed roads and bridges for its entire length. Eight hundred schoolchildren, teachers, and parents on a field trip had to be rescued by army helicopters. What had been a bumper rice crop was wiped out by the twenty-five inches of rain that fell that single day. The storm killed at least 123 people, with another 212 listed as missing and presumed dead. Despite the alerts and widespread foreknowledge of Thelma's approach, many of the missing were fishermen caught in the open sea.[40]

Another casualty of Typhoon Thelma was the SS *Manhattan*. She'd been docked in Yaesu, a port city just west of Pusan, and sustained heavy damage from the storm. The tanker had long skirted the margins of economic profitability even when healthy, and Hudson Waterways Corporation, a subsidiary of Seatrain and her current owner, decided the cost of her repairs was not worth the effort. The company sold the *Manhattan* to Cheerglory Traders of Hong Kong, who had the vessel towed to one of its scrapyards in China.[41] Whether anyone at the demolition facility realized the damaged tanker had once made history is not known. What is certain is that no part of the first commercial vessel to complete the Northwest Passage was saved for its historical value. The ship's wheel, for example, would have made a fine addition to any maritime museum. But it was not to be. In both shipbuilding and oil drilling, economics have always ruled the day, and the recyclable steel of the *Manhattan*'s hull was more valuable to Cheerglory Traders than either nostalgia or tradition. The ship that had survived the arctic ice pack and was once the most famous vessel in the world finally went the way of countless others that sailed the Northwest Passage—crushed and dismantled and ultimately lost to history.

Endnotes

Notes to the Introduction

1. A number of books feature comprehensive accounts of the Trans-Alaska Pipeline, specifically its start of operation in 1977. See Peter A. Coates, *The Trans-Alaska Pipeline Controversy: Technology, Conservation, and the Frontier* (Fairbanks: University of Alaska, 1993); Robert Douglas Mead, *Journeys Down the Line: Building the Trans-Alaska Pipeline* (Garden City, NY: Doubleday & Company, 1978); Jack Roderick, *Crude Dreams: A Personal History of Oil and Politics in Alaska* (Fairbanks: Epicenter Press, 1997).

2. "Berthing Schedule for Oil Tankers," *Valdez Vanguard*, 12 October 1977, 5; "Oil Tanker Schedule in Bay," *Valdez Vanguard*, 26 October 1977, 2.

3. Mead, 513.

4. Dan Lawn, interview by author, 20 May 2011.

5. Mead, 423–26.

6. George Horne, "Giant U.S. Tanker Named in Boston," *New York Times*, 11 January 1962, 66.

7. Humble Oil and Refining Company, "Arctic Tanker Test 1969, Humble's Maiden Northwest Passage Voyage, General Information," SS *Manhattan* Report No. 208 (1969), iii–iv. In 1977, Exxon (previously Humble) organized its collection of project reports and assigned a unique number to each under the heading "SS *Manhattan* Arctic Marine Project." See note at the beginning of bibliography. Reports from this series are hereafter cited in this book as Author, "Title of Report," SS *Manhattan* Report No. xx (date, if known), page(s).

8. William D. Smith, *Northwest Passage* (New York: American Heritage Press, 1970), 15–16.

9. Horne, 66; Mead, 514–17.

10. Smith, *Northwest Passage*, 16.

11. Roxanne Willis, *Alaska's Place in the West: From the Last Frontier to the Last Great Wilderness* (Lawrence: University Press of Kansas, 2010), 94.

12. Roderick, 78–79.

13. Coates, *The Trans-Alaska Pipeline Controversy*, 206–16.

14. Peter A. Coates is one such historian who explores these social contexts in relation to the technological and scientific developments that led to the Trans-Alaska Pipeline. See in particular Coates, *The Trans-Alaska Pipeline Controversy*, chapters 7–8.

15. Leo Marx, "Technology: The Emergence of a Hazardous Concept," *Technology and Culture* 51, no. 3 (July 2010), 577.

16. Quoted in Ken Coates, et al., *Arctic Front: Defending Canada in the Far North* (Toronto: Thomas Allen Publishers, 2008), 97.

17. Merritt R. Helfferich, "The Cruise of the *Manhattan*," *Alaska Geographic* 1, no. 1 (1972), 44.

Notes to Chapter 1

1. Walter J. Hickel, *The Wit and Wisdom of Wally Hickel*, ed. Malcolm B. Roberts (Anchorage: Searchers Press, 1994), 111.

2. Sir John Franklin, *Narrative of a Second Expedition to the Shores of the Polar Sea in the Years 1825, 1826, and 1827* (Philadelphia: Carey, Lea, and Carey, 1828), 139. Some secondary sources refer to Franklin's vessels as boats, others canoes. The distinction merits explanation. Franklin used birch-bark canoes in his first arctic expedition of 1819. He found the canoes suitable for the rivers of arctic Canada but too lightweight for the pounding of the surf in the open sea. Accordingly, for his second expedition, which began in 1825, he commissioned more sturdy vessels made partly of mahogany on frames of ash. He referred to them as "freight canoes," twenty-six-foot-long vessels that could travel under sail or by oar. After testing them in the Thames River prior to the expedition, Franklin proclaimed the vessels "as much like a north canoe as was consistent with the stability and capacity required for their voyage at sea." In his official record of the expedition, however, Franklin consistently refers to the vessels as "boats." Their significant size and the fact they were usually under sail has led most historians to prefer that term. It should be noted that at the time he discovered and named Prudhoe Bay in mid-August 1826, Franklin and his men had lowered the sails and were paddling the vessels along the shoreline. See Ann Savours, *The Search for the Northwest Passage* (New York: St. Martin's Press, 1999), 81–82.

3. Brendan Lehane, *The Northwest Passage* (Alexandria, VA: Time-Life Books, 1981), 110; Savours, 93.

4. Ken Ross, *Environmental Conflict in Alaska* (Boulder: University Press of Colorado, 2000), 145.

5. Charles Brower, *Fifty Years Below Zero: A Lifetime of Adventure in the Far North* (Fairbanks: University of Alaska Press, 1994), 84–85.

6. Quoted in Neil M. Clark, "Ships North to Alaska's Coast," *Montana: The Magazine of Western History* (Fall 1973), 36.

7. Phillip S. Smith et al., *Mineral Resources of Alaska: Report on Progress of Investigations in 1924, Bulletin 783* (Washington, DC: Government Printing Office, 1926), 164–66.

8. Wallace E. Pratt, "Oil Fields in the Arctic," *Harper's*, January 1944, 109. In 1971, three years after the Prudhoe Bay discovery vindicated Pratt's assessment of the Arctic, he was asked about his remarkable foresight. Pratt downplayed the compliment: "Hell's bells. Both the surface and subsurface evidence has been there all along for anyone to see. No question about it. We were bound to make a strike eventually." See W. L. Copithorne, "The Worlds of Wallace Pratt," *The Lamp* 53, no. 3 (Fall 1971), 11–14.

9. Coates, *The Trans-Alaska Pipeline Controversy*, 74–75; Roderick, 41.

10. James Bamberg, *British Petroleum and Global Oil, 1950–1975: The Challenge of Nationalism* (Cambridge: Cambridge University Press, 2000), 188; Roderick, 124.

11. Bamberg, 189.

12. Ibid., 190.

13. Charles S. Jones, *From the Rio Grande to the Arctic: The Story of the Richfield Oil Corporation* (Norman: University of Oklahoma Press, 1972), 81–85.

14. Ibid., 283.

15. Roderick, 79–83; Ross, 145; John Strohmeyer, *Extreme Conditions: Big Oil and the Transformation of Alaska* (Anchorage: Cascade Press, 1997), 45.

16. Roderick, 138.

17. Daniel Yergin, *The Prize: The Epic Quest for Oil, Money, and Power* (New York: Simon & Schuster, 1992), 108–10; Anthony Sampson, *The Seven Sisters: The Great Oil Companies and the World They Made* (New York: Viking Press, 1975), 32–34. Sampson writes that the dissolution of Standard did not quite weaken the smaller companies, but provided the incentive for them to expand and, in the case of Jersey, become an even greater world power. In addition to acquiring Humble, Jersey also turned its attention overseas and eventually secured production in the Middle East, thereby solidifying its base of power internationally. Sampson credits the 1911 breakup with paradoxically spawning a different type of monster. See Sampson, 49–51.

18. William P. Barrett, "Humble Pie," *Forbes*, 19 October 1992, 58–61.

19. Bennett H. Wall, *Growth in a Changing Environment: A History of Standard Oil Company (New Jersey), Exxon Corporation, 1950–1975* (New York: McGraw-Hill, 1988), 23–24.

20. Yergin, 409.

21. Humble Oil and Refining Company, *1954 Annual Report*, 4.

22. Humble Oil and Refining Company, *1955 Annual Report*, 5.

23. Humble Oil and Refining Company, *1956 Annual Report*, 4.

24. *1956 Annual Report*, 12–13; Wall, 134.

25. Wallace E. Pratt, "Petroleum in the North," in *Compass of the World: A Symposium on Political Geography*, eds. Hans W. Weigert and Vilhjalmur Stefansson (New York: MacMillan, 1944), 342–43.

26. Katherine Johnson Ringsmuth, *Beyond the Moon Crater Myth: A New History of the Aniakchak Landscape, A Historic Resource Study for Aniakchak National Monument and Preserve*, U.S. Department of the Interior (2007), 95–97.

27. Roderick, 28–29.

28. Ibid., 29–30.

29. Robert B. Blodgett and Bryan Sralla, "A Major Unconformity Between Permian and Triassic Strata at Cape Kekurnoi, Alaska Peninsula: Old and New Observations on Stratigraphy and Hydrocarbon Potential," U.S. Geological Survey Professional Paper 1739-E (2006), 2–3.

30. Wall, 135–36.

31. Earl Grammer is one of the more notable characters in the history of Alaska oil development for his indefatigable exploration of the Alaska Peninsula. For over four decades he tramped the area, long after his partners (and nearly everyone else) had abandoned the effort. On February 22, 1938, he wrote in his diary, "18 years ago our stampede party

landed at Cold Bay. Of the 17 members, 3 of us are still in this country.... I am the only one who still retains interests in the oil." See Earl Grammer, diary entry, 22 February 1938, Folder 13, Earl Grammer Papers, Alaska and Polar Regions Collections, Rasmuson Library, University of Alaska Fairbanks. Jack Roderick knew Grammer personally in the 1950s and writes about the prospector in his memoir. See Roderick, 19–31.

32. Humble Oil and Refining Company, *1957 Annual Report*, 10; Roderick, 30–31; "Bear Creek No. 1," *Alaska Scouting Service* 5, no. 6 (10 February 1959).

33. "More Exploratory Drilling Seen Needed for Alaska Oil," *Fairbanks Daily News-Miner*, 2 September 1958, 12.

34. In 2006, Blodgett and Sralla reexamined the Bear Creek No. 1 well data and disagreed with Humble's conclusion that the well did not penetrate the Triassic strata. See Blodgett and Sralla, 3–11.

35. Wall, 135.

36. Humble Oil and Refining Company, *1958 Annual Report*, 2–5.

37. "Humble Cuts Staff Here," *Anchorage Daily Times*, 19 July 1960, 1. In an interview sixteen years after the closing of the Anchorage office, Carl Reistle stated that Morgan Davis's reaction to the Bear Creek failure was definitive: "Let's get the hell out of here!" See Wall, 135–36.

38. Wall, 136.

39. *1958 Annual Report*, 5.

40. Wall, 62.

41. Ibid., 134–36.

42. Ibid., 137–38.

43. Jones, 302–15.

44. Roderick, 199–200; Strohmeyer, 55–56; Yergin, 571.

45. Wall, 139.

46. Mead, 79–87. The organization known as TAPS existed from its founding in October 1968 until mid-1970, when it was replaced by the Alyeska Pipeline Service Company. The acronym TAPS has since been used to refer to the pipeline itself, not the company that operates it.

Notes to Chapter 2

1. Sampson, 58.

2. Smith, *Northwest Passage*, 11–12.

3. Stanley B. Haas, "Marine Transport—The Northwest Passage Project," in *Proceedings of the Twentieth Alaska Science Conference*, ed. Eleanor C. Viereck (College, AK: American Association for the Advancement of Science, 1970), 76–78.

4. "Men of the S.S. *Manhattan*" (Humble Oil press release, 3 June 1969), Stanley B. Haas Papers, held by Charla Bauer, Floral City, Florida, copies in author's possession (hereafter cited as SBH).

5. U.S. Senate, Committee on Interior and Insular Affairs, *The Status of the Proposed Trans-Alaska Pipeline*, Part 1, 91st Congress, 1st Session, 9 September 1969, 33–34 (hereafter cited as TAPS Hearings).

6. A. D. Mookhoek and R. L. Vukin, "Arctic Tanker Test: Objectives, Program, Procedures, and Data Acquisition and Usage Systems," SS *Manhattan* Arctic Marine Project, Report No. 207 (15 July 1969), 1.

7. A. H. G. Storrs and T. C. Pullen, "S.S. *Manhattan* in Arctic Waters," *Canadian Geographic Journal* 80, no. 5 (May 1970), 170.

8. Stanley B. Haas, "Arctic Tanker Test Presentation," speech, 30 January 1969, 2–3, SBH.

9. Smith, *Northwest Passage*, 13.

10. German & Milne and Northern Associates, "Arctic Transportation Feasibility Study, Ship Data and Operations," SS *Manhattan* Report No. 334 (undated); German & Milne, "Esso *Manhattan*, Recommendations Covering Alterations Necessary to Fit Vessel for Arctic Service," SS *Manhattan* Report No. 336 (January 1969).

11. Stanley B. Haas, "Through the Northwest Passage," speech, 2, SBH; Smith, *Northwest Passage*, 12–14; Humble Oil and Refining Company, *Through the Northwest Passage*, videorecording, 1970 (hereafter cited as Humble videorecording).

12. Wall, 141.

13. Yergin, 35–44, 96–110.

14. Maurice Cutler, "Voyage Opens Wide Arctic Door," *Oilweek* 20, no. 39 (17 November 1969), 18–19.

15. Stanley B. Haas, "Suggested Ocean Vessel Names," undated memorandum, SBH.

16. "The Fabulous Adventure," *Esso Marine News* 14, no. 2 (1969), ii.

17. Haas, "Arctic Tanker Test Presentation," 1–8; Smith, *Northwest Passage*, 75; Joe Tucker, "Lessons from the Arctic," *Humble Way* 10, no. 1 (1971), 15.

18. Haas, "Arctic Tanker Test Presentation," 3–4, 7 (emphasis in original).

19. Ibid., 8–9.

20. Wall, 142.

21. William O. Gray, interview by author, 8 January 2007.

22. W. O. Gray and R. Maybourn, "*Manhattan*'s Arctic Venture—A Semitechnical History," paper presented at the Society of Naval Architects and Marine Engineers, Spring Meeting/STAR Symposium, Ottawa, Ontario, Canada, 17–19 June 1981, 2.

23. Haas, "Marine Transport—The Northwest Passage Project," 79; Smith, *Northwest Passage*, 16–17.

24. Gray and Maybourn, 4–5.

25. Haas, "Marine Transport—The Northwest Passage Project," 80; Mead, 113; Smith, *Northwest Passage*, 17–18.

26. Humble Oil and Refining Company, "Feasibility of Tanker Operations in Arctic Ice, Volume I," SS *Manhattan* Report No. 315 (undated), 1–3.

27. Humble Oil and Refining Company, "Miscellaneous Notes and Correspondence, SS *Manhattan*, Volume II," SS *Manhattan* Report No. 241 (undated), 1; Virgil F. Keith, "Across the Top," date and publication unknown, 62, SBH.

28. Roderick M. White, "Dynamically Developed Force at the Bow of an Icebreaker," Ph.D. diss., Massachusetts Institute of Technology, September 1965.

29. Helfferich, 44; Keith, 61; Storrs and Pullen, 171; Sydney Wire, "The SS *Manhattan*'s Northwest Passage Voyage," paper presented to Annual Tanker Conference of the Central

Committee on Transportation by Water of the Division of Transportation of the American Petroleum Institute, 27 April 1970, 2, Box 2.207/J60, ExxonMobil Historical Collection, Center for American History, University of Texas at Austin.

30. TAPS Hearings, Part 2, 105.

31. Coates, *The Trans-Alaska Pipeline Controversy*, 177–78; Roderick, 286.

32. Coates, *The Trans-Alaska Pipeline Controversy*, 178–83; Ross, 147, 151; Yergin, 573; Mary Clay Berry, *The Alaska Pipeline: The Politics of Oil and Native Land Claims* (Bloomington: Indiana University Press, 1975), 106.

33. TAPS Hearings, Part 2, 135.

34. TAPS Hearings, Part 1, 29.

35. Berry, 115. Hickel recalled the industry's quest for permits in his 1971 book, *Who Owns America?*: "In the early days of the pipeline proposal, it became evident that Trans Alaska Pipeline System (TAPS), the organization seeking to build the line, was concerned only with getting a permit—not with designing a safe line *first*—before a spadeful of dirt was turned.... We had to turn this attitude around—and we eventually did." See Walter J. Hickel, *Who Owns America?* (Englewood Cliffs, NJ: Prentice-Hall, 1971), 125 (emphasis in original).

36. Hickel, *Who Owns America?*, 125–26; Mead, 87; Terry F. Lenzner, *The Management, Planning and Construction of the Trans-Alaska Pipeline System: Report to the Alaska Pipeline Commission*, State of Alaska Report, 1 August 1977, II-43.

37. Wall, 142; Lenzner, chapter II, 1–60. Terry F. Lenzner was retained by the Alaska Pipeline Commission in 1976–1977 to report on the "costs and charges incurred by the Alyeska Pipeline Service Company [successor to TAPS] during the construction of the Trans-Alaska Pipeline." Of particular interest to the State of Alaska was the extent to which inefficient management and general incompetence on the part of Alyeska contributed to massive cost overruns. Such excessive and unnecessary expenditures could be withheld from the calculation of the pipeline tariff, thereby increasing revenue to the state. Chapter II of Lenzner's report, "TAPS Organization and Management Structure," describes the bureaucratic and inefficient nature of TAPS as it was first organized.

38. Mead, 87.

39. Nubar Gulbenkian, *Pantaraxia* (London: Hutchinson, 1965), 96.

Notes to Chapter 3

1. Pratt, "Oil Fields in the Arctic," 109–12.

2. The first section of this chapter was published in revised form as Ross Coen, "Submarines, Blimps, Trains, and Ships: Transportation Proposals for Prudhoe Bay Crude Oil, 1968–1977," *Oil-Industry History* 4, no. 1 (2003), 55–66.

3. William D. Smith, "Submarine Fleet Urged for Alaskan Oil," *New York Times*, 17 December 1969, 93.

4. Lawrence R. Jacobsen, "Subsea Transport of Arctic Oil—A Technical and Economic Evaluation," paper presented to the Third Annual Offshore Technology Conference, Houston, Texas, 19 April 1971, 95–122; Mead, 164–65.

5. Quoted in Vilhjalmur Stefansson, *Northwest to Fortune* (New York: Duell, Sloan and Pearce, 1958), 333–35.

6. Jacobsen, 97.

7. Coates, *The Trans-Alaska Pipeline Controversy*, 197; Jacobsen, 102; Mead, 164–65; U.S. Department of the Interior, *Draft Environmental Impact Statement for the Trans-Alaska Pipeline Section 102(2)c of the National Environmental Policy Act of 1969* (Washington, DC: Government Printing Office, 1971), 162 (hereafter cited as DEIS).

8. U.S. Department of Commerce, *Arctic Submarine Transportation System—1975: Volume I—Executive Summary* (Washington, DC: Government Printing Office, 1975), 3.1.

9. Ibid., 3.5, 5.2, 6.3.

10. As late as 1984, some still advocated the use of submarine tankers as a "backup" to the Trans-Alaska Pipeline, then in its seventh year of operation. William H. Kumm revived the concept, calling for non-nuclear submarines powered by hydrogen/oxygen fuel cells. Kumm took after his predecessors in the field by citing the cost-effectiveness of such a system as its primary advantage. See William H. Kumm, "Non-nuclear Submarine Could Cost-Effectively Move Arctic Oil and Gas," *Oil & Gas Journal*, 5 March 1984, 76–79.

11. Coates, *The Trans-Alaska Pipeline Controversy*, 198; Mead, 164–65; The Wilderness Society, Environmental Defense Fund, Inc., Friends of the Earth, *Comments on the Environmental Impact Statement for the Trans-Alaska Pipeline*, Volumes I–IV, May 1972 (hereafter cited as *Comments*).

12. *DEIS*, 162; Richard A. Rice, "Comment on the Revised Trans-Alaska Pipeline Impact Statement," *Comments*, Vol. II, Section N; Charles J. Cicchetti, *Alaskan Oil: Alternate Routes and Markets* (Baltimore: Johns Hopkins University Press, 1972), 58–85; E. L. Patton, "Hearing Testimony," booklet produced by Alyeska Pipeline Service Company, February 1971, 7. Even before 1968, Alaska Governor Wally Hickel strongly advocated the construction of a railroad through the Alaskan Arctic and under the Bering Strait to Siberia. Such a link, he argued, would open for development the vast storehouse of natural resources found in northern Alaska, including coal, copper, and iron ore. Hickel also believed that a railroad would lead to large metropolitan areas in the Arctic, a vision he hoped to see realized by the year 2000. Following the Prudhoe Bay strike Hickel again pushed for an arctic railroad, not to transport oil but to serve as the support line for pipeline construction. He formed the NORTH Commission (Northern Operations of Rail Transportation and Highways) and obtained a $750,000 appropriation from the state legislature to begin preliminary work on the concept. As of this writing, a rail link to the North Slope has yet to be established, and Fairbanks remains the northern terminus of the Alaska Railroad. See Hickel, *Who Owns America?*, 187–90; "Alaska Strikes It Rich," *U.S. News & World Report*, 9 December 1968, 48–53.

13. *DEIS*, 164–65.

14. "Alaska Strikes It Rich," 50; William S. Ellis, "Will Oil and Tundra Mix? Alaska's North Slope Hangs in the Balance," *National Geographic* 140, no. 4 (October 1971), 492.

15. Coates, *The Trans-Alaska Pipeline Controversy*, 197; Yergin, 572; "Alternatives to the Pipeline," *Alaska Construction & Oil*, September 1975, 8.

16. *DEIS*, 167.

17. *Comments*, Vol. II, Section O.

18. *Comments*, Vol. II, Section O; *DEIS*, 165–66.

19. Mead, 165.

20. Coates, *The Trans-Alaska Pipeline Controversy*, 21.

21. William O. Gray to Stanley B. Haas, 23 August 1969, SBH.

22. W. O. Gray, "Schedule Meeting at Sun—3 April," memorandum, 9 April 1969, SBH.

23. W. O. Gray to S. B. Haas, 9 April 1969, SBH.

24. Downs Matthews to Elizabeth R. Rogers, 7 July 1969, Box 122, Folder 11, Sierra Club Records, Bancroft Library, University of California, Berkeley.

25. Wall, 132–33.

26. "*Manhattan* Story Told in Video Conference," *Humble News*, July 1969, 8–11. Humble originally planned to host the news conference in New York, Washington, *and* Houston, with additional speakers in all three cities, including Master Roger Steward of the *Manhattan*, U.S. Coast Guard Captain Frederick A. Goettel, and Canadian Department of Transport Captain Thomas C. Pullen. The event was ultimately scaled back, perhaps for logistical reasons. See "Public Relations Plan, Arctic Tanker Test," 10 April 1969, SBH.

27. M. A. Wright, "The 500-Year Dream," speech, 3 June 1969, 3, SBH.

28. Jack F. Bennett, "Moving Arctic Oil to Market," speech, 3 June 1969, 4, SBH.

29. Stanley B. Haas, "The Voyage of the S.S. *Manhattan*," speech, 3 June 1969, 4, SBH.

30. Charles F. Jones, "Future Implications," speech, 3 June 1969, 4, SBH. Charles F. Jones of Humble should not be confused with Charles S. Jones, president of the Richfield Oil Corporation and later board chairman of Atlantic Richfield.

31. Ibid., 4 (emphasis in original).

32. "Project Northwest Passage," press release, 3 June 1969, 3, SBH; Smith, *Northwest Passage*, 18; Storrs and Pullen, 172.

33. Smith, *Northwest Passage*, 41; E. H. W. Platt, "SS *Manhattan* Experiment, Notes on Technical Discussions in U.S.A., Jan/Feb 1969," memorandum, 5 March 1969, 10, SBH.

34. Gray and Maybourn, 12.

35. Smith, *Northwest Passage*, 41–42.

Notes to Chapter 4

1. Eric Nalder, *Tankers Full of Trouble: The Perilous Journey of Alaskan Crude* (New York: Grove Press, 1994), xv.

2. Tom Brown, "Alaska Science Conference Opens," *Anchorage Daily News*, 25 August 1969, 1.

3. Edgar Wayburn, "A Conservationist's Concern About Arctic Development," in *Change in Alaska: People, Petroleum, and Politics*, ed. George W. Rogers (College: University of Alaska Press, 1970), 171 (hereafter cited as Rogers, *Change in Alaska*).

4. For a comprehensive account of the creation of the Arctic National Wildlife Range/Refuge, see Roger Kaye, *Last Great Wilderness: The Campaign to Establish the Arctic National Wildlife Refuge* (Fairbanks: University of Alaska Press, 2006). For a general history of conservation in Alaska, including the roles played by Muir, Sheldon, Leopold, the Muries,

and others, see Douglas Brinkley, *The Quiet World: Saving Alaska's Wilderness Kingdom, 1879–1960* (New York: Harper Collins, 2011).

5. Brown, "Alaska Science Conference Opens," 1.

6. Tom Brown, "The Power of Oil: Conservationist, Oilmen Clash at Conference," *Anchorage Daily News*, 26 August 1969, 1.

7. Tom Brown, "Stevens Blasts the Conservationists," *Anchorage Daily News*, 28 August 1969, 1.

8. For a comprehensive discussion of these themes, see Coates, *The Trans-Alaska Pipeline Controversy*, 28–33, 89–105, 206–16.

9. Keith, 62; Smith, *Northwest Passage*, 11.

10. Humble Oil and Refining Company, "Arctic Tanker Test 1969, Humble's Maiden Northwest Passage Voyage, General Information," SS *Manhattan* Report No. 208 (1969).

11. Lieutenant Commander E. Stolee, "Report on the Voyage in the Canadian Arctic of CCGS *John A. MacDonald*, Summer 1969 (*Manhattan's* Journey)," Canadian Coast Guard report (undated), 51 (hereafter cited as Stolee, 1969 Report).

12. Smith, *Northwest Passage*, 43–44.

13. Roger Benedict, "*Manhattan* Voyage May Be Just Futile Exercise, Says 'Journal,'" *Anchorage Daily Times*, 13 September 1969, 6; Humble videorecording; Bern Keating, "North for Oil: *Manhattan* Makes the Historic Northwest Passage," *National Geographic* 137, no. 3 (March 1970), 383; Joe Rychetnik, "Life on the Tanker *Manhattan*; This Is What It Was Like," *Anchorage Daily News*, 19 September 1969, 4; Terry Shannon and Charles Payzant, *Ride the Ice Down! U.S. and Canadian Icebreakers in Arctic Seas* (San Carlos, CA: Golden Gate Junior Books, 1970), 65.

14. "Dinner Menu, S/S *Manhattan*," menu, 16 September 1969, personal papers of Merritt R. Helfferich (hereafter cited as MRH).

15. "Arctic Tanker Test 1969, SS *Manhattan*, Humble's Maiden Northwest Passage Voyage, General Information," 3–4; Smith, *Northwest Passage*, 56–57.

16. Charles Swithinbank, *Forty Years on Ice: A Lifetime of Exploration and Research in the Polar Regions* (Sussex, England: The Book Guild Ltd., 1998), 42.

17. Smith, *Northwest Passage*, 45.

18. "Maritime Administrator Extends Best Wishes to SS *Manhattan*," press release, 24 August 1969, SBH.

19. "Coast Guard News: 89–69," press release, 23 August 1969, SBH; W. J. Smith to M. A. Wright, 10 March 1969, SBH.

20. Smith, *Northwest Passage*, 94.

21. Lieutenant Colonel Charles J. Fiala, *Alaskan Oil: An Assessment of the North Slope's Implications for Our Strategic Policies Toward Major Producer and Consumer Countries* (Carlisle Barracks, PA: U.S. Army War College, 1970), 25.

22. Christopher Kirkey, "The Arctic Waters Pollution Prevention Initiatives: Canada's Response to an American Challenge," *International Journal of Canadian Studies* 13 (1996), 46.

23. John Kirton and Don Munton, "The *Manhattan* Voyages and Their Aftermath," in *Politics of the Northwest Passage*, ed. Franklyn Griffiths (Kingston, ON: McGill-Queen's University Press, 1987), 72–73 (hereafter cited as Griffiths, *Politics of the Northwest Passage*).

24. Ibid., 76.

25. Kirkey, 47; Brian Meredith, "A Plan for the Arctic: Mr. Trudeau's International Regime," *The Round Table* (1970), 178.

26. U.S. Department of the Interior and U.S. Department of Transportation, *A Report on Pollution of the Nation's Waters by Oil and Other Hazardous Substances* (Washington, DC: Government Printing Office, 1968), 14–15.

27. Robert A. Shinn, *The International Politics of Marine Pollution Control* (New York: Praeger, 1974), 50.

28. Ibid., 64, 111.

29. Ibid., 65–66.

30. John Livingston, *Arctic Oil* (Toronto: Canadian Broadcasting Corporation, 1981), 73–74.

31. Shinn, 67–76.

32. Ibid., 76–77.

33. Shelagh D. Grant, *Polar Imperative: A History of Arctic Sovereignty in North America* (Vancouver: Douglas & McIntyre, 2010), 155–67.

34. D. M. McRae, "The Negotiation of Article 234," in Griffiths, *Politics of the Northwest Passage*, 98.

35. Grant, 230–32.

36. Anne M. Fisher, "Establishing Sovereignty in the Canadian Arctic," *The Musk-ox* 37 (1989), 198–99.

37. Kirton and Munton, 71.

38. Fisher, 199; Donald R. Rothwell, "Australian and Canadian Initiatives in Polar Marine Environmental Protection: A Comparative Review," *Polar Record* 34, no. 191 (1998), 306.

39. Kirton and Munton, 71–73.

40. Jean-Claude Paquet, "Wealth Below the Ice," *La Presse*, 20 October 1969, 30. The original article is in French. The passage quoted here is taken from a translation found in SS *Manhattan* Collection, Record Group 12, Vol. 3855, File 13, Library and Archives Canada, Ottawa.

41. Quoted in Kirton and Munton, 75.

42. Grant, 352–53; Kirton and Munton, 80.

43. Fisher, 199; Rothwell, 313; Shinn, 77.

44. Kirton and Munton, 91.

45. Fisher, 200; Rothwell, 306.

46. Shinn, 79.

47. Grant, 350–52; Kirton and Munton, 69–70; Rothwell, 306; Shinn, 78.

48. Grant, 450.

49. Fisher, 199–200; Thomas C. Pullen and Charles Swithinbank, "Transits of the Northwest Passage, 1906–90," *Polar Record* 27, no. 163 (October 1991), 365–66.

50. McRae, 99.

51. *United Nations Convention on the Law of the Sea*, Part XII, Section 8, Article 234 (10 December 1982), 115–16.

52. Shinn, 77.

53. Quoted in Coates, *Arctic Front*, 98.

54. Joe Clark, "Statement on Sovereignty, 10 September 1985," in *Politics of the Northwest Passage*, 270–71.

55. Coates, *Arctic Front*, 189.

56. Protection of the Arctic Marine Environment, *Arctic Marine Shipping Assessment 2009 Report*, report of the Arctic Council (2009), 50.

57. Ibid, 54.

58. Ibid, 114.

Notes to Chapter 5

1. Hickel, *Who Owns America?*, 140.

2. Lawson W. Brigham, "Icebreaker," in *Encyclopedia of the Arctic*, Vol. 2, ed. Mark Nuttall (New York: Routledge, 2005), 917–19; Pullen and Swithinbank, 365–66; Savours, 326.

3. Edwin A. MacDonald, *Polar Operations* (Annapolis, MD: U.S. Naval Institute, 1969), 34–36.

4. Michael Whitby, "Showing the Flag Across the North: HMCS *Labrador* and the 1954 Transit of the Northwest Passage," *Canadian Naval Review* 2, no. 1 (Spring 2006), 21–24.

5. Keith, 63.

6. Smith, *Northwest Passage*, 68.

7. Stolee, 1969 Report, 96.

8. Captain Paul Fournier, "Report of CCGS *John A. MacDonald* Voyage Through the Northwest Passage and Back with SS *Manhattan*: September–November 1969," Canadian Coast Guard report (undated), 2 (hereafter cited as Fournier, *MacDonald* Report).

9. Bern Keating, *The Northwest Passage: From the Mathew to the Manhattan: 1497 to 1969* (Chicago: Rand McNally & Company, 1970), 143; Keith, 63.

10. Stolee, 1969 Report, 81.

11. Smith, *Northwest Passage*, 76.

12. Keating, *The Northwest Passage*, 143.

13. W. F. Weeks, *On Sea Ice* (Fairbanks: University of Alaska Press, 2010), 331.

14. Fournier, *MacDonald* Report, 2; Keith, 61–63; Smith, *Northwest Passage*, 77.

15. Keating, *The Northwest Passage*, 142.

16. Rychetnik, 4.

17. Keating, *The Northwest Passage*, 143.

18. Smith, *Northwest Passage*, 77.

19. Alan Day, *Historical Dictionary of the Discovery and Exploration of the Northwest Passage* (Lanham, MD: Scarecrow Press, 2006), 229.

20. "News," Humble Oil press release, 3 September 1969, SBH.

21. Helfferich, 47–48.

22. Smith, *Northwest Passage*, 78–79.

23. Ibid., 80.

24. Stolee, 1969 Report, 58.

25. Ibid., 82.

26. "The Norther 1969," ed. Werner Eberhard (yearbook, private collection of Mike Dorsey, Eagle River, Alaska), 6.

27. Rear Admiral R. E. Hammond, Commander 17th Coast Guard District, "OPORDER NO. 202 ALPHA 69: CGC NORTHWIND," U.S. Coast Guard memorandum, 5 May 1969, 1–4, A-1; D. J. McCann, Commanding Officer USCGC *Northwind* (WAGB 282), "Arctic West 1969: Phases I & II," U.S. Coast Guard memorandum, 1 August 1969, 1–3; McCann, "CCGD 17 OPORD 202 ALPHA 69: Artic [*sic*] Tanker Evaluation Project," U.S. Coast Guard memorandum, 6 October 1969, 1–4; W. J. Smith to M. A. Wright, 10 March 1969, SBH. While moored at Thule in mid-August, the *Northwind*'s crew received a cable from Coast Guard Commandant Willard J. Smith that read, in part: "You are about to sail in support of the Arctic Tanker Test. In my estimation this is man's most ambitious undertaking in the Arctic seas. This test is certain to have untold effects on our entire nation. As you undertake this mission in the wake of such famous Arctic explorers as Nansen, Perry [*sic*], Amundson [*sic*], and Byrd, you add another chapter to the Coast Guard polar history." See "The Norther 1969," 55.

28. Keating, *The Northwest Passage*, 144. Captain Paul Fournier's post-expedition report noted that the *MacDonald*'s divers observed that at least eighteen feet of the *Manhattan*'s propeller shafting was unprotected, and the rudders similarly appeared to lack adequate ice protection. He did note, however, that this inspection "was not a detailed one" and no conclusions were to be drawn without further information. See Fournier, *MacDonald* Report, 4.

29. Smith, *Northwest Passage*, 69–70.

30. Ed Clarke, interview by author, 27 October 2009.

31. "News," Humble press release, 11 September 1969, SBH.

32. Smith, *Northwest Passage*, 13–14.

33. Lynton K. Caldwell, "Public Policy for the Environment: Some Guidelines for Alaskans," in Rogers, *Change in Alaska*, 137–38.

34. Lynton Keith Caldwell, *Between Two Worlds: Science, the Environmental Movement and Policy Choice* (New York: Cambridge University Press, 1990), 29.

35. Ibid.

36. Paul T. Heywood, "Arctic Tanker Test, SS *Manhattan*, Analyst's Report," SS *Manhattan* Report No. 214 (January 1970), 22.

37. "The Mission Possible Man," *Humble Way* 10, no. 1 (1971), 13.

38. James H. Galloway, "Petroleum Industry Policies for Protecting the Environment," in Rogers, *Change in Alaska*, 164–65.

39. "The Mission Possible Man," 13.

40. Quoted in Tom Brown, *Oil on Ice: Alaskan Wilderness at the Crossroads* (San Francisco: Sierra Club Books, 1971), 93.

41. John Lear, "Northwest Passage to What?," *Saturday Review*, 1 November 1969, 56.

42. Among the many books and articles on this subject, of particular note are Lewis Mumford, "History: Neglected Clue to Technological Change," *Technology & Culture* 2, no. 3 (1961), 230–36; Trevor Pinch and Wiebe Bijker, "The Social Construction of Facts and Artifacts: Or How the Sociology of Science and the Sociology of Technology Might Benefit Each Other," *Social Studies of Science* 14 (1984), 399–441; Merritt Roe Smith and Leo Marx,

eds., *Does Technology Drive History? The Dilemma of Technological Determinism* (Cambridge, MA: MIT Press, 1994).

43. Coates, *The Trans-Alaska Pipeline Controversy*, 189–90.

44. Eben Hopson, "Mayor Eben Hopson's Warning to the People of the Canadian Arctic," booklet produced by North Slope Borough, 21 September 1976, 10.

45. Quoted in Peter Jull, "Inuit Politics and the Arctic Seas," in Griffiths, *Politics of the Northwest Passage*, 56–7.

46. Haas, "Marine Transport—The Northwest Passage Project," 80.

Notes to Chapter 6

1. Paul Nanton, *Arctic Breakthrough: Franklin's Expeditions 1819–1847* (Toronto: Clarke, Irwin, 1970), 94.

2. Some sources identify five distinct water routes through the Canadian Arctic, others six. See "Arctic Marine Shipping Assessment 2009 Report," report of the Arctic Council, Protection of the Arctic Marine Environment Working Group (2009), 20–21.

3. Graham Rowley, "Bringing the Outside Inside," in Griffiths, *Politics of the Northwest Passage*, 30–31. Note that when referring to McClure Strait, many maps and other sources replace the lowercase "c" in McClure with an apostrophe.

4. Keith, 64; Thomas C. Pullen, "We Smashed Through the Northwest Passage," *Petroleum Today* 11, no. 1 (Winter 1970), 7–8; Mike Dalton, "Helen Bentley First Woman to Trek Northwest Passage," *Fairbanks Daily News-Miner*, 16 September 1969, 3.

5. Quoted in Graham Rowley, "Captain T. C. Pullen, RCN: Polar Navigator," *The Northern Mariner* 2, no. 2 (1992), 42. Rowley cites Pullen's personal papers to which he had access in writing the profile.

6. Downs Matthews and Ian N. Higginson, "Dan Guravich (1918–1997)," *Arctic* 51, no. 2 (June 1998), 181–82.

7. H. Charles Baker, interview with author, 22 January 2007.

8. H. Charles Baker, "Northwest Passage: Voyage of the *Manhattan*," *Ocean Industry* 4, no. 8 (August 1969), 32–33. For a technical description of the *Manhattan*'s communications equipment, see A. D. Mookhoek and W. J. Bielstein, "Problems Associated with the Design of an Arctic Marine Transportation System," paper presented at the Third Annual Offshore Technology Conference, Houston, Texas, 19–21 April 1971, 127–28.

9. Earle Gray, "Arctic Ice Sinks Panarctic Barges," *Oilweek* 20, no. 30 (15 September 1969), 22–23; Tom Kennedy, *Quest: Canada's Search for Arctic Oil* (Edmonton, AB: Reidmore Books, 1988), 11–14.

10. Smith, *Northwest Passage*, 106.

11. Helfferich, 50.

12. The *Northwind*'s stay at Thule was interrupted for three days (August 16–18) for a search-and-rescue operation to the *Southwind*, which had run aground in Baffin Bay. Prior to rendezvous, the *Southwind* managed to free herself. The two ships met forty miles southeast of the grounding site, and after transferring supplies to replace those that had

been ruined in the flooded compartments the *Northwind* returned to Thule. See McCann, "CCGD 17 OPORD 202 ALPHA 69: Artic [*sic*] Tanker Evaluation Project," 1–2, A-3–1.

13. Keith, 66.

14. "News," Humble press release, 8 September 1969, SBH.

15. William D. Smith, interview by author, 7 January 2007.

16. Keating, *The Northwest Passage*, 147.

17. Helfferich, 50; Merritt Helfferich, daily journal, 8 September 1969, 3, MRH (hereafter cited as Helfferich journal); Keith, 66; Smith, *Northwest Passage*, 109–10, 178.

18. Smith, *Northwest Passage*, 111. McCann, "CCGD 17 OPORD 202 ALPHA 69: Artic [*sic*] Tanker Evaluation Project," B-4/1–3.

19. Keith, 66–67.

20. Smith, *Northwest Passage*, 114.

21. Mookhoek and Bielstein, 135, 141.

22. Captain J. W. Moreau, "Problems and Developments in Arctic Alaskan Transportation," *Proceedings of the United States Naval Institute* 96, no. 5 (1970), 115.

23. Keating, "North for Oil," 385.

24. Smith, *Northwest Passage*, 113.

25. Swithinbank, *Forty Years on Ice*, 47.

26. Wire, 4.

27. Stolee, 1969 Report, 83.

28. Ibid., 54.

29. Keith, 67; Joe LaRocca, *Alaska Agonistes: The Age of Petroleum: How Big Oil Bought Alaska* (North East, PA: Rare Books, Ink, 2003), 25–26.

30. Smith, *Northwest Passage*, 115.

31. A post-expedition review of the aerial photography program revealed that the quality of side-looking radar imagery was negatively affected by aircraft movement. The pilots often tried to maintain the given flight path by making small course corrections, which resulted in imagery errors. Even the movement of persons inside the aircraft changed the center of gravity just enough to distort the images. The Coast Guard recommended greater controls on future flights. See Humble Oil and Refining Company, "Miscellaneous Notes and Correspondence: Environmental Data," SS *Manhattan* Report No. 605 (undated), 91.

Notes to Chapter 7

1. "Men of the S.S. *Manhattan*," 5.

2. The first section of this chapter was previously published as Ross Coen, "Alaska's Richest Day: The Prudhoe Bay Lease Sale That Brought $900 Million to the 49th State," *Oil-Industry History* 5, no. 1 (2004), 37–49. For general information about the Prudhoe Bay lease sale, see: Berry, 97–101; H. G. Gallagher, *Etok: A Story of Eskimo Power* (New York: G.P. Putnam's Sons, 1974), 176–87; Keith Harvey Miller, *Prudhoe Bay Governor: Alaska's Keith Miller* (Anchorage: Todd Communications, 1997), 201–4; Claus-M. Naske and Herman Slotnick, *Alaska: A History of the 49th State* (Norman: University of Oklahoma Press, 1987) 248–51; Roderick, 267–81.

3. Roderick, 273.

4. ARCO had previously utilized the same method—drawing a large sheet around the well site—in an attempt to keep confidential the results of the first Prudhoe Bay confirmation well. But, as Gil Mull noted, such attempts were often futile: "When we unscrewed the core head from the drill string, what came out on one of the cores instead of solid rock was just a pile of disaggregated sand, gravel, and oil that ran through the rig floor and into the rig cellar. All the roughnecks could immediately tell what was being found." See Roderick, 220.

5. "Oil Firms Remain Mum on North Slope Finds," *Anchorage Daily Times*, 11 September 1969, 1; "Another Well Set on Slope," *Fairbanks Daily News-Miner*, 10 January 1969, 1.

6. John S. Hedland, "The Public Interest and Competitive Leasing of State Oil and Gas Lands," in Rogers, *Change in Alaska*, 96.

7. Ibid., 93.

8. Gregg Erickson, "Alaska's Petroleum Leasing Policy: A Crisis of Direction," in Rogers, *Change in Alaska*, 102.

9. Ibid., 105.

10. Keith Miller, "The Text of Governor Miller's Speech," *Anchorage Daily News*, 10 September 1969, 4.

11. "The Great Oil Hunt," *Newsweek*, 22 September 1969, 80; Roderick, 276–77.

12. "Native Group to Picket," *Anchorage Daily News*, 10 September 1969, 3. Edwardsen would later achieve some measure of national notoriety both for his dynamic personality and militant stance as an Alaska Native opposed to not only oil development but what he saw as the entire patriarchal legacy of the federal government's relationship with Native Americans. In the hallway outside a Congressional hearing on North Slope oil production, for example, Edwardsen famously shouted to reporters: "If the pigs want to use our land, then THE PIGS MUST PAY THE RENT!" See Gallagher, 19–24 (emphasis in original).

13. Gallagher, 24.

14. Ibid., 179.

15. "Native Pickets Say 'Bad Deal at Tom Kelly's Trading Post,'" *Anchorage Daily News*, 11 September 1969, 3.

16. "Oil Work Nixed By Sierra Club," *Anchorage Daily Times*, 9 September 1969, 2.

17. "The Great Oil Hunt," 81.

18. Joe LaRocca, "Sale Questions Remain," *Fairbanks Daily News-Miner*, 11 September 1969, 1.

19. The *Anchorage Daily Times*, the state's largest newspaper, itself had a record day on September 10, 1969. The paper assigned nine reporters to cover the event, and published four editions that day, two exclusively for street sale and two for home delivery. See "Anchorage Times Sets Record, Too," *Anchorage Daily Times*, 11 September 1969, 1.

20. Linda Billington, "Kelly: 'Lease Sale Total Great!,'" *Anchorage Daily News*, 11 September 1969, 4.

21. Roderick, 279–80.

22. Billington, 4.

23. Jack Roderick, interview by author, 12 January 2004.

24. John Havelock, interview by author, 12 January 2004.

25. "Humble Explains Failure to Obtain Tracts on Slope," *Fairbanks Daily News-Miner*, 12 September 1969, 1.

26. Savours, 224.

27. Jonathan M. Karpoff, "McClure, Sir Robert," in *Encyclopedia of the Arctic*, Vol. 2, ed. Mark Nuttall (New York: Routledge, 2005), 1265–67; Savours, 219–30.

28. Fournier, *MacDonald* Report, 5.

29. Fournier, *MacDonald* Report, 5–6; Helfferich journal, 4–5.

30. Arch A. Smith, "Arctic Tanker Test: Media Operation Plan," memorandum, 17 March 1969, 2, SBH.

31. Smith, *Northwest Passage*, 70–71 (emphasis in original).

32. Stan Haas to Jeanne Haas, undated letter, SBH.

33. Smith, *Northwest Passage*, 117.

34. Joe LaRocca, "Resourcefully Yours…," *Fairbanks Daily News-Miner*, 23 September 1969, A-2.

35. Smith, *Northwest Passage*, 99.

36. Fournier, *MacDonald* Report, 5.

37. Roger W. Benedict, "An Epic Voyage—And Some Questions," *Anchorage Daily News*, 19 September 1969, 4.

38. Quoted in Rowley, "Captain T. C. Pullen, RCN: Polar Navigator," 43.

39. Stan Haas, "Steward," undated memorandum, SBH.

40. Smith, *Northwest Passage*, 134.

41. Swithinbank, *Forty Years on Ice*, 52.

42. Arctic Marine Task Force, "Test Voyage Report, 1970 SS *Manhattan* Full Scale Icebreaking Tests," SS *Manhattan* Report No. 221 (3 August 1970), 81.

43. Ibid., 98.

44. "News," Humble press release, 15 September 1969, 1, SBH; Smith, *Northwest Passage*, 130–31.

45. Storrs and Pullen, 175.

46. Earle Gray, "Oil Can Move via NW Passage," *Oilweek* 20, no. 32 (29 September 1969), 27.

47. Keating, "North for Oil," 386.

48. Ibid., 388.

49. "News," Humble press release, 12 September 1969, SBH; Smith, *Northwest Passage*, 127–29.

50. It bears noting that at least one individual on the *Manhattan* believed the vessel could have made it through McClure Strait, but that what he refers to as two "unpublicized factors" apart from the ice caused Humble to abandon the effort. Joe LaRocca, an Alaska journalist who achieved some renown in the 1960s and 1970s as one of the best investigative reporters on Alaska oil issues, wrote about these factors at the time in his newspaper column and again in a book published in 2003. To quote at length from that book, *Alaska Agonistes*: "Humble's credibility gap widened when its own information sources…found the *Manhattan* significantly delayed by heavy ice which, it had been erroneously reported earlier, did not exist. Fact is, the *Manhattan* was forced to retreat from McClure Strait by two virtually unpublicized factors, both unrelated to its own awesome ice-breaking capabilities.

One involved its ice-crippled Coast Guard escort, the US icebreaker *Northwind*, which could proceed no further after one of its ancient engines broke down. To continue through McClure Strait would have meant abandoning the *Northwind* to an uncertain fate, an unthinkable prospect." Some clarification is in order on this first point. As previously stated in this book, the *Northwind* peeled off from the expedition on September 9–10, in Melville Sound and proceeded independently through Coronation Gulf. Since the *Northwind* was not even in McClure with the *Manhattan* and the *John A. MacDonald* on September 10–12, LaRocca is incorrect to write that her welfare would have been a consideration at that time. Nonetheless, LaRocca's point that the *Manhattan* suffered by not having an additional escort vessel in McClure Strait still holds. His next point: "The second [factor] stemmed from the necessity for meeting pre-arranged deadlines which dictated timely arrivals at Barter Island, Prudhoe Bay and Point Barrow [all in Alaska] in order to rendezvous with an assortment of public and private brass, amid a whirlwind of hoopla and fanfare. What originally purported to be an experimental test voyage responsive principally to the scientific disciplines and soberly reported by an independent press instead degenerated into a gigantic publicity stunt mismanaged remotely by Humble's Houston public relations and communications crew, while both the scientific approach and the independent press reports fell by the wakeside." Humble indeed planned for celebrations and visits from various dignitaries upon the tanker's arrival in Alaska, but the extent to which those schedules influenced the decision-making processes in McClure is only speculative. In personal communication with the author (21 May 2004), LaRocca reiterated his belief that the *Manhattan* failed to make an earnest attempt at McClure Strait, and as such no one can prove either way whether the ice would have prevented the tanker from making the passage. See LaRocca, *Alaska Agonistes*, 25.

51. Fournier, *MacDonald* Report, 7–8; Keith, 68; Smith, *Northwest Passage*, 126–29.

52. Smith, *Northwest Passage*, 132.

53. Fournier, *MacDonald* Report, 7; Helfferich, 53.

54. "News," Humble press release, 11 September 1969, 1, SBH.

55. Fournier, *MacDonald* Report, 9–12.

56. Keith, 68.

57. Keating, "North for Oil," 388; Smith, *Northwest Passage*, 136.

58. Fournier, *MacDonald* Report, 11.

59. "Arctic Oil Tanker/Manhattan Maiden Voyage/Northwest Passage," certificate, 14 September 1969, SBH.

60. T. J. Fuson, who called the *Manhattan* voyage the "happiest experience of my life," died only a month after the end of the expedition. See Smith, *Northwest Passage*, 137, 194.

61. Fournier, *MacDonald* Report, 11.

62. Humble Oil and Refining Company, "Deck Log During 1969 SS MANHATTAN Voyage," SS *Manhattan* Report No. 213 (undated), 45.

63. "News," Humble press release, 15 September 1969, 1, SBH.

64. Robert B. Atwood, "Rep. Pollock Promises Fight for Icebreaker Fleet Buildup," *Anchorage Daily Times*, 17 September 1969, 1.

65. Howard W. Pollock to John A. Volpe, 29 September 1969, Box 5, Folder 111 (*Manhattan Trip*), Howard Pollock Papers, Alaska and Polar Regions Collections, Rasmuson Library, University of Alaska Fairbanks.

66. Helfferich journal, 6.

67. Helfferich, 54.

Notes to Chapter 8

1. Smith, *Mineral Resources of Alaska*, 165.

2. John Wiese, "Will the 'Manhattan' Crack the Ice? Joe's Not So Sure," *Anchorage Daily News*, 9 September 1969, 3.

3. Ibid. The particularly bad ice season of 1913 (to which Bernard refers) trapped the *Karluk*, Vilhjalmur Stefansson's ship on the Canadian Arctic Expedition. The migrating ice pack took the ship all the way to Wrangell Island in the Siberian Arctic before crushing it altogether. Seven men died before rescue teams reached them. See Robert A. Bartlett, *The Karluk's Last Voyage: An Epic of Death and Survival in the Arctic* (New York: Cooper Square Press, 2001); Jennifer Niven, *The Ice Master: The Doomed 1913 Voyage of the* Karluk (New York: Hyperion, 2000); Vilhjalmur Stefansson, *The Friendly Arctic: The Story of Five Years in Polar Regions* (New York: MacMillan, 1921).

4. "News," Humble press release, 17 September 1969, SBH.

5. Smith, *Northwest Passage*, 142–43; Storrs and Pullen, 176.

6. Pullen and Swithinbank, 365. Pullen and Swithinbank list fifty transits for the given time period and acknowledge that of that number some did not pass through Bering Strait. Although the *Manhattan* is one such vessel, the authors nonetheless count both her westward and eastward voyages in 1969 as transits of the Northwest Passage.

7. R. K. Headland, "Ten Decades of Transits of the Northwest Passage," *Polar Geography* 33, nos. 1–2 (March–June 2010), 2.

8. Miller, 204.

9. Upon the successful completion of this maritime first, Captain McCann received congratulatory cables from Captain Thomas C. Pullen and Rear Admiral R. E. Hammond, Commander of the Coast Guard's 17th District. See "The Norther 1969," 56–57.

10. McCann, "CCGD 17 OPORD 202 ALPHA 69: Artic [*sic*] Tanker Evaluation Project," 2–3, A-5/10–13.

11. Fournier, *MacDonald* Report, 15.

12. Ed Clarke, interview by author, 27 October 2009.

13. Tom Brennan, "Golden Barrel Had Dents and Dings," *Anchorage Daily News*, 12 November 2003, B-7.

14. Larry Fanning, "*Manhattan* Gets History's Most Costly Barrel of Oil," *Anchorage Daily News*, 20 September 1969, 1.

15. Helfferich, 54; Smith, *Northwest Passage*, 164–65.

16. E. F. Broderick to S. B. Haas, 18 August 1969, SBH.

17. J. Acquaviva et al., "Arctic Terminal Study," SS *Manhattan* Report No. 501 (15 January 1970), 79–83.

18. Broderick to Haas; Mookhoek and Bielstein, 138; Smith, *Northwest Passage*, 164.

19. Robert L. McCollom and Francis E. Ranft, "Environmental Studies for a Proposed Arctic Marine Terminal," SS *Manhattan* Report No. 603 (undated), 11.

20. Teller offered the services of the Atomic Energy Commission (AEC) to plan such an enterprise, but noted the blast would have to be privately financed. See "Blast Could Make Harbor on Slope," *Anchorage Daily Times*, 25 September 1969, 1. Teller first unveiled this concept a decade earlier in the guise of Project Plowshare, an AEC program designed to achieve peacetime uses of atomic weaponry, and announced plans for a "geographic engineering" blast at Cape Thompson on Alaska's northwest coast. This particular proposal, labeled Project Chariot, met with stiff resistance from the region's indigenous population and environmentalists. The project was later abandoned. For a comprehensive history of the proposal, see Dan O'Neill, *The Firecracker Boys* (New York: St. Martin's Griffin, 1994).

21. Bechtel, Inc., "Feasibility Study, Arctic Slope Terminal and Pipeline System, Volume II," SS *Manhattan* Report No. 506 (December 1969), 89–100.

22. Humble Oil and Refining Company, "Site Reconnaissance, Alternate Marine and Petroleum Storage Terminal, Herschel Island, Canada," SS *Manhattan* Report No. 602 (3 July 1969), 1–13.

23. A. Ronald McKay, "Sea Ice Activity and Pressure Ridge Growth in the Vicinity of Surcharged Grounded Ice Islands UNAK 1 and UNAK 2," SS *Manhattan* Report No. 600 (November 1969), 71.

24. Ibid., 80.

25. Broderick to Haas.

26. "News," Humble press release, 11 September 1969, SBH.

27. Joe LaRocca, "Will *Manhattan*'s Success Spoil the Pipeline?" *Fairbanks Daily News-Miner*, 23 September 1969, A-3.

28. "A Saga—and a Barrel of Arctic Oil," *Anchorage Daily News*, 19 September 1969, 4.

29. Benedict, 4.

30. Smith, *Northwest Passage*, 166.

31. "What Did the *Manhattan* Really Prove?," *Alaska Industry* 1, no. 11 (November 1969), 47.

32. William D. Smith, "Jersey Standard's Leader Meets the Issues Head-on," *New York Times*, 15 December 1968, 9-F.

33. Sampson, 191.

34. Ralph Maybourn, "SS *Manhattan*, Report on Voyage Through the Northwest Passage, September–October 1969," SS *Manhattan* Report No. 210 (October 1969), 1.

35. Wall, 145.

36. Mead, 99.

37. Sampson, 191.

38. Mead, 99–107.

39. Lenzner, II/13–22; Mead, 206.

40. Lenzner, II-24.

41. Richard Mauer, "Blueprint for Disaster: The Spill That Didn't Have to Happen," *Anchorage Daily News*, 5 November 1989, 1.

42. John M. Blair, *The Control of Oil* (New York: Pantheon, 1976), 123.

43. Noam Chomsky, *Year 501: The Conquest Continues* (Boston: South End Press, 1993), 53; Strohmeyer, 83.

44. Mauer, 1.

45. Ibid.

46. Ibid.

47. Joe LaRocca to author, 25 May 2004.

48. Mauer, 1; Mead, 106.

49. Wall, 5.

50. Smith, "Jersey Standard's Leader Meets the Issues Head-on," 9-F.

Notes to Chapter 9

1. The epigram is quoted directly from Smith (*Northwest Passage*, 199), who presumably made a verbatim transcript of the actual document prepared by Pullen and placed in the cairn at Beechey Island. Boker's original poem, however, features the above stanzas in different order. The stanza beginning "The night is" is number twenty of the poem, while the stanza beginning "Bright summer goes" is number eleven. Either Pullen and/or Smith apparently took some creative license in citing this poem for the historic cairn. See George Henry Boker, "A Ballad of Sir John Franklin," in *An American Anthology, 1787–1900: Selections Illustrating the Editor's Critical Review of American Poetry in the Nineteenth Century, Volume 1*, ed. Edmund Clarence Stedman (Grosse Pointe, MI: Scholarly Press, 1968), 262.

2. Helfferich journal, 14. The typewritten manuscript from which this quote is taken is a verbatim transcript of Helfferich's daily log kept in longhand aboard the ship. As such, it contains abbreviations, sentence fragments, and even misspellings of the sort one would expect in a handwritten diary dashed off at the end of a long day. I have corrected misspellings and other errors for the sake of clarity.

3. Savours, 198–202, 314.

4. Smith, *Northwest Passage*, 184–85.

5. Swithinbank, *Forty Years on Ice*, 48–49.

6. Humble Oil and Refining Company, "Feasibility of Tanker Operations in Arctic Ice, Volume II," SS *Manhattan* Report No. 316 (undated), 5–7.

7. Pullen, "We Smashed Through the Northwest Passage," 10.

8. Storrs and Pullen, 177–78.

9. Pullen, "We Smashed Through the Northwest Passage," 10.

10. Stan Haas to Jeanne Haas, 21 October 1969, SBH.

11. Smith, *Northwest Passage*, 185–86.

12. Storrs and Pullen, 178.

13. Pullen, "We Smashed Through the Northwest Passage," 10; Smith, *Northwest Passage*, 186.

14. Smith, *Northwest Passage*, 186–87; Storrs and Pullen, 178.

15. Humble Oil and Refining Company, "Feasibility of Tanker Operations in Arctic Ice, Volume II," 7–40.

16. Fournier, *MacDonald* Report, 50.

17. Cutler, 18–19.

18. Stanley B. Haas, undated speech, SBH. Although undated, the contents of this handwritten document clearly indicate it was the text of remarks Haas prepared for the post-expedition ceremony at Halifax.

19. Smith, *Northwest Passage*, 189–90.

20. Ibid., 187. For a technical description of the hull breach, including subsequent analysis of the properties of the failed steel, see Mookhoek and Bielstein, 134–35.

21. "Sierra Club Wants Development Halted," *Fairbanks Daily News-Miner*, 9 September 1969, 10.

22. Brown, *Oil on Ice*, back cover.

23. Ibid., 17.

24. Thomas C. Pullen, "Expanded Arctic Shipping: Canadian Challenge," *Canadian Forces Sentinel* 7, no. 2 (1971), 34. On November 10, 1969, just two days after the *Manhattan*'s arrival in Halifax, Transport Minister Don Jamieson traveled to the Brussels Conference on Pollution of the Sea by Oil, where he gave a speech outlining Ottawa's position on a number of international conventions then under debate. See Donald Jamieson, "Statement by the Canadian Minister of Transport, The Honorable Donald Jamieson, to the Brussels Conference on Pollution of the Sea by Oil," speech, 10 November 1969, SBH.

25. Stolee, 1969 Report, 39.

26. T. J. Fuson, "SS *Manhattan* news conference, November 12, 1969, New York City," transcript of news conference, held by University of Alberta Library, 9, 17.

27. Pullen, "We Smashed Through the Northwest Passage," 10.

28. William D. Smith, "Triumphant S.S. *Manhattan* Is Welcomed in New York," *New York Times*, 13 November 1969, 74.

Notes to the Epilogue

1. William Langewiesche, *The Outlaw Sea: A World of Freedom, Chaos, and Crime* (New York: North Point Press, 2004), 3.

2. William D. Smith, "*Manhattan*'s 2d Trip Spurs Hope," *New York Times*, 25 May 1970, 66.

3. Paul Fournier commanded the *Louis St. Laurent* at the start of the voyage. On April 12, 1970, just one week into the expedition, however, Fournier became ill and experienced internal bleeding. He was rushed by helicopter first to a hospital in Greenland and later south to Canada, where he made a full recovery. Captain George Burdoch replaced Fournier on April 14 and led the remainder of the expedition. See Lieutenant Commander E. Stolee, "Report on the Voyage in the Canadian Arctic of CCGS *Louis S. St. Laurent*, Spring 1970 (*Manhattan*'s Journey)," Canadian Coast Guard report (undated), 29–31.

4. "Pond Inlet Food Supply Boosted by Ship's Visit," Humble press release, 21 May 1970, SBH.

5. "Second Voyage to Far North Gives Humble Needed Data," *Offshore Technology* 5, no. 6 (June 1970), 17; C. W. M. Swithinbank, "Second Arctic Voyage of SS *Manhattan*, 1970," *Polar Record* 15, no. 96 (September 1970), 355–56.

6. "Humble Decides Economics Favor the Onshore Pipeline over the Icebreaking Tanker for North Slope Operations," *Offshore Technology* 5, no. 12 (December 1970), 17.

7. S. B. Haas to W. F. Robinson and W. J. Bielstein, 18 March 1970, SBH.

8. C. L. Crane, "Icebreaking Model Tests at Helsinki Ice Model Basin for Arctic Tanker Design Project," SS *Manhattan* Report No. 314 (15 December 1970).

9. Seppo Hilden, "Test Report No. 4, Icebreaking Resistance Tests of Four Parametric Series Design Tanker Models to 1:50 Scale," SS *Manhattan* Report No. 305 (19 August 1970), 1–7; Seppo Hilden, "Test Report No. 5, Steering Tests in Level Ice with Five Models to 1:50 Scale, up to July 8, 1970," SS *Manhattan* Report No. 307 (undated), 2–8.

10. Newport News Shipbuilding and Dry Dock Company, "Arctic Tanker Feasibility Design Report, Phase I—Part 1," SS *Manhattan* Report No. 400 (August 1970), 5.

11. J. M. Freymann to J. Wiley Bragg, 19 March 1970, SBH; "Humble Decides Economics Favor the Onshore Pipeline over the Icebreaking Tanker for North Slope Operations," 17.

12. Arctic Marine Task Force, "Test Voyage Report, 1970 SS *Manhattan* Full Scale Icebreaking Tests," 2.

13. "Humble Says Arctic Shipping Feasible But Pipelines May Have Economic Edge," Humble press release, 21 October 1970, SBH.

14. Mead, 518.

15. Smith, *Northwest Passage*, 114–15.

16. Wall, 146.

17. "Humble Lifts Estimate of Cost of Shipping Oil by Northwest Passage," *Wall Street Journal*, 24 September 1969, 12.

18. Wall, 147.

19. Helfferich journal, 14.

20. Cutler, 19.

21. Richard A. Kerr, "A Warmer Arctic Means Change for All," *Science* 297, no. 5586 (30 August 2002), 2.

22. ACIA, *Impacts of a Warming Arctic: Arctic Climate Impact Assessment*. (Cambridge: Cambridge University Press, 2004), i.

23. Ibid., 10.

24. Ibid., 24.

25. National Snow and Ice Data Center, "Models Underestimate Loss of Arctic Sea Ice," press release, 30 April 2007.

26. National Snow and Ice Data Center, "Arctic Sea Ice Shatters All Previous Record Lows," press release, 1 October 2007.

27. Ibid.

28. Ibid.

29. Michael Byers, *Who Owns the Arctic? Understanding Sovereignty Disputes in the North* (Vancouver: Douglas & McIntyre, 2009), 40.

30. Scott R. Stephenson et al., "Divergent Long-Term Trajectories of Human Access to the Arctic," *Nature Climate Change* 1 (June 2011), 156–60.

31. S. D. Rice et al. "The Exxon Valdez Oil Spill," in *Long-Term Ecological Change in the Northern Gulf of Alaska*, ed. R. B. Spies (Amsterdam: Elsevier, 2007), 419–520; J. W. Short et al., "Slightly Weathered Exxon Valdez Oil Persists in Gulf of Alaska Beach Sediments After 16 Years," *Environmental Science & Technology* 41, no. 4 (15 February 2007), 1245–50.

32. Deborah Zabarenko, "Arctic Oil Spill Would Challenge Coast Guard," *Scientific American*, 20 June 2011, available at http://www.scientificamerican.com/article.cfm?id=arctic-oil-spill-would-challenge-coast-guard (accessed 5 July 2011).

33. A representative account of the impacts of climate change to Inuit residents of Nunavut is available in Ed Struzik, *The Big Thaw: Travels in the Melting North* (Mississauga, ON: John Wiley & Sons Canada, Ltd., 2009), 159–82.

34. ACIA, 122.

35. Protection of the Arctic Marine Environment, *Arctic Offshore Oil and Gas Guidelines*, report of the Arctic Council (29 April 2009), 11–12.

36. Quoted in "On Thinning Ice," *Northern Perspectives* 27, no. 2 (Spring 2002), 7.

37. William H. German to S. B. Haas, 12 January 1972, SBH; T. C. Pullen to S. B. Haas, 31 January 1971, SBH; C. H. Rosenthal to Stan Haas, 15 May 1972, SBH. The SBH collection contains dozens of pages of handwritten notes that appear to be drafts of lectures or articles for publication. These notes are untitled and undated, though their content places them somewhere between the cancellation of the icebreaking tanker studies in 1970 and the completion of the Trans-Alaska Pipeline in 1977.

38. Coates, *The Trans-Alaska Pipeline Controversy*, 246–49.

39. Joint Typhoon Warning Center, "1987 Annual Tropical Cyclone Report," Steve J. Fatjo and Frank H. Wells, eds., Report of the Department of the Navy, 19 January 1988, 40–43.

40. "Storm Kills 68 in South Korea," *New York Times*, 17 July 1987, A-3; "Flood Toll Near 100, Seoul Says," *New York Times*, 23 July 1987, A-12.

41. Matt Walker and Katy Bradford, "SS *Manhattan* Goes to the Scrappers," *The Master, Mate & Pilot* 43, no. 4 (July–August 2007), 24.

Bibliography

I n 1977, Exxon (previously Humble Oil and Refining Company) began arranging to release all technical and operational reports from the *Manhattan* voyages to the U.S. Maritime Administration (MARAD). In order to organize the reports in a format suitable for future readers, each was assigned a unique number under the heading "SS *Manhattan* Arctic Marine Project, Report No. xx." Each report retained its original title and authorship. The transfer of all 117 reports to MARAD was completed in March 1979. In January 1982, the entire collection was moved again, this time to the Transport Canada Library in Ottawa, Ontario, where it is housed today. So vital were these reports to the research for this book they are listed here first, ordered alphabetically by author, not sequentially by report number. The reader will note the 117 reports are numbered nonconsecutively from 200 to 605. Not all 117 reports are cited in this book. A complete list is available by contacting the Transport Canada Library.

Other primary sources that enriched this project immeasurably are the personal papers of Stanley B. Haas, Merritt Helfferich, and Mike Dorsey, all held privately by those individuals or their heirs. Copies of all cited documents from those collections are in the author's possession.

Finally, much has been written about the history of oil development in Alaska. The author wishes to acknowledge the many secondary sources used in crafting the narrative of this book. Among the most valuable are those by Peter A. Coates, Merritt Helfferich, Bern Keating, Joe LaRocca, Robert Douglas Mead, Jack Roderick, William D. Smith, John Strohmeyer, and Bennett H. Wall. Full citations appear below. Alaska newspapers, especially the *Anchorage Daily News*, *Anchorage Daily Times*, and *Fairbanks Daily News-Miner*, are a particularly rich source of contemporary accounts of the Prudhoe Bay events of the late 1960s and early 1970s.

SS *Manhattan* Collection, Transport Canada Library, Ottawa, Ontario

Acquaviva, J., et al. "Arctic Terminal Study." SS *Manhattan* Arctic Marine Project, Report No. 501, 15 January 1970.

Arctic Marine Task Force. "Test Voyage Report, 1970 SS *Manhattan* Full Scale Icebreaking Tests." SS *Manhattan* Arctic Marine Project, Report No. 221, 3 August 1970.

Bechtel, Inc. "Feasibility Study, Arctic Slope Terminal and Pipeline System, Volume II." SS *Manhattan* Arctic Marine Project, Report No. 506, December 1969.

Crane, C. L. "Icebreaking Model Tests at Helsinki Ice Model Basin for Arctic Tanker Design Project." SS *Manhattan* Arctic Marine Project, Report No. 314, 15 December 1970.

German & Milne. "Esso *Manhattan*, Recommendations Covering Alterations Necessary to Fit Vessel for Arctic Service." SS *Manhattan* Arctic Marine Project, Report No. 336, January 1969.

German & Milne and Northern Associates. "Arctic Transportation Feasibility Study, Ship Data and Operations." SS *Manhattan* Arctic Marine Project, Report No. 334, undated.

Heywood, Paul T. "Arctic Tanker Test, SS *Manhattan*, Analyst's Report." SS *Manhattan* Arctic Marine Project, Report No. 214, January 1970.

Hilden, Seppo. "Test Report No. 4, Icebreaking Resistance Tests of Four Parametric Series Design Tanker Models to 1:50 Scale." SS *Manhattan* Arctic Marine Project, Report No. 305, 19 August 1970.

———. "Test Report No. 5, Steering Tests in Level Ice with Five Models to 1:50 Scale, up to July 8, 1970." SS *Manhattan* Arctic Marine Project, Report No. 307, undated.

Humble Oil and Refining Company. "Arctic Tanker Test 1969, Humble's Maiden Northwest Passage Voyage, General Information." SS *Manhattan* Arctic Marine Project, Report No. 208, 1969.

———. "Deck Log During 1969 SS MANHATTAN Voyage." SS *Manhattan* Arctic Marine Project, Report No. 213, undated.

———. "Feasibility of Tanker Operations in Arctic Ice, Volume I." SS *Manhattan* Arctic Marine Project, Report No. 315, undated.

———. "Feasibility of Tanker Operations in Arctic Ice, Volume II." SS *Manhattan* Arctic Marine Project, Report No. 316, undated.

———. "Miscellaneous Notes and Correspondence: Environmental Data." SS *Manhattan* Arctic Marine Project, Report No. 605, undated.

———. "Miscellaneous Notes and Correspondence, SS *Manhattan*, Volume II." SS *Manhattan* Arctic Marine Project, Report No. 241, undated.

———. "Site Reconnaissance, Alternate Marine and Petroleum Storage Terminal, Herschel Island, Canada." SS *Manhattan* Arctic Marine Project, Report No. 602, 3 July 1969.

Maybourn, Ralph. "SS *Manhattan*, Report on Voyage Through the Northwest Passage, September–October 1969." SS *Manhattan* Arctic Marine Project, Report No. 210, October 1969.

McCollom, Robert L., and Francis E. Ranft. "Environmental Studies for a Proposed Arctic Marine Terminal." SS *Manhattan* Arctic Marine Project, Report No. 603, undated.

McKay, A. Ronald. "Sea Ice Activity and Pressure Ridge Growth in the Vicinity of Sur-charged Grounded Ice Islands UNAK 1 and UNAK 2." SS *Manhattan* Arctic Marine Project, Report No. 600, November 1969.

Mookhoek, A. D., and R. L. Vukin. "Arctic Tanker Test: Objectives, Program, Procedures, and Data Acquisition and Usage Systems." SS *Manhattan* Arctic Marine Project, Report No. 207, 15 July 1969.

Newport News Shipbuilding and Dry Dock Company. "Arctic Tanker Feasibility Design Report, Phase I—Part 1." SS *Manhattan* Arctic Marine Project, Report No. 400, August 1970.

Archive Collections

Alaska and Polar Regions Collections, Rasmuson Library, University of Alaska Fairbanks
    Earl Grammer Diaries
    Naval Arctic Research Laboratory Records
    Howard Pollock Papers
Bancroft Library, University of California, Berkeley
    Sierra Club Records
Center for American History, University of Texas at Austin
    ExxonMobil Historical Collection
Consortium Library, University of Alaska Anchorage
    Charles Henry Rosenthal Papers
Mike Dorsey Papers, private collection, Eagle River, Alaska
Stanley B. Haas Papers, private collection, held by Charla (Haas) Bauer, Floral City, Florida
Hagley Museum and Library, Wilmington, Delaware
    Sun Shipbuilding and Dry Dock Company Records
Merritt R. Helfferich Papers, private collection, Fairbanks, Alaska
Library and Archives Canada, Ottawa, Ontario
    Dan Guravich Fonds
    SS Manhattan Collection
Smithsonian National Museum of American History, Washington, DC
    Maritime Collections
Suzzallo & Allen Libraries, University of Washington
    Brock Evans Papers

Other Sources

ACIA. *Impacts of a Warming Arctic: Arctic Climate Impact Assessment*. Cambridge: Cam-bridge University Press, 2004.

Alaska Construction & Oil. "Alternatives to the Pipeline." September 1975.

Alaska Industry. "What Did the *Manhattan* Really Prove?" Vol. 1, no. 11 (November 1969).

Alaska Scouting Service. "Bear Creek No. 1." Vol. 5, no. 6 (10 February 1959).

Baker, H. Charles. "Northwest Passage: Voyage of the *Manhattan*." *Ocean Industry* 4, no. 8 (August 1969).

Bamberg, James. *British Petroleum and Global Oil, 1950–1975: The Challenge of Nationalism*. Cambridge: Cambridge University Press, 2000.

Barrett, William P. "Humble Pie." *Forbes*, 19 October 1992.

Bartlett, Robert A. *The* Karluk's *Last Voyage: An Epic of Death and Survival in the Arctic*. New York: Cooper Square Press, 2001.

Berry, Mary Clay. *The Alaska Pipeline: The Politics of Oil and Native Land Claims*. Bloomington: Indiana University Press, 1975.

Blair, John M. *The Control of Oil*. New York: Pantheon, 1976.

Blodgett, Robert B., and Bryan Sralla. "A Major Unconformity Between Permian and Triassic Strata at Cape Kekurnoi, Alaska Peninsula: Old and New Observations on Stratigraphy and Hydrocarbon Potential," U.S. Geological Survey Professional Paper 1739-E, 2006.

Boker, George Henry. "A Ballad of Sir John Franklin." In *An American Anthology, 1787–1900: Selections Illustrating the Editor's Critical Review of American Poetry in the Nineteenth Century, Volume 1*, ed. Edmund Clarence Stedman. Grosse Pointe, MI: Scholarly Press, 1968.

Brigham, Lawson W. "Icebreaker." In *Encyclopedia of the Arctic, Vol. 2*, ed. Mark Nuttall. New York: Routledge, 2005.

Brinkley, Douglas. *The Quiet World: Saving Alaska's Wilderness Kingdom, 1879–1960*. New York: Harper Collins, 2011.

Brower, Charles. *Fifty Years Below Zero: A Lifetime of Adventure in the Far North*. Fairbanks: University of Alaska Press, 1994.

Brown, Tom. *Oil on Ice: Alaskan Wilderness at the Crossroads*. San Francisco: Sierra Club Books, 1971.

Byers, Michael. *Who Owns the Arctic? Understanding Sovereignty Disputes in the North*. Vancouver: Douglas & McIntyre, 2009.

Caldwell, Lynton Keith. *Between Two Worlds: Science, the Environmental Movement and Policy Choice*. New York: Cambridge University Press, 1990.

———. "Public Policy for the Environment: Some Guidelines for Alaskans." In *Change in Alaska: People, Petroleum, and Politics*, ed. George W. Rogers. College: University of Alaska, 1970.

Chomsky, Noam. *Year 501: The Conquest Continues*. Boston: South End Press, 1993.

Cicchetti, Charles J. *Alaskan Oil: Alternative Routes and Markets*. Baltimore: Johns Hopkins University Press, 1972.

Clark, Neil M. "Ships North to Alaska's Coast." *Montana: The Magazine of Western History*, Fall 1973.

Coates, Ken, et al. *Arctic Front: Defending Canada in the Far North*. Toronto: Thomas Allen Publishers, 2008.

Coates, Peter A. *The Trans-Alaska Pipeline Controversy: Technology, Conservation, and the Frontier*. Fairbanks: University of Alaska Press, 1993.

Coen, Ross. "Alaska's Richest Day: The Prudhoe Bay Lease Sale That Brought $900 Million to the 49th State." *Oil-Industry History* 5, no. 1 (2004).

———. "Submarines, Blimps, Trains, and Ships: Transportation Proposals for Prudhoe Bay Crude Oil, 1968–1977." *Oil-Industry History* 4, no. 1 (2003).

Copithorne, W. L. "The Worlds of Wallace Pratt." *The Lamp* 53, no. 3 (Fall 1971).

Cutler, Maurice. "Voyage Opens Wide Arctic Door." *Oilweek* 20, no. 39 (17 November 1969).

Cyriax, Richard J. *Sir John Franklin's Last Arctic Expedition: The Franklin Expedition, a Chapter in the History of the Royal Navy.* London: Methuen & Co., 1939.

Day, Alan. *Historical Dictionary of the Discovery and Exploration of the Northwest Passage.* Lanham, MD: Scarecrow Press, 2006.

Ellis, William S. "Will Oil and Tundra Mix? Alaska's North Slope Hangs in the Balance." *National Geographic* 140, no. 4 (October 1971).

Erickson, Gregg. "Alaska's Petroleum Leasing Policy: A Crisis of Direction." In *Change in Alaska: People, Petroleum, and Politics*, ed. George W. Rogers. College: University of Alaska Press, 1970.

Esso Marine News. "The Fabulous Adventure." Vol. 14, no. 2 (1969).

Fiala, Lieutenant Colonel Charles J. *Alaskan Oil: An Assessment of the North Slope's Implications for Our Strategic Policies Toward Major Producer and Consumer Countries.* Carlisle Barracks, PA: U.S. Army War College, 1970.

Fisher, Anne M. "Establishing Sovereignty in the Canadian Arctic." *The Musk-ox* 37 (1989).

Fournier, Captain Paul. "Report of CCGS *John A. MacDonald* Voyage Through the Northwest Passage and Back with SS *Manhattan*: September–November 1969." Canadian Coast Guard report, undated.

Franklin, Sir John. *Narrative of a Second Expedition to the Shores of the Polar Sea In the Years 1825, 1826, and 1827.* Philadelphia: Carey, Lea, and Carey, 1828.

Gallagher, H. G. *Etok: A Story of Eskimo Power.* New York: G. P. Putnam's Sons, 1974.

Galloway, James H. "Petroleum Industry Policies for Protecting the Environment." In *Change in Alaska: People, Petroleum, and Politics*, ed. George W. Rogers. College: University of Alaska Press, 1970.

Grant, Shelagh D. *Polar Imperative: A History of Arctic Sovereignty in North America.* Vancouver: Douglas & McIntyre, 2010.

Gray, Earle. "Arctic Ice Sinks Panarctic Barges." *Oilweek* 20, no. 30 (15 September 1969).

———. "Oil Can Move via NW Passage." *Oilweek* 20, no. 32 (29 September 1969).

Gray, W. O., and R. Maybourn. "*Manhattan*'s Arctic Venture—A Semitechnical History." Paper presented at the Society of Naval Architects and Marine Engineers, Spring Meeting/STAR Symposium, Ottawa, Ontario, Canada, 17–19 June 1981.

Gulbenkian, Nubar. *Pantaraxia.* London: Hutchinson, 1965.

Haas, Stanley B. "Marine Transport—The Northwest Passage Project." In *Proceedings of the Twentieth Alaska Science Conference*, ed. Eleanor C. Viereck. College, AK: American Association for the Advancement of Science, 1970.

Hammond, Rear Admiral R.E., Commander 17th Coast Guard District. "OPORDER NO. 202 ALPHA 69: CGC NORTHWIND." United States Coast Guard memorandum, 5 May 1969.

Headland, R. K. "Ten Decades of Transits of the Northwest Passage." *Polar Geography* 33, nos. 1–2 (March–June 2010).

Hedland, John S. "The Public Interest and Competitive Leasing of State Oil and Gas Lands." In *Change in Alaska: People, Petroleum, and Politics*, ed. George W. Rogers. College: University of Alaska Press, 1970.

Helfferich, Merritt R. "The Cruise of the *Manhattan*." *Alaska Geographic* 1, no. 1 (1972).

Hickel, Walter J. *Who Owns America?* Englewood Cliffs, NJ: Prentice-Hall, 1971.

———. *The Wit and Wisdom of Wally Hickel*, ed. Malcolm B. Roberts. Anchorage: Searchers Press, 1994.

Hopson, Eben. "Mayor Eben Hopson's Warning to the People of the Canadian Arctic." Booklet produced by North Slope Borough, 21 September 1976.

Humble News. "*Manhattan* Story Told in Video Conference." July 1969.

Humble Oil and Refining Company. *Through the Northwest Passage.* Videorecording, 1970.

———. *1954 Annual Report.*

———. *1955 Annual Report.*

———. *1956 Annual Report.*

———. *1957 Annual Report.*

———. *1958 Annual Report.*

Humble Way. "The Mission Possible Man." Vol. 10, no. 1 (1971).

Jacobsen, Lawrence R. "Subsea Transport of Arctic Oil: A Technical and Economic Evaluation." Paper presented at the Third Annual Offshore Technology Conference, Houston, Texas, 19 April 1971.

Joint Typhoon Warning Center. "1987 Annual Tropical Cyclone Report." Steve J. Fatjo and Frank H. Wells, eds., Report of the Department of the Navy, 19 January 1988.

Jones, Charles S. *From the Rio Grande to the Arctic: The Story of the Richfield Oil Corporation.* Norman: University of Oklahoma Press, 1972.

Jull, Peter. "Inuit Politics and the Arctic Seas." In *Politics of the Northwest Passage*, ed. Franklyn Griffiths. Kingston, ON: McGill-Queen's University Press, 1987.

Karpoff, Jonathan M. "McClure, Sir Robert." In *Encyclopedia of the Arctic*. Vol. 2, ed. Mark Nuttall. New York: Routledge, 2005.

Kaye, Roger. *Last Great Wilderness: The Campaign to Establish the Arctic National Wildlife Refuge.* Fairbanks: University of Alaska Press, 2006.

Keating, Bern. "North for Oil: *Manhattan* Makes the Historic Northwest Passage." *National Geographic* 137, no. 3 (March 1970).

———. *The Northwest Passage: From the Mathew to the Manhattan: 1497 to 1969.* Chicago: Rand McNally & Company, 1970.

Kennedy, Tom. *Quest: Canada's Search for Arctic Oil.* Edmonton, AB: Reidmore Books, 1988.

Kerr, Richard A. "A Warmer Arctic Means Change for All." *Science* 297, no. 5586 (30 August 2002).

Kirkey, Christopher. "The Arctic Waters Pollution Prevention Initiatives: Canada's Response to an American Challenge." *International Journal of Canadian Studies* 13 (1996).

Kirton, John, and Don Munton. "The *Manhattan* Voyages and Their Aftermath." In *Politics of the Northwest Passage*, ed. Franklyn Griffiths. Kingston, ON: McGill-Queen's University Press, 1987.

Kumm, William H. "Non-nuclear Submarine Could Cost-effectively Move Arctic Oil and Gas." *Oil & Gas Journal*, 5 March 1984.

Langewiesche, William. *The Outlaw Sea: A World of Freedom, Chaos, and Crime.* New York: North Point Press, 2004.

LaRocca, Joe. *Alaska Agonistes: The Age of Petroleum: How Big Oil Bought Alaska*. North East, PA: Rare Books, Ink, 2003.

Lear, John. "Northwest Passage to What?" *Saturday Review*, 1 November 1969.

Lehane, Brendan. *The Northwest Passage*. Alexandria, VA: Time-Life Books, 1981.

Lenzner, Terry F. *The Management, Planning and Construction of the Trans-Alaska Pipeline System: Report to the Alaska Pipeline Commission*. State of Alaska Report, 1 August 1977.

Livingston, John. *Arctic Oil*. Toronto: Canadian Broadcasting Corporation, 1981.

MacDonald, Edwin A. *Polar Operations*. Annapolis, MD: U.S. Naval Institute, 1969.

Marx, Leo. "Technology: The Emergence of a Hazardous Concept." *Technology and Culture* 51, no. 3 (July 2010).

Matthews, Downs, and Ian N. Higginson. "Dan Guravich (1918–1997)." *Arctic* 51, no. 2 (June 1998).

McCann, D. J., Commanding Officer USCGC *Northwind* (WAGB 282). "Arctic West 1969: Phases I & II." United States Coast Guard memorandum, 1 August 1969.

———. "CCGD 17 OPORD 202 ALPHA 69: Artic [sic] Tanker Evaluation Project." United States Coast Guard memorandum, 6 October 1969.

McRae, D. M. "The Negotiation of Article 234." In *Politics of the Northwest Passage*, ed. Franklyn Griffiths. Kingston, ON: McGill-Queen's University Press, 1987.

Mead, Robert Douglas. *Journeys Down the Line: Building the Trans-Alaska Pipeline*. Garden City, NY: Doubleday, 1978.

Meredith, Brian. "A Plan for the Arctic: Mr. Trudeau's International Regime." *The Round Table*, 1970.

Miller, Keith Harvey. *Prudhoe Bay Governor: Alaska's Keith Miller*. Anchorage: Todd Communications, 1997.

Mookhoek, A. D., and W. J. Bielstein. "Problems Associated with the Design of an Arctic Marine Transportation System." Paper presented at the Third Annual Offshore Technology Conference, Houston, Texas, 19–21 April 1971.

Moreau, Captain J. W. "Problems and Developments in Arctic Alaskan Transportation." *Proceedings of the United States Naval Institute* 96, no. 5 (1970).

Mumford, Lewis. "History: Neglected Clue to Technological Change." *Technology & Culture* 2, no. 3 (1961).

Nalder, Eric. *Tankers Full of Trouble: The Perilous Journey of Alaskan Crude*. New York: Grove Press, 1994.

Nanton, Paul. *Arctic Breakthrough: Franklin's Expeditions 1819–1847*. Toronto: Clarke, Irwin, 1970.

Naske, Claus-M., and Herman E. Slotnick. *Alaska: A History of the 49th State*. Norman: University of Oklahoma Press, 1987.

National Snow and Ice Data Center. "Arctic Sea Ice Shatters All Previous Record Lows." Press release, 1 October 2007.

———. "Models Underestimate Loss of Arctic Sea Ice." Press release, 30 April 2007.

Newsweek. "The Great Oil Hunt." 22 September 1969.

Niven, Jennifer. *The Ice Master: The Doomed 1913 Voyage of the* Karluk. New York: Hyperion, 2000.

Northern Perspectives. "On Thinning Ice." Vol. 27, no. 2 (Spring 2002).

Offshore Technology. "Humble Decides Economics Favor the Onshore Pipeline over the Icebreaking Tanker for North Slope Operations." December 1970.

———. "Second Voyage to Far North Gives Humble Needed Data." June 1970.

O'Neill, Dan. *The Firecracker Boys.* New York: St. Martin's Griffin, 1994.

Patton, E. L. "Hearing Testimony." Booklet produced by Alyeska Pipeline Service Company, February 1971.

Pinch, Trevor, and Wiebe Bijker. "The Social Construction of Facts and Artifacts: Or How the Sociology of Science and the Sociology of Technology Might Benefit Each Other." *Social Studies of Science* 14 (1984).

Pratt, Wallace E. "Oil Fields in the Arctic." *Harper's*, January 1944.

———. "Petroleum in the North." In *Compass of the World: A Symposium on Political Geography*, eds. Hans W. Weigert and Vilhjalmur Stefansson. New York: MacMillan, 1944.

Protection of the Arctic Marine Environment. *Arctic Marine Shipping Assessment 2009 Report.* Report of the Arctic Council, 2009.

———. *Arctic Offshore Oil and Gas Guidelines.* Report of the Arctic Council, 29 April 2009.

Pullen, Thomas C. "Expanded Arctic Shipping: Canadian Challenge." *Canadian Forces Sentinel* 7, no. 2 (1971).

———. "We Smashed Through the Northwest Passage." *Petroleum Today* 11, no. 1 (Winter 1970).

Pullen, Thomas, and Charles Swithinbank. "Transits of the Northwest Passage, 1906–90." *Polar Record* 27, no. 163 (October 1991).

Rice, S. D., et al. "The Exxon Valdez Oil Spill." In *Long-Term Ecological Change in the Northern Gulf of Alaska*, ed. R. B. Spies. Amsterdam: Elsevier, 2007.

Ringsmuth, Katherine Johnson. *Beyond the Moon Crater Myth: A New History of the Aniakchak Landscape, A Historic Resource Study for Aniakchak National Monument and Preserve.* U.S. Department of the Interior report, 2007.

Roderick, Jack. *Crude Dreams: A Personal History of Oil and Politics in Alaska.* Fairbanks: Epicenter Press, 1997.

Ross, Ken. *Environmental Conflict in Alaska.* Boulder: University Press of Colorado, 2000.

Rothwell, Donald R. "Australian and Canadian Initiatives in Polar Marine Environmental Protection: A Comparative Review." *Polar Record* 34, no. 191 (1998).

Rowley, Graham. "Bringing the Outside Inside." In *Politics of the Northwest Passage*, ed. Franklyn Griffiths. Kingston, ON: McGill-Queen's University Press, 1987.

———. "Captain T. C. Pullen, RCN: Polar Navigator." *The Northern Mariner* 2, no. 2 (1992).

Sampson, Anthony. *The Seven Sisters: The Great Oil Companies and the World They Made.* New York: Viking Press, 1975.

Savours, Ann. *The Search for the Northwest Passage.* New York: St. Martin's Press, 1999.

Shannon, Terry, and Charles Payzant. *Ride the Ice Down! U.S. and Canadian Icebreakers in Arctic Seas.* San Carlos, CA: Golden Gate Junior Books, 1970.

Shinn, Robert A. *The International Politics of Marine Pollution Control.* New York: Praeger, 1974.

Short, J. W., et al. "Slightly Weathered Exxon Valdez Oil Persists in Gulf of Alaska Beach Sediments After 16 years." *Environmental Science & Technology* 41, no. 4 (15 February 2007).

Smith, Merritt Roe, and Leo Marx, eds. *Does Technology Drive History? The Dilemma of Technological Determinism*. Cambridge, MA: MIT Press, 1994.

Smith, Phillip S., et al. *Mineral Resources of Alaska: Report on Progress of Investigations in 1924, Bulletin 783*. Washington, DC: Government Printing Office, 1926.

Smith, William D. *Northwest Passage*. New York: American Heritage Press, 1970.

Stefansson, Vilhjalmur. *The Friendly Arctic: The Story of Five Years in Polar Regions*. New York: MacMillan, 1921.

———. *Northwest to Fortune*. New York: Duell, Sloan and Pearce, 1958.

Stephenson, Scott R., et al. "Divergent Long-Term Trajectories of Human Access to the Arctic." *Nature Climate Change* 1 (June 2011).

Stolee, Lieutenant Commander E. "Report on the Voyage in the Canadian Arctic of CCGS *John A. MacDonald*, Summer 1969 (*Manhattan*'s Journey)." Canadian Coast Guard report, undated.

———. "Report on the Voyage in the Canadian Arctic of CCGS *Louis S. St. Laurent*, Spring 1970 (*Manhattan*'s Journey)." Canadian Coast Guard report, undated.

Storrs, A. H. G., and T. C. Pullen. "S.S. *Manhattan* in Arctic Waters." *Canadian Geographic Journal* 80, no. 5 (May 1970).

Strohmeyer, John. *Extreme Conditions: Big Oil and the Transformation of Alaska*. Anchorage: Cascade Press, 1997.

Struzik, Ed. *The Big Thaw: Travels in the Melting North*. Mississauga, ON: John Wiley & Sons Canada, Ltd., 2009.

Swithinbank, Charles. *Forty Years on Ice: A Lifetime of Exploration and Research in the Polar Regions*. Sussex, England: The Book Guild Ltd., 1998.

Swithinbank, C. W. M. "Second Arctic Voyage of SS *Manhattan*, 1970." *Polar Record* 15, no. 96 (September 1970).

Tucker, Joe. "Lessons from the Arctic." *Humble Way* 10, no. 1 (1971).

United Nations Convention on the Law of the Sea. 10 December 1982.

U.S. News & World Report. "Alaska Strikes It Rich." 9 December 1968.

U.S. Senate, Committee on Interior and Insular Affairs. *The Status of the Proposed Trans-Alaska Pipeline*, 91st Congress, 1st Session. Washington, DC: Government Printing Office, 1969.

U.S. Department of Commerce. *Arctic Submarine Transportation System—1975: Volume I—Executive Summary*. Washington, DC: Government Printing Office, 1975.

U.S. Department of the Interior. *Draft Environmental Impact Statement for the Trans-Alaska Pipeline, Section 102(2)(c) of the National Environmental Policy Act of 1969*. Washington, DC: Government Printing Office, 1971.

U.S. Department of the Interior and U.S. Department of Transportation. *A Report on Pollution of the Nation's Waters by Oil and Other Hazardous Substances*. Washington, DC: Government Printing Office, 1968.

Walker, Matt, and Katy Bradford. "SS *Manhattan* Goes to the Scrappers." *The Master, Mate & Pilot* 43, no. 4 (July–August 2007).

Wall, Bennett H. *Growth in a Changing Environment: A History of Standard Oil Company (New Jersey), Exxon Corporation, 1950–1975*. New York: McGraw-Hill, 1988.

Wayburn, Edgar. "A Conservationist's Concern About Arctic Development." In *Change in Alaska: People, Petroleum, and Politics*, ed. George W. Rogers. College: University of Alaska Press, 1970.

Weeks, W. F. *On Sea Ice*. Fairbanks: University of Alaska Press, 2010.

Whitby, Michael. "Showing the Flag Across the North: HMCS *Labrador* and the 1954 Transit of the Northwest Passage." *Canadian Naval Review* 2, no. 1 (Spring 2006).

White, Roderick M. "Dynamically Developed Force at the Bow of an Icebreaker." Unpublished Ph.D. diss., Massachusetts Institute of Technology, September 1965.

Wilderness Society, Environmental Defense Fund, Inc., Friends of the Earth. *Comments on the Environmental Impact Statement for the Trans-Alaska Pipeline, Vol. I–IV*. Self-published, 1972.

Willis, Roxanne. *Alaska's Place in the West: From the Last Frontier to the Last Great Wilderness*. Lawrence: University Press of Kansas, 2010.

Yergin, Daniel. *The Prize: The Epic Quest for Oil, Money, and Power*. New York: Simon & Schuster, 1991.

Zabarenko, Deborah. "Arctic Oil Spill Would Challenge Coast Guard." *Scientific American*, 20 June 2011. http://www.scientificamerican.com/article.cfm?id=arctic-oil-spill-would-challenge-coast-guard (accessed 5 July 2011).

Index

Note: Italicized page numbers indicate photographs and maps, which are located between pages 120 and 121.

W

Wall, Bennett H., 21–22, 141
Wärtsilä Shipyard, 37, 159–160
Washington conference, Humble Oil and
    Refining, 30–34
water sky, 127
Watson, Ian, 66
Wayburn, Edgar, 59–61, 115, 153
"Wealth Below the Ice" (*La Presse*), 72
Weeks, W. F., 158
whaling station proposal, for Cumberland
    Gulf on Baffin Island, 70
White, Roderick M., 39–40
wildcatting for crude oil, 5
Wilderness Society, 47
Wilkins, Bishop John, 46
Willis, Roxanne, 5
Wolf, David P., 95
world oil markets, volatility of, 17–18
World War II, demand for petroleum
    following end of, 17
Wright, Don, 115, 159
Wright, Michael A., 52–53, 141, 163

Y

Yermak (icebreaker), 80

Z

Zeien, Charlie, 51